Politics'
Strangest
Characters

Other titles in this series

Boxing's Strangest Fights
Bridge's Strangest Games
Cricket's Strangest Matches
Fishing's Strangest Days
Football's Strangest Matches
Golf's Strangest Rounds
Horse-racing's Strangest Races
The Law's Strangest Cases
Medicine's Strangest Cases
Motor-racing's Strangest Races
Rugby's Strangest Matches
Shooting's Strangest Days
Tennis's Strangest Matches

Politics' Strangest Characters

Curious and colourful characters
from over 250 years

NEIL HAMILTON

ROBSON BOOKS

First published in Great Britain in 2003 by Robson Books,
Bramley Road, London W10 6SP.

A member of **Chrysalis** Books plc

British Library Cataloguing in Publication Data
A catalogue record for this title is available from the British Library.

ISBN 1 86105 526 9

Typeset by FiSH Books, London WC1
Printed in Great Britain by Bell & Bain Ltd, Glasgow

Dedicated to Gerald Howarth,
(Conservative MP for Cannock and Burntwood 1983–92;
Aldershot 1997–)
whose eccentricity
is
to believe in fidelity to persons and principles
– especially in adversity.

Contents

Introduction

Dame Edith Sitwell was well known as a poet, but the public knew her better for her strange appearance. Cloaked and bejewelled, her head crowned with 'bird-king's hat', her neck swathed in a gold Aztec collar and delicate, ringed fingers festooned with huge aquamarine rocks, she announced in a TV interview that, if she appeared in a normal coat and skirt, 'people would doubt the existence of the Almighty'.

In her book *English Eccentrics* she declared, 'Eccentricity exists particularly in the English, and partly I think because of that peculiar and satisfactory knowledge of infallibility which is the hallmark and birthright of the British nation.' About thirty years ago I read somewhere and wrote down an evocative litany on Britain's traditional veneration for its eccentricities:

for soldiers who march around in hats a yard high and made of hair;
for talking dogs and performing fleas;
for a system of democracy that has not one written rule;
for commanders who lead their soldiers into battle with a walking-stick;
for dukes who exhort the nation to 'pull its finger out';
for police who pursue armed thugs with whistles, truncheons and a grave demeanour;
for institutions like the House of Lords;
for tattooed ladies and two-headed cows;
for trade unionists who cling resolutely to the aspirations of

the Tolpuddle Martyrs;
for the hordes who write angry letters when a TV newsreader appears wearing a floral tie;
for old Cheltenham ladies who devote their lives to saving the cats of Venice;
for the lengthy correspondence in *The Times* discussing the appearance of blue sky over London this summer;
for all the splendid inanities and contradictions which go towards making Britain the most civilised country on earth.

After a generation of change, some of these strange characteristics have fallen by the wayside. Who today cares what newsreaders wear? The bobby on the beat now drives a souped-up patrol car and whistles are a remote memory of a more innocent age. Fred Kite, the shop-steward caricature played by Peter Sellers in *I'm All Right Jack*, a reality in the 1960s, is now extinct. The House of Lords has been despoiled. But otherwise many of the 'splendid inanities and contradictions' flourish still.

British political history teems with strange characters. Indeed, the contents of this book prove Britain's pre-eminent claim to be the World's Leading Political Asylum.

THE STRANGENESS OF PARLIAMENT

LONDON, 1547–PRESENT

The House of Commons has many eccentricities. When I was elected in 1983 I was surprised that no one gave me a certificate to prove the fact. No-one officially told me what to do next or even when to turn up. However, I presented myself at Westminster at the Serjeant at Arms' Office where I was given everything he thought necessary to perform my new functions as an MP.

Outside the Members' Entrance I was shown the mounting block where, like the Duke of Wellington in his dotage, I could mount my horse if I needed help to reach my stirrups. More usefully, I was also shown my coat-hanger, to which someone had helpfully tied a short piece of red ribbon. This was so that I could hang my sword on arrival at the House, it being unparliamentary nowadays for anyone other than the Serjeant at Arms to take an offensive weapon (other than a speech) into the Chamber. However, there is no prohibition on spurs, which may still be worn in the Chamber – but only by County Members, not Borough Members!

In the Chamber itself I saw that precautions had been taken to reduce the risk of a fight if a Member did somehow, in defiance of the rules, manage to smuggle in a sword undetected. A red line had been inserted into the green carpet in front of each front bench. The distance dividing them is two sword-lengths and it is out of order for an MP to cross the red line when he is speaking.

On the table lying between the red lines I saw two bronze plinths, on which the Mace rests when the House is in session. Indeed, another of the Commons' eccentricities is that, whilst the Speaker's presence is not necessary for business to be transacted, nothing can be done if the Mace is absent. In the nineteenth century the Commons attended a naval review at Spithead and the Members came back to London by two special trains. The official who had the key to the Mace cupboard travelled in the second train, which arrived back an hour late. The House had to wait for him to unlock the Mace before it could begin its business for the day.

Then, like a schoolboy again, I was given a locker, of dimensions approximately two feet by eighteen inches. That was the limit of my office accommodation. I could not immediately have either a room or even a telephone (apart from public call boxes). Times have changed, however, and now MPs are busily engaged in providing themselves with sumptuous office suites costing the taxpayer over £1 million each.

The Serjeant at Arms places the Mace on the table.

However nugatory the office facilities were in 1983, at least supplies of stationery were not stinted. I learned, however, that even this had once been a sensitive issue – until relatively recently MPs could demand only twelve sheets of writing paper free on any one sitting day and had to pay for any extra. This official meanness could be circumvented by attending to correspondence in the Library, where there was effectively no restriction, as the librarians refilled the stationery racks regularly.

However, even this seemingly anodyne matter could sometimes bubble up into heated political controversy. The crests on the writing paper in the 1960s were either blue or red (to indicate party affiliation). On one famous occasion the Librarian was held to be showing party prejudice because the staff had unwittingly distributed too many sheets of paper of one colour and not enough of the other!

Perhaps even more strange than the failure to provide an office for everyone was the surprising fact that there are not even enough seats for all MPs in the Chamber. Whereas there were 650 MPs, only 346 could find space on the green benches on the Floor of the House itself (actually 345, as Cyril Smith required two spaces).

Another eighty or so could be seated in side galleries above the Chamber, from which it is also technically possible to make a speech, although this has not been done in living memory. In 1980 the inconvenience of these seats was used to advantage by Dr Ian Paisley (MP for Antrim North 1970–) and his two Democratic Unionist colleagues, who disrupted the proceedings following the assassination of the Rev. Robert Bradford (Official Unionist MP for Belfast South 1974–82). The Serjeant at Arms' long arm could not reach them from his place down below in the Chamber and it took many minutes for him to clamber, in knee-breeches and clanking sword, up the staircase into the gallery.

Theoretically all MPs are equal and can choose to sit where they like in the Chamber. If a Member is prepared to face the opprobrium involved he may even occupy the seat usually taken by the Prime Minister. One formidable backbench eccentric, Dame Irene Ward (Conservative MP for Wallsend 1931–45,

Tynemouth 1950–74) once did. In the 1962–3 session, enraged by
the failure of her own Government's economic policy as it
affected her beloved North-East, she insisted on plonking her
bulky form in the place from which Harold Macmillan expected
shortly to answer a debate. It was with some difficulty that she
was persuaded by the Chief Whip to move along, but only after
making her point.

The tradition of seating in parallel rows separated by a
gangway is a relic of the arrangement of the choir stalls in the old
St Stephen's chapel, where the Commons sat when they first
appropriated it for a debating chamber in 1547.

The Chamber in both Houses is strange by the standards of
most legislatures. Members speak from their places and not from
a platform or tribune. Instead of a hemicycle with desks the
seating takes the form of parallel rows of benches, from which
the tradition has arisen of Government and Opposition Members
sitting opposite. The only time they turn their backs on one
another is during prayers, when both sides face the wall behind
them – supposedly because the benches make it impossible to
pray facing across the Chamber if you are wearing your sword,
a problem of limited modern significance. Every day starts in the
same way – the Speaker's chaplain enters in procession with the
Speaker, looks around him at the Members and prays for the
future of the country.

A novice Member was supposedly once shown around the
Chamber by an old hand and said, pointing to the other side of
the House 'So that is where the enemy sit?' This elicited the
response, 'No. Those who sit opposite are your political
opponents. You will find that your enemies sit behind you.'

This story is, no doubt, apocryphal but a similar experience
did occur to Jeremy Hanley (Conservative MP for Richmond
1983–97). When first elected he fell into conversation with Dr
Ian Paisley and expressed surprise to find him and the other
Democratic Unionists sitting next to him on the Government
side of the House (unlike the Official Unionists, who sat
opposite). Hanley said, 'Excellent to see you! I never realised
that you were on our side.' Paisley replied with thunderous

voice but twinkling eye, 'Young man, never confuse sitting on your side with being on your side!'

The only method of reserving a seat is for a Member to attend prayers, having left a card with his name written on it on the designated seat in advance. Formerly, it was the custom to leave one's hat on a seat for this purpose but, of course, few Members wear hats today.

In Victorian times tall hats were worn at most times, except when entering, leaving or actually addressing the House. In 1900 the hat-wearing rules were set out as follows:

> At all times remove your hat on entering the House and put it on upon taking your seat; remove it again on rising for

Prayers in the House of Commons.

In the days when Members wore hats, they used them to reserve their chosen seat.

whatever purpose. If the MP asks a Question he will stand with his hat off and he may receive the Minister's answer seated and with his hat on. If, on a Division, he should have to challenge the ruling of the Chair, he will sit and put his hat on. If he wishes to address the Speaker on a Point of Order not connected with a Division, he will do so standing with his hat off. When he leaves the Chamber to participate in a Division he will take his hat off, but will vote with it on. If the Queen sends a Message to be read from the Chair the Member will uncover. In short, how to take his seat, how to behave at Prayers and what to do with his hat form between them the ABC of the Parliamentary scholar.

In 1892 a scuffle occurred because the ferocious Ulster Conservative, Col. Saunderson (MP for North Armagh 1885–1906), finding a strange hat on his accustomed seat, absent-mindedly sat down upon it and squashed it. J. S. Wallace (Liberal MP for Limehouse 1892–5), the flattened hat's furious owner, then tried to drag the colonel out of his seat. Henry Lucy, a Parliamentary sketch-writer, recalled 'the colonel stands six feet high, is all bone and muscle and was born fighting. He gently but firmly laid Mr Wallace on his back and resumed his seat.' Stern action by the Speaker was avoided only by Saunderson's agreement to replace the hat.

If someone left his hat on a seat, it must indicate he would soon return, it being inconceivable that anyone would either walk around or leave the Palace of Westminster without it. So, an informal system of seat reservation developed. However, the more enterprising Members soon realised that, by bringing two silk hats to the House, they could obey etiquette by wearing one whilst reserving their seat with the other.

On the introduction of the Home Rule Bill in 1892 Members appeared as early as 5 a.m. to reserve seats. Dr Tanner (Irish Nationalist MP for Mid Cork 1885–1906), having no hat, tried to claim his place by taking off his coat and leaving it as a marker but, as there was no precedent, it was disallowed. Austen Chamberlain, the Liberal Unionist Whip (MP for Worcestershire East 1892–1914, Birmingham West 1914–37), reportedly drove into New Palace Yard in a four-wheeled carriage filled with second-hand hats, which he arranged on the benches below the gangway 'pegging-out' claims on behalf of his friends. The prayer-card was introduced to avoid hat congestion.

When in 1919 Lady Astor (Conservative MP for Plymouth Sutton 1919–45) became the first woman MP to take her seat *The Times* pointed out that no such event had occurred since

Wallace's hat is flattened by Col. Saunderson.

abbesses had sat in the Saxon Witenagemot and ruminated portentously upon the important problems which this might cause. Was it conceivable that she should sit hugger-mugger on the benches with all those men? And should she wear a hat or not? The Speaker gave special consideration to this latter important question and issued his judgment of Solomon: male Members would still be forbidden to address the House whilst behatted, but lady Members could do as they pleased.

As the twentieth century wore on hats became increasingly rare. By the 1950s only two MPs appeared in their silk toppers in the painting commissioned by the House of a full Chamber. However, it still remained necessary to wear a hat (technically to be 'seated and covered') to raise a Point of Order during a Division. Two collapsible opera hats were kept by the Serjeant at Arms especially for the purpose, as it was 'disorderly' to wear a handkerchief or an Order Paper as a substitute. The House likes its humour to be kept simple and never tires of its repetitive jokes, so this familiar event invariably met with uncontrollable hilarity.

Often, several Members wished to raise Points of Order in rapid succession, causing the opera hat to race around the Chamber like a relay baton, a scene described by John Biffen, a former Leader of the House, as 'Members displaying the nervous excitement of children playing the Christmas game of pass the parcel'. He also speculated on what might happen if a practising Sikh were to be elected – would he be obliged 'to perch this bizarre headgear on top of his turban'?

Having mastered the intricacies of these essential rules, one is ready to open one's mouth. The first great Parliamentary debate after the election is on the Queen's Speech. The Commons hears it in the Lords and then returns to begin a week-long discussion on the Government's programme for the session. But there is, first, another eccentric pantomime to be gone through.

Since 1727 the first business has always been the First Reading of the Outlawries Bill – this is strange because it is a Bill which no Member presents, has never been printed and never makes any further progress. Similarly, in the House of Lords, the Select

Vestries Bill is read a first time and then forgotten. This apparently pointless exercise has occurred year in and year out and in effect preserves Parliament's right to debate anything it chooses, placing its own priorities above those of the Monarch contained in the Royal Summons calling Parliament together.

In debate MPs are supposed to maintain civility to one another. This means avoiding 'unparliamentary' remarks, the criteria for identifying which sometimes appears upon examination to be rather strange also. 'Erskine May', the bible of Parliamentary procedure, carries a list of abusive, coarse and insulting expressions which the Speaker has banned over the centuries.

Obviously an MP must not accuse another of lying, a rule circumvented by Sir Winston Churchill when he charged an MP with telling 'a terminological inexactitude'. Other insults to be avoided are blackguard, cad, dog, guttersnipe, hooligan, hypocrite, behaving like a jackass, lousy, murderer, pharisee, cheeky young pup, impertinent puppy, rat, ruffian, stool-pigeon, swine, traitor. The list is not closed and 'git' has recently been added to it.

It is difficult to discern any principle distinguishing which epithets are acceptable and which are not. For example, 'Nosey Parker' was banned in 1955, whereas Tony Banks (Labour MP for Newham North West 1983–97, West Ham 1997–) was allowed to call Terry Dicks (neanderthal Conservative MP for Hayes & Harlington 1983–97) 'a pig's bladder on a stick'. Similarly, it was ruled all right to repeat in the House the Norwegian Agriculture Minister's description of John Selwyn Gummer (Conservative MP for Lewisham West 1970–4, Eye 1979–83, Suffolk Coastal 1983–) as 'drittsek', despite the fact that the English equivalent (shitbag) would most definitely be classed as an extremely 'unparliamentary expression'.

Animal-house behaviour is now largely confined to that most meaningless constitutional charade, Prime Minister's Questions, but the House is a pale shadow of the riotous assembly it was in the eighteenth and nineteenth centuries. Perhaps the worst example of a Parliamentary brawl occurred in July 1893, at the end of the Committee Stage of the Home Rule Bill. It was sparked off by T. P. O'Connor (Irish Nationalist MP for Liverpool, Scotland 1885–1929) calling Joseph Chamberlain a 'Judas'.

The weather was hot and the political atmosphere like a highly charged powder-keg. T. P.'s taunt acted as a detonator. In the mayhem that ensued dozens of Members grappled with one another in an unprecedented fracas. In the words of J. L. Garvin, Chamberlain's biographer, 'one could see the teeth set, the eyes flashing, faces aflame with wrath and a thicket of closed fists beating about in wild confusion'.

But in the midst of the battle the House of Commons' priorities had to be observed. 'The appearance amid the throng of the Serjeant at Arms was portentous and seemed to show that things were desperate indeed. But his sternest remonstrance was addressed to a member standing up below the gangway, watching the fight. "I beg your pardon," said the Serjeant at Arms gently, "but you're standing up with your hat on, which you know is a breach of order."'

When order was eventually restored a ludicrous incident brought the evening to a close. On the next business being called

A fracas erupts in the House.

the Clerk of the House read it out in such a whimsical tone of voice and with so much emphasis that the whole House burst out into laughter. The next business happened to be 'Pistols Bill – Second Reading!'

It may appear to be strange that Members must refer to each other by their constituencies and not their names. But this is all part of the elaborate rules developed to impart civility to debate. All MPs are 'honourable' unless members of the Privy Council, in which case they are 'right honourable'. Senior barristers (but not solicitors) are also 'learned', officers (but not lower ranks) are 'gallant'. The sons of dukes and marquesses are all 'noble Lords', but not the son of an earl unless he bears a courtesy title as the eldest surviving son. Every daughter of an earl, however, is a 'noble Lady'.

The upshot of all this is that the son of a duke, who had been an officer, a QC and a Privy Counsellor would be addressed as 'the right hon., learned, gallant and noble Lord, the Member for Blankshire'. The eccentricities of this system may be a little confusing. Lord Dunglass became MP for Lanark in 1931, but was obliged to leave for the House of Lords in 1950 on the death of his father, the Earl of Home. However, he was re-elected to the Commons in 1963, having disclaimed his peerage, when he became Sir (rather than plain Mr) Alec Douglas-Home, on account of being a Knight of the Thistle.

A diverting discussion on the strange complications of aristocratic nomenclature took place in the Commons on 7 February 1972. Viscount Lambton (Conservative MP for Berwick-upon-Tweed 1950–73) succeeded his father as Earl of Durham in 1970 but did not wish to go to the Lords and disclaimed his peerages. The effect of this in the Commons was that 'the noble Lord', Lord Lambton, became the plain 'hon. Member', Mr Antony Lambton.

However, he wished to continue using the name by which he had always been known – the 'courtesy title' of Viscount Lambton which he had, of course, disclaimed along with his earldom. The Speaker sympathetically announced he could be called Lord Lambton in the House and described as such in all Parliamentary papers. Members had the right 'to be called in the House what they wish to be called and as they are called in their constituencies.' Lambton had described himself on the ballot paper as 'Antony Claud Frederick Lambton, commonly called Lord Lambton' and was elected as such. Hansard records general mirth when the Speaker went on to say, 'There are several hon. Members in this House who are called by names which are not their own'.

This immediately brought forth a storm of outrage from Labour MPs. The republican scourge of the royal family, Willie Hamilton (Labour MP for West Fife 1950–74, Fife Central 1974–87), denounced 'the irrelevant nonsense that takes place in this House far too often'. Lambton, he declared, was simply trying to have his cake and eat it. 'If he is to be known in that way I want to be called Lord Fife from now on.' The Speaker suavely replied that as soon as he was known as such in his constituency he would consider the matter.

Another left-winger, Eric Heffer (Labour MP for Liverpool Walton 1964-91), then took up another grievance: 'Could all MPs who served in the armed forces, who were not officers but

Charles Bradlaugh languishing in the Prison Room. He was put there for one night in 1880 for attempting to take his seat without taking the oath.

members of the lower ranks, like myself, henceforth be called "gallant".' It was about time we got away from this snobbery in the House. To tumultuous cheers he declared, 'From now on, I want to be referred to as the "gallant Gentleman from Walton." ' '

David Steel (Liberal MP for Roxburgh, Selkirk & Peebles 1965–83; Tweeddale, Ettrick & Lauderdale 1983–97) followed, complaining: 'Why should the epithet "learned" be confined to members of the legal profession? Are not those who consider themselves to be learned entitled to be so called?'

John Wilkinson (Conservative MP for Bradford West 1970–4, Ruislip Northwood 1979–) then posed a knotty problem for the Speaker. Was it not irrelevant that Lambton was called 'Lord' in his constituency? 'Another parliamentary candidate was Screaming Lord Sutch. If returned to this House would he have had the title of Lord Sutch?' The Speaker wisely decided to resolve that question when Sutch was elected and that it was time to move on.

Whilst all these eccentricities are more or less amusing, there are other eccentricities that are not. One of the privileges of Membership of Parliament is freedom from civil arrest. This was once an important advantage as a means of avoiding debtor's prison. In 1807 a man named Mills who was in debt to the tune of £23,000 bought a rotten borough for £1000 and avoided imprisonment. In 1826 a man elected MP for Beverley whilst in prison for debt was released by Order of the Speaker.

Both Houses also retain powers to punish breaches of privilege and contempts. The Lords and the Commons may imprison anyone for any reason, but whereas the Lords, as a Court of Record, can imprison indefinitely the Commons can do so only until the end of the Session. There is a prison room in the Clock Tower to which the recalcitrants are sent, but no-one has been imprisoned there since Charles Bradlaugh (MP for Northampton 1880–91) in 1880 and it is now used as a staff rest room.

In years gone by these draconian powers have sometimes been used in trivial cases. A man was imprisoned by the Commons for poaching Admiral Griffiths MP's fish, another for cutting down a Member's tree and another for arresting an

MP's tailor for debt! In 1827 the House of Lords reacted strongly when a member of the public sued one of its attendants for the loss of an umbrella which disappeared after it was committed to his charge. The disgruntled owner was awarded £1 0s 4d damages but Lord Chancellor Eldon summoned him to the Bar of the House and threatened him with imprisonment unless he refunded the money and apologised. But these days it is unlikely that the Commons would visit such injustice upon anyone other than one of its own Members.

JOHN WILKES

MP FOR AYLESBURY 1757–64,
MIDDLESEX 1768–9, 1774–90

and SIR FRANCIS DASHWOOD

MP FOR NEW ROMNEY 1741–61,
WEYMOUTH & MELCOMBE REGIS 1761–2,
AFTERWARDS 8TH LORD LE DESPENCER

'Thank you. I have no small vices.'

One of the most colourful political adventurers ever to become a Member of Parliament, John Wilkes took everything he did to reckless extremes. Four times expelled from the House of Commons, he was re-elected by his constituents immediately thereafter. He wrote and published obscene poems, leading to his most unlikely achievement: to get a bishop to read one to a shocked House of Lords. The Bishop of Gloucester had thought it would discredit Wilkes to recite this litany of filth. Wilkes enjoyed the improbable scene but was imprisoned in the Tower of London for seditious libel and obscenity whilst the House ordered the poems to be burnt by the public hangman.

He was outlawed and yet, not long afterwards, elected Lord Mayor of London and once again re-elected to Parliament. Horace Walpole wrote of this amazing series of events: 'Thus, after so much persecution by the Court, after so many attempts on his life, after a long imprisonment in a gaol, after all his crimes and indiscretions, did this extraordinary man, of more extraordinary fortune, attain the highest office in so grave and important a city as the Capital of England.'

Wilkes was an Olympic-class debauchee, who scandalised even the dissolute eighteenth century by his excesses. He was introduced to this life by an even greater libertine, Thomas Potter, an MP whose father was Archbishop of Canterbury. In a letter of 1752 Potter urged him to join an expedition to Bath 'if you prefer young women and whores to old women and wives, if you prefer toying away hours with little Sattin Back to the evening conferences of your Mother-in-law... but above all if the heavenly-inspired passion called Lust have not deserted you'.

At Medmenham Abbey in Buckinghamshire he was introduced to the Hell-fire Club, a society of sots and sex maniacs whose high priest was Sir Francis Dashwood MP, Colonel of the Buckinghamshire Militia. He was a cultivated and remarkable man, a Fellow of the Royal Society, an Oxford DCL and a founder of the Society of Dilettanti (which Horace Walpole unfairly described as 'a club of which the nominal qualification is having been in Italy, and the real one being drunk'). But Dashwood was also profligate and profane. Expelled from Italy for scandalous conduct, he also achieved the astonishing feat of making love to the Empress Anne of Russia whilst disguised as King Charles XII of Sweden.

Dashwood delighted in architectural puns and jokes. In his grounds at West Wickham he erected a round, upright pillar and a narrow bush-shaded door to a temple, the sexual symbolism of which was obvious. He built a hollow globe atop the parish church, which he used for drinking sessions with Wilkes and others. The church bore the Latin inscription 'MEMENTO', (lacking the usual 'MORI'). Dashwood told inquirers the missing word was 'MERI' – so worshippers were actually being exhorted, not to remember their mortality, but 'Don't forget the drink'.

His gardens also boasted a statue of Priapus (the god of lasciviousness and obscenity, characterised by an erect phallus).

This statue carried the motto: 'PENI TENTO NON PENITENTI'. Wilkes said this emphasised that the favourite doctrine of the Abbey was certainly not penitence ('peni tento' means 'I feel my penis').

But Dashwood's greatest practical joke was the Order of Medmenham Monks – a sacrilegious club devoted to sexual depravity and popularly known as the Hell-fire Club. Dashwood conceived the idea after attending a service in the Vatican Sistine Chapel, where the worshippers pretended to scourge themselves for their sins with whips. Dashwood saw that they lashed themselves very lightly and decided to teach them a lesson for hypocrisy. He hid a horsewhip under a greatcoat one Good Friday and, when the lights dimmed for the flagellation, thrashed his real whip about him with gusto. Screams of pain suddenly rent the air. The real worshippers soon cottoned on to what was happening and Dashwood had to run for his life.

Wilkes was one of his twelve 'Franciscans', ostensibly so-called so they could pass off their excesses as anti-Catholic mockery (but actually a pun on Sir Francis' name). In fact they were all atheists, agnostics or deists. The 'ceremonies' seem to have been largely public fornications – a girl would be laid naked upon a bed disguised as an altar and sexual intercourse took place to the accompaniment of 'prayers' and incantations by the assembled voyeur 'monks'.

Some of the fraternity were inclined to invest the anti-religious element of these activities with too much gravity. They recited blasphemous prayers in an attempt to shock themselves, like naughty schoolboys scrawling rude words on lavatory walls. Wilkes had no truck with this nonsense. On one celebrated occasion and despite having no religious belief, they announced that they would try a prayer to the Devil. Wilkes decided to play a practical joke.

He procured a baboon, swathed it in red garments, strapped horns on its head and shut it up in a cupboard in the 'chapel'. When Lord Orford began his Satanic incantations, Wilkes pulled a cord. This released the baboon, which leapt screeching out of the cupboard onto the backs of the terrified devil-worshippers and then scampered out of the window. Wilkes was convulsed with laughter; everyone else nearly died of shock.

Wilkes purchased his Parliamentary seat at Aylesbury in 1757, spending £7,000 on an unopposed return. In the metropolis he quickly fell in with 'women of easy virtue and men of studied vice'. However, he did not gamble, drink excessively or smoke. He once politely declined an offer of snuff, saying 'Thank you, I have no small vices.'

Despite his ugliness (he was extremely boss-eyed) he appears to have been irresistible to women. A fellow libertine, Lord Sandwich, told him, 'You will die either on the gallows or of the pox.' Wilkes replied blandly, 'That, my Lord, depends upon whether I embrace your Lordship's principles or your mistress.'

Prof. Steven Watson says he 'distinguished himself by always going to the ultimate extreme in all adventures. In the Hell-fire Club or in politics his recklessness was apparent, for he scorned

John Wilkes by Hogarth.

the decent concealment, the hypocrisy, the cloudy phrases in which weaker men sought safety.'

Despite eschewing the heavy gambling which ruined so many contemporaries, life among the fast set was expensive and Wilkes soon found himself in financial difficulties, living increasingly on his wits. Always in debt, he relied on borrowings from a Jewish moneylender called Silva. These debts he treated with supreme insouciance. A crisis developed throughout the summer of 1760, when many of his IOUs and banker's drafts fell due. He temporised and delayed and eventually asked Silva to bring all the outstanding notes and drafts to a meeting.

When they met Wilkes asked him whether he had brought everything. 'All, sir.' 'Drafts and notes?' 'Everything.' 'Let me see – ten days after date – one month after date – six weeks after date. You are sure these are all?' 'Every one, Mr Wilkes.' 'That's well,' said Wilkes, tearing them all into tiny fragments. He then gave Silva a fresh note for a distant date, advising him, 'You would do better to take your chance on getting the money eventually than sue me and get nothing.'

He entered Parliament in 1757, supporting the Prime Minister, Pitt the Elder, more from desire to become Ambassador to Constantinople or Governor of Quebec than any point of principle. Then, in 1760, everything changed. George III became King and, wishing to govern more actively than George I or II, quickly replaced the political giant, Pitt, with a Scottish nonentity, the Earl of Bute.

The Scots were very unpopular amongst the English, understandably since it was less than twenty years since Bonnie Prince Charlie had frightened the life out of them. Dr Johnson's prejudices were typical of the period:

Seeing Scotland, Madam, is only seeing a worse England.

Sir, it is not so much to be lamented that Old England is lost, as that the Scotch have found it.

[On Lord Mansfield, a Scot educated in England] Much may be made of a Scotchman if he be caught young.

The noblest prospect a Scotchman ever sees is the high
road that leads him to England!

Wilkes blamed Bute for his failure to gain preferment. He
determined to capitalise upon his Scottish unpopularity and
make him the butt of ridicule, founding a satirical newspaper
called *The North Briton* for the purpose. Bute did not last long
but Wilkes delighted in being the 'Lord Gnome' of the 1760s,
taunting and lampooning the Establishment. On a visit to Paris,
Mme. de Pompadour asked him 'How far, then, does the liberty
of the press extend in England?' to which he replied, 'That,
Madame, is what I am trying to find out!'

In the famous issue No. 45 of *The North Briton* (23 April
1763) he published a violent slander on the King, accusing him
of lying in his speech from the throne at the behest of his
Government. The law officers advised the arrest of the culprit
and prosecution for seditious libel. But there was a problem in
framing the warrant, as Wilkes had taken good care to make the
publication anonymous. The Secretary of State, Lord Halifax,
solved this difficulty by issuing a general warrant, naming no
one but ordering the arrest of 'all concerned in the publication'
and seizure of their papers.

When the King's Messenger, Watson, told Wilkes he had
come to arrest him, Wilkes demanded to see the warrant. Seeing
there was no name on it he rejected it as 'a warrant against the
whole English nation!' and asked the hapless official
mischievously, 'Tell me, Mr Watson, why you serve it on me,
rather than on the Lord Chancellor, or one of the Secretaries of
State, or Lord Bute or Lord Coke next door? Why on me?'
Watson, hiding behind his orders, declined to argue.

Wilkes then sent his publisher, John Almon, off for a writ of
habeas corpus from the Court of Common Pleas – a move which
shows Wilkes' cleverness and cunning. The Common Pleas had no
jurisdiction in such cases and the application ought to have been
made to the Court of King's Bench. But Wilkes knew that Sir
Charles Pratt, Chief Justice of the Common Pleas, was a strong
Opposition Whig and would be sympathetic to him – whereas Lord

Mansfield, Lord Chief Justice in the King's Bench, was a Tory Scot from whom he could expect no favour.

Whilst waiting for his habeas corpus, Wilkes delayed the Messengers by obfuscation and they sent for further orders. Halifax sent a note asking Wilkes to visit him at his house, just a few steps down the street. Wilkes replied sardonically that, as they had not been formally introduced, he could not call on him. By the time written orders for Wilkes' arrest arrived from Halifax, Wilkes' house had filled with a noisy clamour of friends. Frightened by Wilkes' confidence and belligerence, the Messengers sent for reinforcements, constables, and even threatened to send for a regiment of Guards to enforce the warrant.

Eventually, Wilkes was forced to go to Halifax's house, only a few yards distant. But, to make his plight more public, Wilkes insisted on calling his sedan chair, in which he made a stately procession accompanied by hordes of raucous supporters.

Halifax, prepared for Wilkes' arrival, sat behind an imposing table together with the other Secretary of State, Lord Egremont, supported by Under-Secretaries, the Treasury Solicitor and various other flunkeys. Wilkes returned his civility with insolence and refused point blank to answer questions. When Halifax demanded to know if Wilkes was the author of *The North Briton* he responded, 'What your Lordship knows, it would be a great impertinence for me to repeat. What you do not know, I will never inform you.' Then, with great bravado, he threatened: 'On the first day of the new Session I shall rise in my place and impeach you both for the outrage you have committed, in my person, against the liberties of the people.'

Halifax replied smugly that he had acted on the best legal advice and tried to question Wilkes further. Wilkes, however, would not play: 'My Lord, I suspect that you are lost in a dark and difficult path, and seek a light to guide you along it. Your Lordship may rest assured, not a single ray will come from me.'

Halifax and Egremont grew testy and Halifax ended the interview by asking whether Wilkes preferred to go to the Tower or to Newgate. Wilkes replied coolly, 'I thank your Lordship, but I never receive an obligation but from a friend. I demand justice, and immediate liberty, as an Englishman who has offended no law of my country.' Turning to Egremont, he sneered, 'My only request is to be confined in the cell where your Lordship's father was imprisoned as a Jacobite. If that is not possible, pray let me have one which has never been occupied by a Scotchman, provided such a cell can be found; for I have no wish to catch the itch.'

Wilkes was taken to another room, where he found some of his friends arguing with the Treasury Solicitor. They said they had seen the Chief Justice issue a writ of habeas corpus addressed to Blackmore and Watson, the two King's Messengers who had seized Wilkes. In order to evade the writ, the authorities promptly transferred Wilkes to the custody of other Messengers, the first of four such underhand moves.

Wilkes was then carted off to the Tower and kept in solitary confinement. But he was able to turn this to his advantage too. The Secretaries of State had given no orders to deny him pens and paper and, ever the adroit propagandist, he set about informing the outside world of his plight, making an unpopular Government fall headlong into even greater odium and contempt.

Eventually he appeared before the court. A vast multitude thronged Westminster Hall and, having sniffed the heady air of democratic adulation, he used the opportunity to make a demagogic speech ostensibly to the judge, but actually to the crowd. He turned a bungled attack by Ministers on the violent language of a political opponent into an attack on 'the liberty of all peers and gentlemen and, what touches me more sensibly, that of all the middling and inferior set of people'. Wilkes was freed on grounds of Parliamentary privilege. The mob, ten thousand strong, went wild and ecstatically but precariously carried him home in procession, huzza-ing and bellowing 'Wilkes and Liberty' all the way.

Once indoors, and fresh from his public humiliation of the Government, Wilkes gleefully applied himself to adding insult to injury. He wrote to Halifax and Egremont: 'Under your Lordships' warrant I find that my house has been robbed and am informed that the stolen goods are in the possession of one or both of your Lordships. I therefore insist that you do forthwith return them.' For good measure he then went to Bow Street and tried to take out a warrant to search their own houses for his papers.

The Ministers, who were foolish enough to reply in intemperate terms, told him he would be prosecuted by the Attorney-General and refused to return his papers until they had decided which were proofs of his guilt. Wilkes was delighted and published the correspondence in the form of a flysheet which was posted all over London, further inflaming the mob.

Wilkes' extreme behaviour now began to project his eccentricity in full measure – only a real eccentric would have invited such alarming risks with such merriment and glee. It was but a foretaste of the extraordinary events yet to unfold. He determined to carry the war into the enemy's territory and reprint the offending articles but, finding no printer brave enough, he set up a printing press for the purpose in his own house. He also sued the Secretaries of State and their underlings personally for wrongful arrest, search and seizure. Chief Justice Pratt, in a landmark judgment for liberty, ruled general warrants illegal and the London jury awarded Wilkes the huge sum of £1000 damages against the Under-Secretary in the first of dozens of cases (encouraged by Wilkes) by others who had also felt the heavy hand of the Government.

Wilkes' provocative actions incited the Government to persecute him by every means. The Commons voted No. 45 a seditious libel and ordered it to be publicly burnt. The Lords accused him additionally of publishing a pornographic poem, 'The Essay on Woman', (actually written by Thomas Potter, son of the Archbishop of Canterbury and privately printed by Wilkes but never published). This last charge was brought, with particularly cynical hypocrisy, by Lord Sandwich – one of the most debauched of Wilkes' fellow members of the Hell-fire Club – and supported by false evidence obtained by bribery. Dashwood, proprietor of the Hell-fire Club and by now Lord le Despencer, commented audibly after Sandwich's speech that it was the first time he had heard Satan preaching against sin.

The Commons then voted that Parliamentary privilege did not cover seditious libel, thus exposing Wilkes to criminal prosecution. He found it expedient to slip away to France for a time and, in January 1764, was expelled for the first time from the House. Jaunty as ever though, he excused himself from a card game because 'I am so ignorant I cannot tell a King from a Knave.' In another jest he said, 'I love my King so well that I hope never to see another.' His trial for seditious libel and obscenity came on whilst he was abroad and, as he did not appear, he was outlawed.

In 1768, having made several vain attempts to get the sentence reversed, Wilkes suddenly announced his candidature for the City of London in the General Election. He came seventh and bottom of the poll, but the campaign demonstrated the raucous support he could expect from the public at large. He immediately announced his candidature for Middlesex, whose election took place five days after the City election.

In an ordinary county the forty-shilling freeholders (the county electors) voted as the local gentry ordered, but in Middlesex the local government system had broken down with the increasing urbanisation of a shifting and violent population. The Middlesex electors were restless, radical and, unlike the City, not divided into organised groups.

Wilkes presented himself as a tribune of the people persecuted by an unpopular Government. The election was extremely drunken and disorderly and he rapidly assumed the leadership of the mob. The windows of the houses of Wilkes' enemies, Bute and Egremont, were all smashed. The Duke of Northumberland was forced to supply them with liquor and drink Wilkes' health. All the windows from west to east were illuminated to please them, or else they were broken.

Wilkes had a ready reply for any heckler. To one who told him he would rather vote for the Devil than John Wilkes, he replied, 'And, if your friend is not standing?' His picture adorned every public house and many were hung as an inn-sign. He enjoyed telling a story against himself, of how he walked behind an old lady who looked up at one of them and said, 'Aye, he swings everywhere but where he ought!'

At the hustings he tried to bandy civilities with one of the rival candidates, Sir William Beauchamp Proctor, the erstwhile MP who resented Wilkes' intervention. Pointing at the mob of his supporters Wilkes observed humorously, 'I wonder, Sir, if there are more fools or knaves down there?' Proctor replied with menace, 'I will tell them what you say and they will put an end to you.' Wilkes then settled his hash: 'It is yourself who would be put an end to: for I would tell them it is a falsehood and they would destroy you in the twinkling of an eye.'

On election day vast crowds accompanied electors in triumphant procession from London to the polling booth at Brentford. Wilkes scored a runaway victory and the mob took ecstatic control of the streets, ensuring that 'Wilkes and Liberty' or 'No. 45' was chalked on every carriage and every house. Benjamin Franklin observed that for fifteen miles out of London not a door, window or shutter remained unmarked and this even continued here and there all the way to Winchester sixty-four miles away. The Austrian Ambassador, Count de Seilern, 'the most stately and ceremonious of men', was forced out cf his coach and ignominiously held with his legs in the air while the figures '45' were chalked on the soles of his shoes – an insult which led to an official protest, although the Minister found it hard not to laugh at the gravity with which the protest at such a ludicrous happening was made.

All the while, of course, Wilkes was still an outlaw and, typically, his first act after his election was to insist that he be arrested, much to the discomfiture of the Government, which was most reluctant to grapple once more with so intractably obstreperous an individual. In fact, it was looking for a way out. But, knowing that the King would not hear of a pardon, and also that the mob might be moved to insurrection by an arrest, it settled for a policy of masterly inactivity and did nothing.

Wilkes, however, was determined on martyrdom. He knew that, once in prison again, obloquy for the Government, public sympathy for him and his capacity to whip up the mob would all be maximised. So, on the very first day of the legal term he surrendered himself before a nervous Lord Chief Justice

Mansfield in the Court of King's Bench. He listened impassively to Wilkes' defence but refused either to sentence him or cancel his outlawry on the ridiculous grounds that, as Wilkes was an outlaw, he could take no notice of him! He should first ask the Attorney-General to arrest him on a writ of 'capias utlagatum' (warrant to arrest an outlaw at large) and then come back.

Ridicule was Wilkes' strongest weapon against the over-mighty State and he knew plenty of ways to make the Government look foolish. He got himself arrested by a sheriff's officer and then wrote to inform the Attorney-General that, as he would not do his duty, he had effectively arrested himself!

Wilkes was then quickly brought before the Court and committed to the King's Bench prison. But by now the situation was totally out of hand. The prison coach was intercepted by the vast throng of Wilkites, the horses taken out, the police expelled and Wilkes was drawn up and down the city by an uproarious whooping and cheering crowd. He 'protested' that he was the King's prisoner and this was all most irregular. Eventually he was taken to a tavern for refreshment and, late at night, managed to get away to knock up the prison governor and demand admission!

Weeks passed and the prison was daily besieged by thousands of Wilkites, their excitement kept up by a well-organised plan of action worked out by an informal council of war held daily in Wilkes' cell. When Wilkes appeared before Mansfield again, the judge cancelled the outlawry on the absurd grounds that the writ had been made out 'at the County Court for the County of Middlesex' rather than 'at the County Court of Middlesex for the County of Middlesex'. Mansfield, transparently afraid of the consequences of condemning Wilkes, had fled from responsibility.

This put Wilkes back to where he was in 1764, but he still had to face the original charges of seditious libel and obscenity. Wilkes had been tried and condemned in his absence, so all Mansfield had to do was pass sentence – a £500 fine for each publication and twenty-two months' imprisonment.

Smarting from their public ridicule, the Government determined on strong action. The Secretary for War in exasperation ordered the troops around the prison to stop at nothing to keep order. A party of Scots Guards fired on the crowd, killing several innocent bystanders and, worse still, pursued a stone-thrower, mistook another boy for him and foolishly killed him – an event instantly dubbed in folklore as the 'St George's Fields Massacre'. An inquest jury found the soldier who fired the shot guilty of murder and two others guilty of abetting. A grand jury at Guildford Assizes, packed with Government supporters, threw out the charges, but Wilkes scored another victory, publishing pamphlets accusing the Government of using Scotch butchers to intimidate free-born Englishmen.

Months of disorder then ensued, exacerbated by economic distress and strikes – explosive forces which, when combined with Wilkes' inflammatory squibs, created a dangerous instability. Prison for Wilkes was not an effective cage. He lacked for nothing – had excellent rooms and servants, was able to use the shops, coffee-house and tavern which existed inside the walls and enjoyed an unlimited supply of visitors. Admirers all over the country and even across the Atlantic sent lavish gifts of food, drink and tobacco. Other necessaries were also forthcoming – women as sightseers, conversationalists and providers of more basic services, both amateur and professional.

Despite incarceration, he was now an MP again and irrepressibly bent on further mischief. He contemptuously spurned the deal offered by the Prime Minister, the Duke of Grafton, whereby the Government would not interfere with his taking his seat if he agreed to be quiet – in particular, agreeing to abandon any idea of questioning the legality of his past treatment.

His belligerent response was, immediately upon the opening of the new session, to present a general petition to Parliament against the whole of his treatment. To this was added another petition, complaining of Mansfield's bias in a case brought against him for libelling the Secretary of State, Lord Weymouth, for his role in inciting the St George's Fields Massacre. To nobody's surprise the House rejected the petitions, which were adjudged scandalous and seditious. The Government then obtained his expulsion from the House on the triple grounds of libelling the King and the Government, and publishing an obscene poem.

Wilkes was not in the least abashed by this turn of events. Indeed, he rather welcomed further martyrdom. Eighteenth-century politics was largely an affair of faction and Wilkes was able to rely on the support of great men like Shelburne and Chatham who were now in opposition. The immediate consequence was his election as an Alderman of the City and then re-election to Parliament for Middlesex unopposed and at no expense to himself. Two thousand Wilkite electors presented themselves at Brentford on polling day in case they were needed and Wilkes' unopposed return was received with rapture, with illuminated and musical celebratory processions taking place all over London.

Idiotically, Grafton had not contemplated the possibility of the people re-electing Wilkes in the by-election caused by his expulsion. Wilkes' exuberance now knew no bounds and, far from being defeated and discouraged, every new blow by the Government was returned with greater insolence and defiance. He told the electors of Middlesex: 'If Ministers can once usurp the power of declaring who shall not be your representative, the next step is very easy and will follow speedily. It is that of telling you whom you shall send to Parliament.'

Stung into rage by Wilkes' success, the House voted the very next day to expel him yet again and to declare him 'incapable of being elected a Member'. This foolish move made a serious difficulty worse as it cut off any avenue of retreat for the Government. The effect was to make it a contempt of Parliament for anyone to nominate, vote for or even to receive votes for Wilkes. Everyone, including the Returning Officers for Middlesex, stood in danger of being sent to Newgate. This threat was so extreme as to be unenforceable against the numbers and interests to which it applied. Hence, the House and the

Government contrived to make themselves look even more foolish and impotent than before.

A third time Wilkes defied the House and stood again for election. This time the Government had difficulty in finding a candidate to oppose him and, when one was found, after enduring an hour of personal abuse and aspersions upon his legitimacy at the hustings, not a single elector could be found who was willing to nominate him. Amid laughter and rejoicing Wilkes was then elected for the third time. The following day the House of Commons obstinately expelled Wilkes yet again and ordered yet another election.

In this fourth election candidates were procured to stand against him. Foremost amongst them as the main Government protagonist was Colonel Luttrell, already sitting as MP for Bosinney, a Cornish pocket borough of Lord Bute's with only twenty-five voters. Luttrell had a reputation for personal violence, bilking his mistresses and seducing the innocent – having kidnapped an eleven-year-old girl, debauched her and avoided prosecution by bribing witnesses to swear she was already a prostitute. He was also accused of lapse of taste for turning up at Mrs Cornelys' masque dressed as a corpse, complete with shroud and a coffin decorated with a plate recording that its occupant had died of venereal disease contracted in his hostess's house. Finally, he was on the worst of terms with his father, Lord Irnham, whose challenge to a duel he had once refused on grounds that 'Lord Irnham was not a gentleman'!

Wilkes was elected with the runaway majority of 1,143 to 296, only for the House immediately to expel him a fourth time and then take the further extreme step of declaring that Luttrell was duly elected. Burke called it 'the fifth act of a tragi-comedy acted by His Majesty's servants, at the desire of several persons of quality, for the benefit of Mr Wilkes and at the expense of the constitution'. Supporters of Wilkes then toured the country to drum up popular support and a public fund was set up to pay his enormous debts whilst he still languished in prison. From this unlikely position Wilkes had achieved his object – monopolising the political system for two solid years, undermining the whole

Establishment, from the King downwards, and establishing himself as the undisputed leader of democracy.

At this point there could well have been a revolution if only Wilkes had been a revolutionary. But he was not. He wanted to restore the constitution not overthrow it. He would harry the King and his Ministers but always keep 'just to windward of the law'. He was also far too much of a hedonist to crave power, with its concomitant responsibility. Where apple carts were concerned his instinct was to upset them not drive them.

In 1770 Wilkes was released from prison and, now denied a place in Parliament, he sought a power base instead in the City of London, becoming an alderman and Master of the Joiners' Company. From this vantage point he chose his next battleground – freedom of the press. Relishing a further assault on the Commons, he took up the cudgels on behalf of three printers summoned to the Bar of the House for the temerity of publishing reports of its debates without permission. The House theoretically forbade such reports so as to protect MPs from the indecencies of democratic pressure. But, in practice, this proscription had been ignored to such an extent that even as strong a Tory upholder of the established order as Dr Johnson scratched a hack living from writing Parliamentary reports. Johnson, however, did not actually break the rules, as he generally did not bother to attend a debate before putting pen to paper and, in concocting the supposed speeches, he 'took care that the Whig dogs should not have the best of it'.

But the ferment caused by Wilkes' exertions revived democratic fears. Summoned by the Speaker, the printers made themselves scarce. A Speaker's warrant was then issued for their arrest and a Commons messenger sent to the City to execute it. Battle was now joined, the messenger himself was arrested, charged with assault and brought before the sitting magistrate – none other than Alderman Wilkes himself. He was duly remanded and not released until the Deputy Serjeant at Arms angrily arrived to stand bail for him.

The Commons were stung once more by Wilkes' impudence into an ill-advised violent reaction. Brass Crosby (the Lord

Mayor) and two aldermen, Wilkes and Oliver, were summoned to the Bar of the House to answer for their insolence. Wilkes, unabashed, refused to accept the summons unless it was made out to him as MP for Middlesex and sent an insolent reply to the Speaker to that effect.

Wilkes was a mad dog and the House had no wish to be bitten again. Prudently, it was decided to take action only against Crosby and Oliver, both of whom were MPs. North hoped to avoid a popular disturbance by bringing them to Westminster by water. But Crosby determined to milk the situation for all it was worth. He arrived at Palace Yard in his state coach, drawn and escorted by an enormous mob. Riddled with gout, he hobbled to his place and rose to wave in the Speaker's face the City charter and the City magistrates' oaths, bellowing out, 'I could not have acted otherwise without violating my oath and my duty and shall always glory in having done so, be the consequences what they will.'

Several days of bitter debate ensued, attended by riots outside the House, in which Lord North was dragged from his smashed coach, his hat pulled to pieces and sold for souvenirs, while the portly Charles James Fox was rolled in the gutter. At the end Crosby and Oliver were sent to the Tower for contempt. But that was not the end.

Wilkes, openly boasting of originating the fracas, was thought by the Government too hot to handle. But he was not prepared to indulge their cowardice and primed a radical MP to propose that he be summoned to the Bar. Furthermore, in order to maximise the potential uproar, he moved from Westminster to the City, where his arrest would create most trouble. Faced with this defiance and at last learning by bitter experience, the Government beat a hasty if ignominious retreat. Wilkes was summoned to appear before them on 8 April and then the Commons speedily voted to adjourn until the 9th!

Crosby and Oliver were then automatically released from the Tower by the House rising and the printers were not further proceeded against. Thus, the Commons effectively retired in defeat, exhausted by Wilkes' endurance and ingenuity in provoking them to fight battles on boggy ground from which they could not extricate themselves with either dignity or honour. His incessant bastinados painfully disrupted the timetable of the House, which sat regularly until three or four in the morning discussing his affairs, dividing time after time after time. For these tumultuous affairs the House would be full, whereas barely half a House could be mustered for debates on the serious developments in America. The Speaker, Sir John Cust, was also a victim. Having no deputy, he was obliged to remain in his chair sometimes for sixteen hours at a stretch. As a result of the stress induced by Wilkes he developed various internal disorders, of which he died whilst still a comparatively young man in 1770.

Wilkes now turned his attentions to the City and resolved to become Lord Mayor. By the curious electoral system, the members of the City livery companies had to present two candidates from whom the court of aldermen would choose one. However, Wilkes had fallen out with several powerful aldermen, not least because it was easier for him to keep hot coals in his mouth than a witticism, which might often be at the expense of more pompous and slow-witted City colleagues. Despite topping the poll he was vetoed twice.

It looked as though the Luttrell case was about to be repeated in the City. Wilkes responded with traditional intransigence by announcing that, if so, he would be a perpetual candidate, choosing annually a new running mate and, if he could not become Lord Mayor himself, at least he should dictate who would. In 1774 Wilkes stood and topped the poll a third time, with the current Lord Mayor, Frederick Bull, again as his running-mate. The narrow majority of anti-Wilkites on the court of aldermen prepared to frustrate Wilkes yet again by re-electing Bull.

But Wilkes' fertile brain had anticipated them and the reason for his choosing Bull a second time quickly became apparent. He brought out an Act of the City's Common Council from the reign of Henry VIII and read it to them. This forbade the aldermen from electing the same person two years running. As Bull was ineligible, Wilkes won by default, an event which was greeted once more with rumbustious acclaim by the mob on the streets.

To cap everything, within a few weeks Parliament was dissolved and Wilkes was at last re-elected for Middlesex, accompanied by a dozen Wilkites for various constituencies.

Horace Walpole reflected on this amazing switchback journey:

> Does there not seem to be a fatality attending the Court whenever they meddle with that man? What instance is there of such a demagogue maintaining a war against a King, Ministries, Courts of Law, a whole legislature and all Scotland for nine years together? Wilkes in prison is chosen Member of Parliament and then Alderman of London. His colleagues betray him, desert him, expose him and he becomes Sheriff of London. I believe if he was to be hanged he would be made King of England.

The truth of the matter was that his popularity arose as much from the stupidity of his opponents as from his undoubted skill in capitalising upon it. In his hour of victory Wilkes said of his outlawry in 1764, 'If the King had sent me a pardon and £1000 to Paris, I should have accepted them, but I am obliged to him for not having ruined me.'

Ultimately success put him out of business. Deprived of his martyrdom and the leadership of the mob, he was nothing and, as things turned out, he was ruined by respectability. For several years Wilkes made constructive proposals for reforms which had to wait yet a half century and more to be adopted, but speechifying in a serious way in the House of Commons was not his forte.

By a startling paradox his political career was effectively ended by his opposition to an outbreak of mob violence led by an intractable demagogue. The anti-Catholic riots of 1780, led by his fellow MP Lord George Gordon, enveloped the City in flames. Wilkes strongly disapproved of religious intolerance and recognised that the riot must be put down or else the City would be razed to the ground.

Here the two traditional foundations of Wilkes' support at last parted company. The City merchants, frightened by the holocaust, clamoured for the riots to be suppressed regardless of the cost to the rioters, and were cured for some time of support for any popular agitation, however noble the cause. The mob, on the other hand, with cheerful intolerance, persecuted Catholics and enjoyed the destruction as a street festival.

The mob were Wilkites almost to a man but they cared nothing for Wilkes' principled tolerance. As an alderman, he was partly responsible for law and order in the City and his decision to quell the rioting by firing on the mob destroyed his erstwhile power base on the streets.

Wilkes became immediately, in his own words, 'an extinct volcano' and thereafter did little positive other than propose the rescinding of the resolution of 1769, which had expelled him as 'subversive of the rights of the whole body of this Kingdom'. At last in 1782 he succeeded in getting a majority and his last ambition was achieved.

Disgusted by the cynicism of a Government of irreconcilable opposites led by Fox and North, Wilkes gave support to Pitt the Younger who became the King's First Minister in 1784. Thus, in not the least eccentric development in Wilkes' career, he was transformed into a tacit supporter of the King. Before too long Wilkes was seen in conversation with George III amongst other supporters at his levees. The Wilkites and official Whigs could not conceal their indignation.

At Carlton House Wilkes also attended upon the Prince of Wales, who detested his father. Called upon to give a toast after dinner Wilkes proposed 'The King – Long life to him.' The Prince was astonished and annoyed and asked Wilkes, 'Since when have you been so anxious over my parent's health?' 'Since I had the pleasure of Your Royal Highness' acquaintance!' he replied sweetly with a bow.

Wilkes' eccentricity lay in his absolute fearlessness and his positive aversion to reasonableness. Indeed, he always positively chose the most reckless and dangerous option, which inevitably enabled him to take the slow-witted enemy by surprise. He gloried in contrariness and advised a Parliamentary aspirant: 'Be as impudent as you can and say whatever comes uppermost.'

He affected a hardened cynicism and spoke of his constituents as 'those Middlesex fools'. He once whispered to the Speaker, 'I've come to present a Petition from a set of the greatest scoundrels on earth.' Yet, within seconds, he was rising to his feet and unctuously declaring, 'Sir, I hold in my hand a Petition from a most intelligent, independent and enlightened body of men . . .'

Again, in speaking to his own motion to rescind all the Commons' resolutions regarding the Middlesex election, he asserted that by proposing his expulsion Lord North had committed high treason against Magna Carta, but assured North in an audible aside, 'I only said that to please the fellows who follow me.'

He never could resist the temptation to flout convention or poke fun, even at his own acolytes, and was a curious mixture of opposites. Cultivated and civilised, he surrounded himself with diamonds of a rougher sort, who often served as butts for his barbed wit. Once watching with amusement an alderman attack a steak with plebeian vigour he joked: 'See the difference between the City and a Bear Garden. There the bear is brought to the stake; here the steak is brought to the bear.'

At another City banquet a fellow diner pulled off his wig, put on his nightcap and asked Wilkes if it looked all right, eliciting the charming reply: 'Very well, Sir, but it would be better pulled right over your face.' When another said pleasantly how remarkable that he should have been born in the first minutes of New Year's Day, Wilkes riposted, 'Not at all, for you could have been conceived only on April the first!'

It was his wicked wit which transformed him from a mere nuisance into a danger to tyranny, but he always remained paradoxical and unpredictable. The best epitome of his most serious political eccentricity lies in his own words. George III asked him one day a question about Serjeant Glynn, who had defended him in his great constitutional law cases and was later his colleague as MP for Middlesex. Wilkes twinkled and said, 'Oh, Sir, he was a Wilkite – which, as Your Majesty knows, I never was.'

ANTHONY HENLEY

MP FOR SOUTHAMPTON 1729–41

'I have found another constituency to buy.'

The great merit of the eighteenth-century practice of buying
seats in Parliament was that it produced many MPs of robustly
independent character. Today the role of an MP is largely
reduced to that of a glorified social welfare officer, most MPs
being slaves to their constituency correspondence and
'surgeries'. Two centuries ago this was unheard of.

Votes were then solicited only at infrequent elections and, in a
'rotten borough', it was not necessary to have any contact with
the residents at all – all that was required was to secure the
support of the patron or corporation who controlled it. Today,
MPs treat even the most minor or tiresome single-interest
pressure group with exaggerated respect. But, in the days of the
unreformed Parliaments before 1832, MPs demanded respect
from, rather than gave it to, their constituencies.

Anthony Henley stands out even among eighteenth-century
MPs for his eccentric independence in relation to his electors. In
the 1730s he received a respectful request from them that he vote
against some tax change proposed in the Budget. This was his
response:

Gentlemen,
I have received your letter about the Excise and I am
surprised at your insolence in writing to me at all. You know,

as I know, that I bought this constituency. You know and I know that I am now determined to sell it, and you know, what you think I don't know – that you are looking out for another buyer. And I know what you certainly don't know – that I have found another constituency to buy.

About what you said about the Excise: may God's curse light upon you and may it make your women as open and as free to the excise officers as your wives and daughters have always been to me whilst I have represented your scoundrel corporation.

I have the honour to be, my dear Sirs, ever your obliged humble servant,

ANTHONY HENLEY

Anthony Henley.

1ST MARCHIONESS OF SALISBURY

1750–1835

'Damn you, my Lady! Jump!'

In the famous Westminster election of 1784 Lady Salisbury was the Tory equivalent of Georgiana, Duchess of Devonshire. A woman of spirit, she was conscious of her rank and wished others to know it too. She was not up to kissing butchers, and so was less successful in wooing the voters than the duchess.

Nevertheless, she shocked the strait-laced by her hunting, free-spoken talk, extravagance and gambling. She shocked conventional opinion by holding card-parties on Sunday evenings and concert parties earlier in the day to conflict with the times of Hatfield church services. The Rector of Hatfield himself often fell victim to their attractions. Just before the service was due to begin, he would look up and down the street to see if anyone was coming. If not, he would quickly lock the door and beetle off to face the music.

Occasionally Lady Salisbury did go to church, for social reasons. Arriving late at the Chapel Royal in London once, she found the place full. One of her daughters asked: 'Where shall we go, Mamma?' 'Home again, to be sure,' she replied, 'if we cannot get in, it is no fault of ours – we have done the civil thing.'

At Hatfield church on another occasion she heard the story of Adam and Eve for the first time. She was outraged to learn that Adam had blamed Eve when rebuked by God for eating of the Tree of Knowledge. When she heard Adam's excuse: 'The woman tempted me and I did eat,' she exclaimed in a loud voice, 'A shabby fellow, indeed.'

At the Handel Festival, held in Westminster Abbey in the presence of George III and Queen Charlotte, she arrived late and sat in the box erected for the Lord Chamberlain's party. Shortly afterwards, the music was interrupted by a loud hammering and banging. The King asked what on earth was happening – to be told that Lady Salisbury, finding her box divided in two by an inconvenient partition, had sent for the Abbey carpenters to dismantle it at once.

She resolutely refused to accept the infirmities of age, surrounded herself with young people and modelled her dress and behaviour on theirs. At the age of eighty she still insisted on going out hunting. Though her spirit was willing, the flesh was increasingly weak. To avoid falling off her horse, she had herself strapped onto it. The horse, in turn, was attached by a leading-rein to a groom, because she was too blind to see where it was going. Every time they came to a hedge the groom would shout out 'Damn you, my Lady! Jump!' and over they went.

Her death was as spectacular as her life. Late one evening a servant dashed in to tell young Lord Salisbury that clouds of smoke were pouring out of his mother's bedroom in the West Wing. They ran out to find it in a blaze, whipped up by a high wind. They tried again and again to fight their way through the flames but the fire was too fierce. It raged for several hours, until the wind suddenly changed and it could finally be got under control. By then the West Wing was a shell of rubble and all that remained of Lady Salisbury was a few charred bones.

At the inquest it was thought that the fire had started at the top of her head. She had habitually worn her hair piled high and decorated with feathers, after the fashion of her youth. Getting up from a table, this highly combustible tower on top of her head must have caught in a chandelier and started the blaze that consumed her.

CHARLES JAMES FOX

MP FOR MIDHURST 1768–74, MALMESBURY
1774–80, KIRKWALL BURGHS 1784–5,
WESTMINSTER 1780–1806

*'Fox was never normal. When he did not rise above
accepted standards, he fell below them.'*

Charles James Fox combined a great, if chaotic, political career
with a personal life which was eccentric even by the standards of
eighteenth-century rakes. A prince of excess in an age of glorious
self-indulgence, immediately upon coming of age he applied
himself systematically to dissipating one of the largest fortunes
of his age.

Born to position as well as wealth, his father, Lord Holland,
was a key member of the governments of the 1750s and 1760s.
So he had no difficulty in parachuting young Charles into
Parliament in 1768 as MP for Midhurst. He was only nineteen,
eighteen months short of the legal qualification for election.
An indulgent House of Commons conveniently ignored the
fact that, as an 'infant', he was technically ineligible to sit.

Constituents were even less of a problem – for the simple
reason that his constituency had not a single resident voter. The
right to vote in Midhurst depended on occupying one of a
handful of specific smallholdings. No human being lived on any
of them and each was distinguishable amongst the surrounding
pasture and stubble only by a large stone set up on its end in the
middle as a marker.

Every one had been bought up by a single proprietor, Lord
Montagu. Whenever an election loomed he temporarily assigned

a few tenements to his servants, told them whom to nominate as the town's two MPs and after the 'election' they assigned the land back to him. Hence Fox was duly 'elected' without ever having visited his constituency – indeed at the time he was too busy amusing himself on the Grand Tour in Italy, where he remained for another six months.

However, he immediately made his reputation as an extempore orator and by the age of twenty-one had become the youngest member of the Government. But although one of the most gifted, he was also one of the idlest men of his age and took to heart his father's maxim: 'Never do today what you can put off till tomorrow, or ever do yourself what you can get anyone else to do for you.'

Lord Holland anticipated by two centuries the theories of child development which became fashionable in the 1960s. 'Young people,' he said, 'are always in the right and old people in the wrong.' So, if Charles wished to stamp on his father's gold watch, wash his hands in a bowl of cream at dinner or deliberately smudge the ink on Government papers, his father would just sigh indulgently, 'Very well. If you must, I suppose you must.'

At Oxford Charles combined serious study with heavy gambling and whoring. At the age of eighteen he wrote to his cousin, 'I have had one pox and one clap this summer. I believe I am the most unlucky rascal in the universe.' The following summer he was in Nice, 'perhaps the dullest town in the world, and what is a terrible thing, there are no whores...my poxes and claps have weakened me a good deal, but by means of the cold bath I recover apace.'

In the eighteenth century, politics was a very different profession from today. In those days there was real money to be made. Lord Holland acquired fabulous riches from the office of Paymaster-General. As he was responsible for the whole of the money voted by Parliament for the land forces of the Crown, vast sums of money passed through his hands. These he could, quite legitimately, treat as though he were a private banker, pocketing the interest on the bank deposits and also, if he invested any of the money successfully, keeping any capital profits made. The scale of the operation was colossal. As Paymaster during the Seven Years' War, £49.5 million washed through his accounts – equivalent to nearly a third of the national debt. Some of it was still in the hands of his executors nine years after his death and eighteen years after he had resigned.

How different from the practice of a more recent Paymaster-General, Geoffrey Robinson – who, far from using the office to amass a vast private fortune for himself at the public expense, took no salary at all and appeared to be paying for the rest of the Government out of his own pocket! Lord Holland spent years in office quite lawfully lining his own pockets, whereas Robinson was hounded out for digging into them!

Holland decided Eton was not providing the fourteen-year-old Charles with a broad enough education. So he sent him to Spa for four months to learn how to gamble, with five guineas a night to lose at the tables. On his return to Eton Charles spread the fever of gambling like an epidemic, prompting Pitt the Elder to remark: 'Holland educated his children without the least regard to morality and with such extravagant vulgar indulgence that the great change which has taken place among our youth has been dated from his son's going to Eton.'

In adult life Fox showed he had fully mastered the art of reckless profligacy for which his education had uniquely fitted him. On one occasion he played faro at Almack's club for twenty-two consecutive hours, from 7 p.m. on Tuesday till 5 p.m. on Wednesday, losing on balance £11,000. On Thursday, after speaking and voting in a debate on the Thirty-Nine Articles (where Horace Walpole noted, unsurprisingly, he 'did not shine'), he went to dinner at past 11 p.m. He then sat up all night drinking at White's until seven the next morning, when he crossed the road to Almack's, winning back £6,000 before leaving for Newmarket between three and four on Friday afternoon.

In only three or four years he demolished a vast fortune. At Almack's the play was very deep – there was usually £10,000 on the table and 50 guineas often the minimum stake. Even after two hundred years' inflation (multiply the figures by 200) some individuals' losses beggar belief. One profligate lost £70,000 and his carriages in one night, after which Fox proposed to pay him an annuity from the pool on condition that he left cards alone. Where money was concerned Fox suffered from powerful centrifugal forces. He and his brother, Stephen, once lost £32,000 in three nights.

Had he gambled on his knowledge and skill he might have made a good living. He was a superlative whist player and an excellent judge of form on the turf, frequently returning from Newmarket £10–15,000 up. But ease of winning seemed to mar the excitement. He preferred games of pure chance, like faro, where his losses were so huge that his sizeable winnings elsewhere disappeared like droplets into a raging torrent.

He was quite bloodless about financial catastrophe. After one particularly disastrous night at Almack's he had lost so much money that a close friend thought he might commit suicide and followed him home to his lodgings as a precaution. Far from slitting his throat, he was astonished to find Fox calmly engrossed in reading Herodotus in ancient Greek. There was no answer to his cheery riposte: 'Well, what would you have a man do, who has lost his last shilling?'

Charles was a second son but, whilst his elder brother remained childless, the security of being heir presumptive to the Holland millions was comforting enough to lenders and he had no trouble borrowing to finance his losses. So great was the throng of duns at Fox's house every day that a special room had to be set aside for them which, in a sarcastic reference to omnipresent Jewish moneylenders, he dubbed his 'Jerusalem Chamber'.

Then, in 1773, disaster struck. His elder brother produced a son and heir. This caused consternation in the ranks of Charles' creditors because it destroyed his reversionary inheritance. However, he just joked on hearing the news, 'Brother Ste's son is a second Messiah, born for the destruction of the Jews!'

Those who had previously queued so solicitously to lend now struggled desperately to salvage whatever they could. Every creditor jumped upon him – and not just the professional loan sharks. His friends who had stood him security and would now be crippled; tradesmen, servants, even sedan-chairmen whose shillings he had cadged on the way home from a nocturnal revel – all faced ruin themselves with the apocalyptic destruction of his credit.

Lord Holland, recognising his culpability in promoting his son's spendthrift habits, stepped in. He gave instructions 'to sell and dispose of my long annuities and so much of my other stock, estates and effects, as will be sufficient to pay and discharge the debts of my son the Honble. Charles James Fox, not exceeding the sum of £100,000'. But even this staggering estimate proved wildly optimistic and inadequate. The debts finally weighed in at over £140,000 – equivalent to perhaps £30 million today. Charles was twenty-four years old.

In 1774 Fox was obliged to exchange Midhurst for Malmesbury. As one of his biographers pointed out, this was 'a more democratic constituency, where the ratio of MPs to voters was 2 to 13'. By 1780 he had fallen out with his patron at Malmesbury on account of a transfer of political loyalties, but a new patron offered him a safe seat at Bridgwater. He accepted this but preferred, if possible, to sit for the most democratic (because most populous) seat in the country, Westminster.

A hotly contested election in the eighteenth century was a long orgy of noise, drunkenness, corruption, bullying and general rowdiness. He threw himself enthusiastically into electioneering, publishing daily squibs and haranguing crowds at every opportunity. He turned himself into 'The Man of the People' and was uproariously elected.

Four years later another election was called. The Westminster election of 1784 surpassed all others in rowdiness and noise. Charges of lying, bribery, fraud and violence were made on both sides. Bands and processions constantly marched and counter-marched. They fought daily with fists and sticks. In one battle 'a gang of fellows, headed by naval officers and carrying His Majesty's colours' (as Foxites described them) met in pitched battle with 'Irish chairmen and pickpockets' (as described by Government agents). In another, a constable who had harmed no one was killed and each party strove energetically to fix the blame on the 'banditti of ruffians' on the other side.

Today all voting takes place on one day. Before modern transport and communications, it might extend over several weeks, as travelling to the polling booth could be a lengthy undertaking with a far-flung constituency. At Westminster in 1784 the poll was open for forty days.

Until the eleventh day, when Fox was 318 votes behind, he lost ground. Then his fortune turned, due to the energetic canvassing of the Duchess of Devonshire and her sister, Lady Duncannon. The duchess wore a hat draped with fox-tails and covered herself from head to toe in buff and blue, the colours which Fox adopted from Washington's uniform and defiantly wore in the Commons throughout the American war. She flew around from 8 a.m. till dark, bringing tradesmen and navvies to the poll, swapping kisses for votes where necessary. Fox's friends gathered every day to support him, including the Prince of Wales, who appeared with a badge of laurel and a fox's brush, escorted by a guard of prizefighters.

A week before the poll closed Pitt, leader of the Tories, was given the Freedom of the City of London and entertained afterwards at a City dinner presided over by John Wilkes. On his return to Westminster he was led along by a spirited mob of supporters, attracting more and more along the way. The uproarious procession turned up St James's Street from Pall Mall, at which point the leading marchers decided to try to force the occupants of Brooks's club (the HQ of Fox and the Whigs) to illuminate their windows in Pitt's honour.

The club held a council of war and determined to resist. The club servants were gathered and sent to attack the mob from the front door with bludgeons and broken chair poles whilst club members hurled missiles at them from the upper windows. A violent battle then ensued with Foxites shouting 'Fox and popular government.' The Pittites retaliated with 'Pitt and the Constitution' whilst enthusiastically smashing the windows of the Temple of Whiggism. Beating a hasty retreat from the mêlée Pitt escaped into the calmer waters of the Tory citadel, White's club, opposite whilst his carriage was smashed into splinters by the enthusiasts of Fox.

Fox himself was suspected of having directed the riot, but was able to rebut the charge with not only a cast-iron alibi appropriate to his rackety lifestyle but a witness too: 'I was in bed with Mrs Armistead – who is ready to substantiate the fact on oath.'

On the fortieth day the poll was closed. The result was: Hood 6,694, Fox 6,234, Wray 5,998. Fox was re-elected with Hood. But there then followed another exhausting part of the proceedings – chairing the Member. The procession set off from the hustings at St Paul's Covent Garden to Charing Cross, along Pall Mall and St James's Street, up Piccadilly, round Berkeley Square and into Devonshire House courtyard. It was an impressive sight:

Heralds on horseback
Twenty four Marrow-bones and Cleavers
The Arms of Westminster
Thirty Freemen of Westminster
Martial Music
Committees of the Seven Parishes with white wands,
following their respective banners and attended by
numberless
Gentlemen of the Several Districts
Squadron of Gentlemen on Horseback in the Blue and
Buff uniform
Trumpets
Flag. The RIGHTS of the COMMONS
Grand Band of Music
Flag. THE MAN OF THE PEOPLE
Marshals on Foot
TRIUMPHAL CHAIR
Decorated with laurels in which was seated
The Right Hon. CHARLES JAMES FOX
Trumpets
Flag. The WHIG CAUSE
Second squadron of Horse
Liberty Boys of Newport Market
Mr FOX's Carriage crowned with Laurels

Banner. Sacred to Female Patriotism!
Blue standard inscribed
INDEPENDENCE
State Carriages of the Graces
The Duchesses of PORTLAND and DEVONSHIRE
drawn by six horses superbly caparisoned, with six
running
footmen attendant on each
Gentlemen's servants, closing the Procession, two and two
etc.

At Devonshire House the Prince of Wales waited on a specially erected platform, from which Fox thanked his six thousand supporters. Then on to dinner at Willis's Rooms, where more speeches were made, new songs 'full of applicable points' were sung and the night 'spent with unusual exhilaration'.

On the next day the Prince of Wales held a morning fete at Carlton House. After a breakfast in marquees decorated with devices 'equally expressive of the political principles and the gallantry of his Highness' the company danced in the garden, pleasurably conscious that the sounds of their rejoicings were audible in the Mall, where the King was passing in state to open the new Parliament.

The celebrations were a litle premature. Wray petitioned against the result, preventing Fox from taking his seat. Fox, however, had the foresight to guard against this possibility by securing election simultaneously for Kirkwall Burghs, where he was returned unopposed. So, although he had triumphed in Parliament's home constituency of Westminster, he actually took his seat in the new Parliament for the most distant constituency of all – despite never in his life getting closer to it than a jaunt to Doncaster races for the St Leger.

In hotly contested elections petitions were common. Personation and sharp practice were rife and a scrutiny could be protracted and expensive, as it involved not just a simple recount but an examination of the electoral qualifications of all the voters. In Old Sarum, with only seven voters or Midhurst, with apparently none at all, this was no problem. But in Westminster, with many thousands, it meant chaos and confusion. The matter was debated in the House several times, the Government's majority steadily dropping. After eight months and an eighth of the poll scrutinised (with costs of £10,000 to each party), Fox's supporters outvoted the Government and stopped it with Fox's vote reduced from 6,234 to 6,126 and Wray's from 5,998 to 5,895, a net difference of five!

Fox was not a successful politician – he was handicapped by honesty and lack of self-control. He was also short, fat, swarthy and unwashed. Horace Walpole described him in 1783: '...he rose very late, he had a levee of his followers and of the Gaming Club at Brooks's, all his disciples. His bristly, black person and shagged breast quite open, and rarely purefied by any ablutions, was wrapped in a foul linen night-gown and his bushy hair dishevelled.'

Ill-groomed, impulsive, gregarious and libidinous, he was in every respect the opposite of his great rival, Pitt the Younger. Fox's private life was a squalid public debauch. George III loathed him for corrupting the morals of the Prince of Wales, to whom he had introduced his mistresses and whose favours he had even invited him to share.

Like his private life, Fox's Parliamentary career staggered chaotically around like a drunkard. At the start, his speeches lauded the perfection and inviolability of the constitution. In 1771 he declared, 'What acquaintance have the people at large with the arcana of political rectitude, with the connexions of Kingdoms, the resources of national strength, the abilities of Ministers, or even with their own dispositions. I pay no regard whatever to the voice of the people.' He even canvassed in Middlesex for Luttrell against Wilkes, defending the rights of Parliament against the people. Yet ten years later he was proclaiming himself the voice of the people.

When elected in 1768 he was a supporter of Lord North, who put him in the Government at the age of twenty. Yet within a short time he had resigned to oppose a measure which virtually no one could care a fig about, the Royal Marriages Bill (which compelled all the descendants of George II to seek the King's consent before marrying). Reinstated soon afterwards, Fox provoked an unnecessary crisis by arrogantly forcing the Government into another unwanted Wilkite confrontation over freedom of the press. This led to a highly embarrassing House of Commons defeat, in which Lord North, then Prime Minister, was obliged unwillingly to support Fox but simultaneously advised all other Ministers to vote the other way.

In the 1770s Fox became a vitriolic opponent of Lord North, yet in 1782 he formed a shameless alliance with him despite their political convictions remaining diametrically opposed. Then, with the advent of Pitt, Fox emerged as the champion of the liberty of the subject and the press, apparently reversing all his earlier opinions so vehemently expressed in the struggle with Wilkes.

His political career was as strange as his personality. He was a junior Minister for two short periods, the first ending in unnecessary resignation and the second in dismissal unnecessarily provoked. Following that came a period in implacable opposition to the Prime Minister, Lord North, whom he had recently just as vigorously supported. Then, having destroyed North as a serious political figure, he formed an alliance with him to share temporarily the political leadership of the country.

Christopher Hobhouse, his most readable biographer, concluded that 'Fox was never normal. When he did not rise above the accepted standards of conduct, he fell below them.' Facile in debate, with an extemporary oratorical ability amounting to genius, he was also as incorrigibly idle as he was reckless. With public gifts as great as his personal failings, he united 'all that makes a statesman with all that can undo a politician'. Never bearing grudges or ill-will himself, he did not understand that others more thin-skinned could not forgive the violence of his language of criticism. His personality was a mass of contradictions and his personal judgements were abysmal. 'He was a bad hater, for he hated the wrong people. His best friendships were his worst mistakes.'

In 1806 both great rivals died, first Pitt and then Fox, each worn out by decades of alcoholic abuse. Pitt was only forty-seven, Fox fifty-seven. Pitt succumbed to cirrhosis of the liver and renal failure, a consequence of studious consumption of several bottles of port a day. Fox died of dropsy, his corpulent frame horribly distended by a lifetime of heroic self-indulgence.

Charles James Fox as Demosthenes.

LORD GEORGE GORDON

MP FOR LUDGERSHALL 1774–80

'He had got a twist in his head.'

Horace Walpole dismissed the entire Gordon family: 'They were and are all mad.' Lord George's mother, the Duchess of Gordon, had been a precocious eccentric – she habitually galloped madly down Edinburgh High Street on the back of a capering pig. Later, she married off three of her daughters to dukes and a fourth to a future marquess, gaily assuring him that there was 'not a drop of Gordon blood in Louisa's body'.

Her mother-in-law, wife of the 3rd Duke, was a Gordon by blood as well as marriage – increasing a tendency to insanity. She was described as looking like 'a raw-boned Scotch metaphysician that has got a red face by drinking water'. On her husband's early demise she conceived a violent passion for King Stanislas Poniatowski of Poland, whose grandmother had been a Gordon. Despite never having met him before, she invited him for tea.

She then sent for her two youngest children and dressed them up as cupids, each with a bow and a quiver full of silver arrows. When the King was shown into the drawing room he was assailed by a hail of arrows, one of which hit him on the head, narrowly missing his eye. The Duchess gazed on the scene from a sofa, where she was artistically reclining in a state of reverie. Lord George's première as a madcap had begun.

At the age of eight he became an ensign in his father's regiment, the 89th Foot, being promoted lieutenant at age ten.

However, upon leaving Eton, he joined the Navy as a midshipman. He discovered early the truth of Dr Johnson's dictum, 'No man will be a sailor who has contrivance enough to get himself into jail; for being in a ship is being in a jail, with the chance of getting drowned. The man in jail has more room, better food and commonly better company.'

He did not endear himself to the officers by complaining on behalf of the men, within days of first boarding his ship, that a consignment of ship's biscuits was infested with weevils and that the purser and naval suppliers were incompetent and probably dishonest.

Lord George Gordon.

In the West Indies he was horrified at the conditions in which the slaves lived on the sugar plantations and, in America, was impressed by its more meritocratic society. His attitudes resulting in a perpetually blocked promotion, he resolved to turn to politics and decided to seek election for Inverness-shire. He cultivated the constituency so assiduously and successfully that the sitting Member, General Fraser, became thoroughly alarmed. His father, Lord Lovat, was induced to speak to Gordon's brother, the Duke, to get him to stand down.

A compromise solution was arrived at – buy him a different seat, which would, in any case, be both cheaper and less troublesome than bribing all the voters of Inverness-shire. Thus, General Fraser arranged with George Selwyn, its owner, and Lord Melbourne, one of its two MPs, to buy the pocket borough of Ludgershall in Wiltshire. As all the votes in Ludgershall were included in the purchase Lord George did not need to visit it and the news of his election was brought to him whilst he was dining with his brother in London.

He said nothing in the Commons for three years. But, in due course, fluent though incoherent, he discovered that the more he spoke the more he enjoyed it. He cut a striking figure with long, lank hair and clad in puritan black with violently clashing plaid trousers. At first he was ranged against the Government, in due course he became completely erratic, vehemently attacking Lord North and the King's Friends one day and the next doing the same to the Opposition. His watchword was 'The Ministers have lost the confidence of the people and the Opposition have not found it.'

In 1779 he visited Scotland and was enthusiastically taken up by the various Protestant Associations founded to oppose a Bill which sought to abolish some of the legal penalties imposed on Roman Catholics. His language became increasingly wild and violent. He claimed in the Commons that the Scots were ripe for rebellion – 'they would prefer death to slavery and perish with arms in their hands or prevail in the contest'. In another speech he declared, '120,000 men at my back are convinced in their own minds the King is a papist'.

A frenetic atmosphere quickly developed, in which any preposterous rumour could be accepted as Gospel truth. Twenty thousand Jesuits were supposed to be hidden in a network of tunnels under the south bank of the Thames, ready at a moment's notice upon the order from Rome, to blow up the bed and banks of the river and flood London! In Southwark it was said that a band of Benedictine monks disguised as Irish sedan-chairmen had poisoned all the flour in the area and, for days, no one would touch any bread unless it had first been tested on a dog.

The Roman Catholic Bishop Hay returned to his house in Edinburgh to find a crowd setting fire to his chapel. He enquired of a woman spectator what was going on and received the alarming reply: 'We are burning the Popish chapel and we only wish we had the bishop to throw into the fire.'

On 24 January 1780 he spoke again in the House and insisted on reading out the whole of a long pamphlet 'much to the dislike of the House which, from near 200 Members, soon thinned to less than 50.' He attempted to repeat the exercise in the following day's debate, saying it was 'really so excellent that it ought to be read every day of the week'. The Speaker called him to order for 'tedious repetition', so Gordon changed tack and read out instead long extracts from newspapers. When he started for the second time to read the Declaratory Act of 1718 all the Members left the Chamber.

On 15 February he tried to embark upon another long harangue, but was prevailed upon to desist when told that the Speaker was too ill to endure it. He was, at this time, becoming more and more deranged in his utterances – on 8 March he announced that he had '160,000 men in Scotland at his command and that, if the King did not keep his coronation oath, they would do more than take away his Civil List revenue, they were determined to cut off his head'.

He demanded an audience of the King in January 1780, which the indulgent monarch granted despite the growing violence and derangement of Gordon's speeches. Gordon then proceeded to read aloud from a long pamphlet. Horace Walpole recorded the event:

The King had the patience to hear him do so for above an hour, till it was so dark that the lecturer could not see. His Majesty then desired to be excused and said he would finish the piece himself. 'Well,' said the lunatic apostle, 'but you must give me your honour that you will read it out.' The King promised, but was forced to pledge his honour. It is to be hoped that this man is so mad that it will soon come to perfection.

In the debate on 11 April 1780 Gordon was in the middle of a gabbled discourse on the state of popery in Ireland in 1626 when he was interrupted by Charles Turner: 'I cannot sit still and hear the noble lord run on at that rate. The noble lord is perpetually interrupting business and introducing matters directly personal. He had got a twist in his head, a certain whirligig which ran away with him if anything relative to religion was mentioned. I cannot bear to see the noble lord render himself a laughing stock and become the make-game of the whole House.'

Gordon paid no attention, continued by reading out extracts from yet another newspaper and told the House that his supporters 'had not yet determined to murder the King and put him to death; they only considered they were absolved from their allegiance'.

On 26 May he gave notice that he would present to Parliament the petition of the Protestant Association against religious toleration for Roman Catholics. A few days later he told a rapturous meeting of the Association that he was not a man to do things by halves and that he would not present the petition unless accompanied by a demonstration of at least twenty thousand men.

This reckless and extravagant demand was greeted with wild enthusiasm and arrangements were made for placing advertisements and publishing handbills to attract the largest possible crowd. Accordingly, on 2 June a vast concourse sixty thousand strong gathered in St George's Fields (now the site of Waterloo station) and marched in three columns, converging on the House of Commons from different directions via London, Blackfriars and Westminster Bridges.

A Westminster schoolboy described the crowd as

occupying every avenue to the Houses of Parliament, the whole of Westminster Bridge and extending to the northern end of Parliament Street. The greater part of it was composed of persons decently dressed, who appeared to be excited by extravagance, by a species of fanatical phrenzy. They talked of dying in the good cause, and manifested all the violence of the disposition imbibed under the banner of Presbyterianism. They had long lank heads of hair, meagre countenances, fiery eyes and they uttered deep ejaculations; in short, displaying all the outward and visible signs of hypocrisy and starvation.

The vast but peaceable gathering was augmented on its journey by hordes of ruffians, street-boys, pickpockets, prostitutes and drunken trouble-makers of all sorts. Orders were given by some unknown person to stop all unpopular members of the House of Lords, force them to put blue cockades on their hats and shout 'No Popery' twice before being allowed to continue.

First to arrive was the aged Lord Bathurst, Lord President of the Council and former Lord Chancellor. He was pulled from his carriage, hit across the face, pelted with mud and jeered at for being 'the Pope and a silly old woman'. The Duke of Northumberland's secretary, on account of his pale countenance and sombre black clothes, was mistaken for a Jesuit, dragged from his coach, kicked and beaten. Lord Mansfield, the Lord Chief Justice, had all his carriage windows smashed and his wig torn from his head. The Bishops of Lincoln and Lichfield had their gowns torn off and they were plastered with mud and excrement. From inside his coach Lord North had his hat grabbed. The enterprising thief then cut it into pieces and sold them for a shilling each.

The respectable part of the crowd, horrified at such excesses, began to drift away, leaving a precipitate of the most ignorant, bigoted and violent Protestant demonstrators to which were allied the criminals and ruffians, whose only interest lay in plunder and havoc. Samuel Romilly, believing 'there is much to be learned by studying human nature, even in its most humiliating and disgusting form', mingled with the crowd. He said they were 'the lowest rabble; men who without doubt, not only had never heard any of the arguments for or against toleration, but who were utterly ignorant of the very purpose of the petition. A miserable fanatic accosted me, questioning where my cockade was. When I very civilly informed him it had dropped out of my hat in the crowd, he told me that the reign of the Romans had lasted too long!'

The demonstration was undoubtedly illegal under the Tumultuous Petitioning Act of 1661. As it had been well advertised, the Government had anticipated trouble and orders were sent through Lord North to the magistrates of Westminster to quell any tumults which might take place. Unfortunately, the absent-minded Premier put the order in his pocket and promptly forgot it until two o'clock on the day, by which time the rabble were so numerous as to be uncontrollable.

The atmosphere in the Lords was alarming, as the mob surged and tried to batter down the doors. In the Commons, the position was even worse. The day had started calmly enough with consideration of amendments to the Hair Powder Bill. Then as the din grew from without, Members were forced to shout at each other in order to be heard. Eventually, Gordon rose to present his petition, signed by 120,000 and praying for the repeal of the Toleration Act passed the previous year, which horrified 'a populace determined to stand up for their rights against the pernicious effects of a religion, subversive of all liberty, inimical to all purity of morals, begotten by fraud and superstition and teeming with absurdity, persecution and the most diabolical cruelty'.

He moved that the petition should be considered immediately and a heated debate ensued, fuelled by indignation at the clamour and disorder outside. During its course Gordon, intoxicated by the frenzy which he had released, ran excitedly in and out of the Chamber and Lobby to report progress to the demonstrators: 'Lord North calls you a mob.' 'Mr Burke is now speaking. He is no friend to your petition,' and so on.

The Speaker's Chaplain pleaded with him to disperse the crowd, but he refused on grounds that any delay in dealing with the petition might cause it to be lost, if there were an imminent Dissolution of Parliament. Gordon thereupon went out to incite the mob once more, provoking Col. Holroyd, another Member, to tell him: 'My lord, at first I thought you were only mad; and was going to move that you might be sent to Bedlam; now I see there is much more malice than madness in this business. If you go once more to the mob I assure you upon the faith of Parliament I will instantly move that you be committed to the Tower.'

Other Members laid their hands on their swords and threatened to use them if the rabble tried to gain entry to the House itself. But Gordon was now in such transports of hysteria that nothing could induce him to reasonableness. He was drunk with the plaudits of the multitude and delirious with the belief that he led them as the general of an army of righteousness.

For six hours the debate continued amidst the hubbub. At 8 p.m. the vote was taken. Of the 196 MPs who had managed to reach the House only six voted with Gordon and his fellow teller, Alderman Bull. This crushing defeat provoked scenes of even greater menace and disorder and at this point the decision was taken to send for a party of Foot and Horse Guards to restore order.

Unfortunately, the effect was not as intended and seemed to incite the mob even more. The Foot Guards had their hats knocked off and their bottoms poked with sticks. One observer recorded that the crowd was

> wedged into such firm and compact masses that the cavalry were actually compelled to recede and return in a full gallop, in order to give their career sufficient force to penetrate them. The consequence was that after the cavalry had passed through them, the mob lay in the most ludicrous manner one over another like a pack of cards and the only accident of which I heard was a fractured leg.

This surprisingly improved the humour of the crowd, which agreed to disperse on condition that the soldiery were returned to barracks.

This was not the end, but only the curtain-raiser of the rioting. For six days thereafter the mob controlled the streets, looting, burning and pillaging. The Protestant Association issued appeals for calm and order and Gordon offered his services to Lord North. It was all to no avail. The complete collapse of civil order was swiftly followed by a collapse of civil authority. No magistrates could be found to read the Riot Act, without which it was erroneously thought that military action was unlawful. The streets were, therefore, given over to an orgy of arson, drunkenness and confusion. Newgate Prison was attacked and burnt and all the prisoners released. The houses of Lord Chief Justice Mansfield and the Archbishop of York were sacked. Hundreds of rioters were killed.

With the politicians apparently in a state of paralysis, the King insisted upon a proclamation enjoining all to help restore tranquillity and ordering troops to fire on the mob if felonies were being committed in their sight. Troops were rushed to London from all parts of the country. On 9 June Gordon was arrested and imprisoned in the Tower to await trial on charges of high treason.

His trial did not take place until February 1781. As a result of masterly cross-examination of prosecution witnesses by Kenyon and a brilliant closing speech by Erskine, both the leading counsel of their day, the jury acquitted him. Meanwhile, a General Election had taken place in September 1780, in which Gordon was unable to stand. Out of Parliament, he harboured hopes of a return but was overtaken by greater and greater eccentricity.

In 1781 he accepted nomination in a by-election in the City of London. But fear of further rioting had made him unelectable and he withdrew. He never stood for Parliament again but was always available as an orator for any Whig candidate who asked him. Like Wilkes he was more effective as a speaker before a crowd than in the Commons. But his name was more a liability than an asset, as most voters were property-owners and viewed with the greatest alarm mob violence fuelled by demagoguery. By contrast, the audiences with whom Gordon held greatest sway were largely voteless. Few candidates, therefore, called on his services – although Fox did in the Westminster election of 1784.

In May 1785 Gordon became convinced the Pope had sent two Jesuits to England to poison him and he wrote to the Foreign Secretary to demand protection. In August he wrote to Emperor Joseph II of Austria informing him that 'if you had paid due attention to the remarks I made on your ordinance against the Jews on 14 March 1782 you and your subjects would not be in such a state of distraction and plague as at this hour'

In 1788 he was prosecuted on two charges of libel. One involved a pamphlet he published on behalf of the prisoners of Newgate and which was alleged to be a libel on 'the Judges and Administration of the Laws of England'. The other involved two paragraphs he had inserted in the *Public Advertiser* attacking Queen Marie Antoinette of France and the French Ambassador.

Neither Kenyon nor Erskine was available to defend him so he made the disastrous error of defending himself.

He started his defence with an interminable and incoherent speech which included a lengthy summary of the history of English criminal law from the reign of King Athelstan. He had been persuaded to study these laws, he said, when a servant of his had been sent out to buy a fowl costing three shillings. The servant had said it cost 4s 6d and, having defrauded him of 1s 6d, had committed a capital offence. He had refused to hand the man over to the authorities because he had 'looked into the law of God and found it required no man's blood' and also believed capital punishment did not deter crime, a view which he 'communicated to His Majesty's Judges'. He had gone to Lord Mansfield, who would not receive him. Then he went to Mr Justice Gould, 'who had tears in his eyes' when he was talking about it and recommended he put his thoughts on paper. He went to the Recorder, who told him Parliament should take it up. He also went to Sheriff le Mesurier for permission to talk to condemned convicts. But, having tried to persuade him, he sent him away saying 'Pooh, Pooh! I shall not attend to it at all.'

At this point the judge intervened to ask what relevance any of this had to the charges against him. Gordon apologised and then carried on as before.

He tried to subpoena Mrs Fitzherbert (the morganatic wife of the Prince of Wales), with whom he had had a conversation in Paris two years before. What purpose this could have served was obscure as he was unable to get her into the witness box, having been thrown out of her house by her servants and threatened with a whipping by her brothers.

The property-owning jury were stupefied. Only cranks were interested in penal reform and no man's property would be safe without the draconian penalties then exacted for even the smallest thefts. After an inept and irrelevant defence the jury had no difficulty in convicting Gordon on both counts. The judge postponed sentence until the following day. But, having been released without bail overnight, he took the opportunity to disappear and for seven months he could not be found.

In that period he had converted to Judaism and was apprehended in the Jewish quarter of Birmingham wearing a straggly black beard and dirty gaberdine coat topped by a large-brimmed black hat similar to those worn by Polish merchants. In Birmingham he had been circumcised and according to the chronicler, Wraxall, 'preserved with great care the sanguinary proofs of his having undergone the amputation'.

He was brought back to London for sentence – three years for the prison libel and two years to run consecutively for the French libel. Additionally he had to find £10,000 in sureties for his good behaviour for the following fourteen years.

He was able to buy a room of his own in prison and employed two maidservants. His habits were regular – rising punctually at eight each morning, he read the newspapers over breakfast. Then he dealt with his voluminous correspondence until noon, when he received his numerous visitors.

His cell was often so crowded there was no room to sit, even on the floor. He would see anyone and had many interesting guests, including a 'young lady from Oxford Street' who came to tell him that, although she was pregnant, she was a virgin. She had been very miserable until the Archangel Gabriel appeared to her in a vision and told her the end of the world was at hand, commanding her to convey the news to Lord George Gordon!

Dinner was served punctually at 2 p.m. and he rarely entertained fewer than eight. The food was simple but good. His guests had beer or wine, whilst he always drank porter. After dinner he lit his pipe and serious discussion would take place on politics, religion or social problems. Dukes would sit down with Italian barbers, Jewish shopkeepers, ladies of rank and fashion, MPs, soldiers, American merchants and Polish noblemen. There were no rules of precedence or protocol. The only prohibition was on unorthodox Jews who trimmed their beards or uncovered their heads.

In January 1793 he became eligible for release. But he could not (or perhaps did not try to) find the £10,000 sureties required to secure it. He died of jail fever the following November.

BOB MACKRETH

MP FOR CASTLE RISING 1774–84, ASHBURTON 1784–1802

'If three thirds of the men of Law were sent to Botany Bay it would be the greatest blessing.'

Mackreth became an MP by a most eccentric means. The right to vote in Castle Rising was vested in the holders of a handful of 'burgage tenements', the majority of which were owned by the lord of the manor, Lord Orford. In 1774, as he controlled the majority of the votes, he was asked by the Returning Officer whom he wished to nominate as the Member.

Having recently recovered from a bout of insanity and with no eligible candidate to hand, he nominated the first person who came into his head, Bob Mackreth – a waiter and billiard-marker in his club, Arthur's, in St James's. However, as he was not sure of his nominee's Christian name, the nomination was declared void. Undaunted by this initial setback, his Lordship persisted in the nomination, a fresh election was held and, once Mackreth's Christian name had been ascertained, he was duly elected and took his seat.

Orford no doubt enjoyed the prank of returning an ex-waiter to Parliament. His son, Horace Walpole, wrote in a letter: 'The interlude of Mackreth had caused so much offence that, after running the gauntlet, he has been persuaded to be modest and give up his seat.' However, Mackreth thought again, for Walpole added a postscript: 'Mackreth is determined to continue a Member, like the rest of the world.' Nevertheless, Walpole appears not to have continued the patronage after the death of his father in 1781.

By then Mackreth had amassed a considerable fortune as a usurer, lending money to young aristocratic spendthrifts. In 1786 he came badly unstuck. James Fox Lane pleaded before the Master of the Rolls that Mackreth, who 'supplied young persons of rank and fortune, or expectation of fortune, with money when in distress' had defrauded him of his inheritance, worth £1300 a year, whilst he was still a minor. Mackreth was ordered to repay £20,000, a judgment which was confirmed on appeal to the House of Lords who 'imposed the highest costs ever given in a similar case'.

Mackreth's jaundiced conclusion was, 'I had rather be in the prison of an Inquisition than have anything to do with the Court of Chancery. As the Law is now administered, it is a pest to society and the ruin of three parts of the Kingdom. If three thirds of the men of Law were sent to Botany Bay it would be the greatest blessing that providence could bestow upon mankind. The Law is become what the Church was four or five centuries ago – a curse to the country.'

Six years later in Lincoln's Inn Fields he bumped into Sir John Scott (afterwards Lord Chancellor Eldon), who had been Fox Lane's counsel. Having called him 'a liar and a scoundrel', he challenged him to a duel. Scott, however, refused to rise to the bait and contented himself with preferring an indictment against Mackreth, who was fined £100 and imprisoned for six weeks.

SIR WILLIAM PAXTON

MP FOR CARMARTHEN 1803–6, CARMARTHENSHIRE 1806–7

'Paxton's folly.'

Sir William Paxton was a 'nabob' who had made his fortune in India. He returned to Britain and wished to cement his position by becoming an MP. He bought a country seat at Middleton Hall, near Carmarthen and, in the 1802 General Election, declared himself a candidate for the county seat. His campaign has become famous for its eccentric profligacy.

His expenses are said to have amounted, over fifteen days of polling, to the enormous sum of £15,690 4s 2d, spent not on improving literature but on providing unlimited entertainment in the taverns and ale houses of Carmarthen for the two and a half thousand or so voters. Paxton is said to have paid for 11,070 breakfasts, 36,901 dinners, 684 suppers, 25,275 gallons of ale, 11,068 bottles of spirits, 8,879 bottles of porter, 460 bottles of sherry, 509 bottles of cider, milk punch (eighteen guineas), ribbons (£786) and 4,521 separate charges for horse hire. After all this he lost by 1,267 votes to 1,222!

The following year he had better luck, being returned unopposed in a by-election for the borough seat of Carmarthen. Then in 1806 he transferred to the coveted county seat, once more being elected unopposed. However, in the General Election of 1807 he was opposed, and lost again.

JOHN MYTTON

MP FOR SHREWSBURY 1819–20

'What! Never been upset in a gig? What a damned slow fellow you've been all your life.'

'Mad Jack' Mytton, squire of Halston in Shropshire, is more celebrated for his feats in the hunting field than Parliament. In fact it is probably a surprise, even to those familiar with his madcap exploits, that he had any political career at all.

Showing his form early, he agreed to attend Oxford University but only on condition that he would be expected to study nothing but the racing calendar and the Stud Book. To sustain him in these academic studies he ordered to be sent on ahead of him and await his arrival, three pipes (i.e. 315 gallons!) of port.

From an early age he drank five bottles of port in the morning and, on two occasions when none was available, drank bottles of eau de Cologne 'to forestall the bad effect of night air'. He eventually became completely immune to the intoxicating effect of port and substituted brandy and quicksilver instead.

His physical endurance was legendary. He had an iron constitution and refused to wear warm clothes even in the most arctic conditions. He always wore the thinnest of silk stockings under very thin leather boots, so that in winter his feet were nearly always wet. His hunting breeches were unlined and he wore only one small waistcoat which was nearly always open. He could often be spotted stripped to a thin shirt, lying in deep snow awaiting the arrival of wildfowl at dusk. On one occasion he was observed running stark naked over heavy ice in pursuit of some ducks.

He was utterly fearless physically, with a recklessness bordering on insanity when driving a carriage. During one roller-coaster journey one petrified passenger begged him to slow down for fear of being upset. Mytton enquired nonchalantly, 'Were you ever hurt, then, by being upset in a gig?' 'No, thank God, for I never was upset in one,' came the reply. Astonished at this unaccountable omission he exclaimed, 'What! Never been upset in a gig? What a damned slow fellow you must have been all your life.' With that, he promptly filled the gap in his passenger's experience by running his nearside wheel up a bank, turning the vehicle over and pitching them both out onto the road.

On another occasion he went out to dinner, driving his horses in tandem. He was drawn into a discussion after dinner about this method of harnessing horses, which some of the guests held to be inherently unsafe as no one had any control over the leader, who was not confined by pole or shafts. Mytton at once bet them £25 that he would drive his tandem that night across country for

John Mytton taking his horse the shortest way home.

A large brown bear is Mytton's mount for the evening.

Nothing but a thin shirt to keep out the cold as Mytton goes shooting in midwinter.

a mile and a half, crossing a sunken fence, a deep drain and two quickset hedges. An eyewitness recorded the scene:

> The first obstacle was the sunk fence, into which, as might be expected, he was landed. But, the opposite side being on a gradual slope from top to bottom, the carriage and its

extraordinary inmate were drawn out without receiving injury. Nowise disconcerted, he sent his team on to the next fence – the wide drain – and such was the pace he went at that it was cleared by a yard or more. But the jerk pitched Mytton onto the wheeler's back; but by crawling over the dashing leather he regained his seat and again got the horses back in the proper direction, taking the two remaining fences in gallant style, got safe into the turnpike road and pocketed the cash!

Other madcap escapades followed. He bought some more horses from a dealer called Clarke and put one of them into a gig, tandem, to see if he would make a good leader. 'Do you think he is a good timber-jumper?' he asked poor Clarke, who was now sitting beside him in a state of some consternation. Without waiting for a reply Mytton shouted, 'We'll try him,' and gave the horse his head in front of a turnpike gate. The horse performed admirably, clearing the gate – but leaving Mytton, Clarke and the carriage spreadeagled in confusion on the other side.

He once bet a friend that he could get home fifteen minutes ahead of him. To win the wager, he drove the horse the shortest distance between the two points – in a straight line directly through Halston lake. He completely ignored the fact that he could not swim and that if he had been thrown in the water he would undoubtedly have drowned. On another occasion he was curious to discover whether or not his horse would fall if he galloped full tilt over a rabbit warren. It did and the horse rolled over him, nearly killing him into the bargain.

However uncaring he was of the fate of the human body, Mytton was extremely kind to animals. If cold and wet through after a canter on a miserable winter's day, he would often stop at a cottage and demand a fire to be lit indoors so that he and the horse could warm themselves side by side before continuing. His kindness was sometimes overpowering. On one occasion a poor mount collapsed and died because Mytton, out of the kindness of his heart, had tried to warm him by pouring a bottle of mulled port down the horse's throat.

He undoubtedly had a way with horses. He bragged to a group of friends that one particular filly was remarkably clever and that, when she won the Oaks, she would put the prize money into his pocket. Then to prove how exceptional the horse was, he lay down underneath her, putting her hind foot into his pocket and tickling her stomach.

He also owned sixty cats, each of which was dressed in livery suitable to its breed. But dogs he loved even more and he was reputed to have maintained over two thousand at any one time. One day a favourite bulldog of his called Tizer was involved in a ferocious fight with a friend's pet in Mytton's own drawing-room. Mytton was not in the least concerned except that, when it looked as though Tizer was going to come off second best, he stepped in to save his own prized pet. He then seized the other dog's nose in his teeth and held on until it submitted.

Incurably adventurous, Mytton once abandoned the horse as a steed – riding instead right into his dining room, dressed in full hunting costume on a large brown bear. Dinner was on the table and the entertaining spectacle went down splendidly until the squire suddenly dug his spurs into the bear's side. The animal promptly bit him through the calf of his leg and inflicted a serious wound.

Mytton did not hold this attack against the bear, whose company he continued to enjoy. On a later occasion he put a drunken Shropshire horse-dealer to bed – accompanied by the bear and two bulldogs. The man died soon after. He had also suffered from a prank which was Mytton's favourite way of dealing with bores – secretly putting red-hot coals in their pockets!

He frequently played practical jokes on his friends. He once invited a doctor and a parson to a convivial dinner with him. After waving them off home Mytton disguised himself as a highwayman and, by taking a short cut, intercepted them as they ambled along the road. Firing a brace of pistols loaded with blanks, he called on them to stand and deliver. Terrified out of their wits, they galloped off down the Oswestry road, with Mytton in hot pursuit. He later declared that neither had ever ridden so fast in their lives.

If Mytton was balked in any way, he was quite prepared to settle matters with his fists. Squire he may have been, but he was quite untroubled by mixing it with the 'lower orders'. When a burly Welsh miner tried to head off his hounds Mytton challenged him to a bare-knuckle fight. Twenty rounds later the exhausted miner threw in the towel. Mytton, however, took it all in good part, congratulated the loser on putting up a fine performance and sent him off with half a sovereign.

He had no idea whatever of the value of money and, in the last fifteen years of his life, more than £500,000 drained through his hands like water through a sieve. His wardrobe contained 152 pairs of breeches and trousers (with coats and waistcoats in proportion), 700 pairs of boots and slippers, over a thousand hats and nearly three thousand shirts.

On one occasion, returning from a successful day at Doncaster races, he counted out on the seat of his carriage several thousand pounds in winnings. He then fell asleep and, when he woke up, discovered that the entire pile of money had disappeared, blown out of the windows by the wind. He considered this a capital joke.

In 1819 Mytton decided to follow the family tradition and seek election to Parliament for Shrewsbury, the county town. This was also an expensive undertaking – not least because one method of canvassing was to ride around the town wearing a coat with gold buttons, a £10 note attached to each for the voters to snatch at! His opponent, Panton Corbett, retaliated by walking the streets with pockets stuffed with gold which he ostentatiously jingled.

Mytton promised at his adoption meeting as Tory candidate 'I shall never be biased by any party or private views. I shall fear that the follies of my youth have, in some instances, created in the public mind an impression unfavourable to my interest. But I trust, gentlemen, that my future conduct will be such as to remove those impressions.' This was a forlorn hope, but sufficient to secure his election by 384 votes to 287.

He was chaired around the town in the traditional manner, but departed from tradition when he arrived outside the Lion hotel, where he leapt out of the chair and through the window. Unfortunately he had not waited for it to be opened and delivered his speech of thanks covered in the wreckage of broken glass and window frame.

It was June before the House first met and, although Mytton's intentions were probably rather better than those which accompanied him to Oxford, he was not likely to shine as a Parliamentarian. As it happened the weather was warm, the old House of Commons Chamber soporific and the debate dull. No man was ever so congenitally incapable of sitting and listening for hours to seemingly endless linguistic shadow-boxing.

Mytton's patience expired in short order. He was only twenty-three years old and life had much more to offer than this. Despite the economic and political convulsions through which the country was passing in the aftermath of the Napoleonic Wars, Mytton preferred to converse with his horses and dogs, not politicians. He charged post-haste back to Shropshire, never to be seen at Westminster again. Six months later, in January 1820, George III's death precipitated another General Election and Mytton's brief and inglorious Parliamentary career expired with the King.

In a letter to his constituents he blandly announced, 'Finding a proper and punctual attention to your interests and that of the country at large is incompatible with my present pursuits, it is not my intention to become a candidate for your suffrages.'

The 1820s were, for Mytton, a rake's progress of lunatic profligacy. It was impossible to reason with him and the family's financial advisers despaired. Typical was this exchange with a disgruntled relative who pleaded with him not to sell an estate because it had been in the family for such a long time: 'How long?' asked Mytton. 'About five hundred years.' 'The devil it has! Then it is high time it should go out of it.'

At length he was forced to flee the country to escape his creditors. On his way to bed one night whilst lodging at Calais, he was seized by an attack of hiccups. Being of a practical frame of mind, Mytton decided the best cure would be a sudden fright – whereupon he seized a lighted candle and set fire to his nightshirt which, being cotton, burst immediately into flames. He was saved only because two compatriots knocked him down and rolled over him to put out the flames. Mytton's only reaction was to note with satisfaction, 'The hiccup is gone, by God!' and, appallingly burnt, he staggered into bed.

Eventually he returned home to face the music. He was arrested almost immediately and sent to the King's Bench, a debtor's prison. He had abused his body so liberally that it was worn out at only thirty eight. He had painful ulcers, the agony of which he expunged by soaking himself in alcohol. Soon afterwards he suffered a stroke which brought on delirium tremens, from which he was relieved by a fatal brain haemorrhage.

COL. CHARLES DE LAET WALDO SIBTHORP

MP FOR LINCOLN 1826–32, 1835–55

*'I would advise persons living near the park to keep
a sharp look-out after their silver forks and spoons
and servant maids.'*

Sibthorp was arguably the most reactionary MP who ever lived.
Over thirty years he set a standard of reaction, nationalism and
xenophobia unrivalled in Parliamentary history. In some respects
he even made Lord Eldon look like a 'wet'. 'Progress' of any kind
was absolute anathema to him and, even in his own day, he was
regarded as a considerable eccentric. If he had been present at the
Creation he would undoubtedly have urged God to think again
and conserve the formless void.

Sibthorp was God's gift to caricaturists and a constant butt of
ridicule in virtually all the early volumes of *Punch*. An American
academic has counted 345 references to him between 1841 and
1855 and over fifty cartoons.

According to the *Dictionary of National Biography*:

In Parliament he belonged to the ultra-Tory and ultra-
Protestant party and was the embodiment of old-fashioned
prejudice. Partly by his uncompromising opinions, partly
by his blunt expressions and partly by an eccentricity that
did less than justice to his real abilities, he made himself for

Col. Sibthorp on the Crystal Palace: 'Would to God that a heavy hailstorm or a visitation lightning would put a stop to the further progress of that work.'

many years rather a notorious than a respected figure in political life.

We also have a lively pen-portrait of Sibthorp in 1835, drawn by Charles Dickens in one of his *Sketches by Boz*:

You see this ferocious-looking personage, with a complexion almost as sallow as his linen, and whose large black mustachios would give him the appearance of a figure in a hair-dresser's window, if his countenance possessed one ray of the intelligence communicated to those waxen caricatures of the human face divine. He is a militia-man, with a brain slightly damaged and (quite unintentionally) the most amusing man in the House. Can anything be more absurd than the burlesque grandeur of his air, as he strides up to the lobby, his eyes rolling like those of a Turk's head in a cheap Dutch clock? He never appears without that bundle of dirty papers under his arm – they are generally supposed to be the miscellaneous estimates for 1804, or some equally important documents. He is very punctual in his attendance at the House and his self-satisfied 'He-ar He-ar' is not unfrequently the signal for a general titter.

This is the man who once actually sent a messenger up to the Strangers' Gallery in the old House of Commons to enquire the name of a gentleman who was using an eye-glass in order that he might complain to the Speaker that the individual in question was quizzing him! On another occasion he repaired to Bellamy's kitchen – a refreshment room where persons who are not Members are admitted on sufferance, as it were – and, perceiving two or three gentlemen at supper, who he was aware were not Members and could not in that place very well resent his insolence, he indulged in the exquisite pleasantry and gentlemanly facetiousness of sitting with his booted leg on the table at which they were supping!

Sibthorp was a grotesque, his deep-set fanatically gleaming eyes framed by a luxuriant moustache and whiskers rarely troubled by scissors, comb or brush. His fingers were laden with 'sparkling brilliants' and the overall effect was said to be 'like the debris of what must once have been a magnifico...a majestic air of tawdry grandeur...you behold a sallow and bearded Turk.'

Though only forty-three when first elected, he dressed in a style already antique, sporting the long coat and Wellington boots of the Regency, accompanied by an enormous gold quizzing-glass dangling on a stout chain, an item more appropriate to a period fifty years before that. An anachronism from the outset, he instantly became a 'character' in the House and was guaranteed to provoke a mixture of groans and laughter every time he rose to speak.

His opinions were as anachronistic as his dress. Reform, he told the House, was 'a thing which he detested as he detested the devil' and innovation he denounced as 'at best a dangerous thing; and he had seen in his own time so many dangerous results from innovations – for instance the Reform Bill, which had done everything to cause revolution – railroads, and other dangerous novelties – that he felt disposed to oppose everything savouring of innovation.' The apogee of antediluvian prejudice was probably reached when he informed astonished Parliamentarians that he 'disapproved of the new patent water-closets and much preferred the old system'.

He also opposed, needless to say, the new sanitary boards set up to provide burgeoning urban areas with a modern sewerage system. He denounced the inquisitorial powers of inspectors 'which would almost authorise them to go to the house of the Lord Mayor of York and see what he had for dinner, and whether he went sober to bed, which he was sure the rt. hon. gentleman always did.'

Sibthorp distinguished himself at the beginning of his political career by implacable hostility to Roman Catholic emancipation and 'any attempts to subvert that glorious fabric, our matchless constitution'. On 2 March 1828 he presented a number of petitions from Lincoln against the Emancipation Bill, declaring: 'All these petitions come from persons of real John Bull feeling; and, as an agriculturist, I would say that their desire was to have the real British breed and no cross one from the Popish.'

Loud laughter met his claim on 6 March that the 'detestable Bill was calculated to sap the foundations of the constitution' but he 'cared as little for their smiles as he did for their frowns and should treat both with the utmost contempt. If they wished to know what he thought of their laughter he would tell them: 'risu inepto nulla res ineptior est' ['Untimely grinning is the silliest sin' – Catullus].' He viewed the conduct of Ministers as a political apostasy that disgraced them.

On 16 March he declared 'the Bill excited considerable apprehension in Lincolnshire; where the humbler classes, instead of cultivating their grounds, had turned politicians'. Sibthorp was followed by his reactionary colleague, General Peachy, who referred to a reformist placard which had been circulated in Taunton. It read 'None are against Catholic emancipation but interested parsons and bigots; but they are for tithes, oppression etc.' To Sibthorp's enthusiastic approval he then announced, 'This is the way I should use this miserable and contemptible placard.' Amid laughter and cheers, he tore it into pieces and flung the fragments on the floor of the House.

A proposal to make a grant of £9,000 to the Roman Catholic seminary at Maynooth produced a fit of Sibthorpian apoplexy and on 22 May 1829 he excoriated the supposedly Tory Government for 'introducing a system for the encouragement and protection of beings who were little better than devils incarnate'.

Anti-Catholicism remained a violent passion throughout his Parliamentary life and when, in 1850, Pius IX restored the Roman Catholic hierarchy in England Sibthorp furiously denounced it: 'Cardinal Wiseman was certainly a dangerous person and, when he made his appearance here with his new authority from the Pope, ought to have been at once sent out of the country.' As an afterthought he then threw in that the Prime Minister, Lord John Russell, was 'not much better'.

The more violent his denunciations, however, the more he was treated as a figure of fun. An Irish Member gibed that, rather than submit to be shaved, Sibthorp would see the Tories, Constitution and all scattered to the winds. His reply gives a true flavour of his oratorical style:

> I tell the rt. hon. Gentleman [Sir Robert Peel, ostensibly leader of Sibthorp's own party] that I will never support him. I'll never support any man who acts contrary to the duty that he owes to his Sovereign, to the people and, last of all, and greatest of all, to his God. I never will support any man who does this, and though the hon. and learned Gentleman told me I would sooner sacrifice my principles than I would be shaved – I tell that hon. and learned Gentleman that I had not only rather be shaved, but have my head shaved off, than forget I am a Protestant, born a Protestant, bred a Protestant, educated

a Protestant – and God grant that I may die with similar feelings and in that faith.

Sibthorp detested Peel for his religious tolerance, but equally for his apostate conversion to Free Trade. Sibthorp, an extensive landowner in five counties, naturally belonged to the most extreme faction of agricultural protectionists. In 1844 he assured the House that Lincolnshire agricultural labourers were 'perfectly content with everything but the movements of the Anti-Corn Law League' and, after the repeal of the Corn Laws in 1846, he never ceased to complain that agriculture was severely depressed and farm workers had been driven to the edge of starvation.

Though a Tory of the blackest hue throughout his life, the colonel wisely had no faith in Tory leaders (like Wellington, Peel and Disraeli) to stand firm on Tory principles. Whilst abominating all its measures, he often said he preferred a Liberal Government to a Tory because there was less 'deceit and hypocrisy' in the former than the latter.

In addition to change of every description he particularly hated all foreigners and 'abroad'. There was only one acceptable reason to go abroad – to put foreigners in their place by acts of war. On 1 March 1830 he called for an account of the number of passports issued in the previous five years, together with the names of those to whom they had been issued and the countries of destination. Absenteeism from the country was a great evil and he thought that, if absentees were taxed, 'it would cause £4,000,000 to be spent at home that was currently spent abroad'.

In 1840 he strongly disapproved of Queen Victoria's marriage to Prince Albert, a foreigner. Acting on this prejudice, he successfully proposed that a planned £50,000 annuity to the Prince should be reduced to only £30,000. Much to the surprise of Lord Melbourne, the Prime Minister, who had assured the Queen that the £50,000 would go through without difficulty, Sibthorp triumphed with a majority of 104, one of the few occasions when he was on the winning side. *Fraser's Magazine* wrote that 'Colonel Sibthorp was a study... Not Sir Robert Peel himself when the Government was within his grasp could be more proudly conscious of his position. His bearing, his air of grandeur, were sublime . . . The best part of the affair consisted in the patronising manners he assumed towards the Conservative leaders.' The Queen never forgave this humiliation and refused to visit Lincoln so long as Sibthorp was one of its MPs.

Sibthorp was an advocate of the most rigid economy, although military spending did tend to be an Achilles heel. Paradoxically, although living in an age of unparalleled plenty, he spoke as though the country teetered on the verge of bankruptcy. In 1831 (and again in 1851) he opposed spending large amounts of money remodelling royal residences, denouncing the exorbitant demands of the works at Windsor Castle and Buckingham Palace as 'unwarrantable luxuries and superfluous extravagances'. There had been an overrun of £71,000 on the £500,000 provided for in the estimates.

In 1850 he also inveighed against spending any more money on the new Houses of Parliament. 'What was the edifice after all? A piece of mere frippery and flummery, not fit to accommodate the Members of that House and much more

Sibthorp was also a vehement opponent of railways.

suitable in style for a harem than a place of meeting for a grave and important legislative body.' So much for the masterpiece of Pugin and Barry!

He opposed everywhere the grant of pensions (including to Queen Victoria's mother) or high salaries for officials whether at home or abroad and insisted on cutting spending to the bone so as to keep taxes to the irreducible minimum. He opposed virtually all tax increases and only once or twice found a good reason for a new tax – in 1840 he welcomed a new tax, but only for the highly desirable effect it would have in making the incumbent Ministry more unpopular!

Democracy the colonel especially abominated. He violently obstructed the extension of the franchise and the disfranchising of rotten boroughs. He was totally against outlawing bribery and other means of influencing voters. This, he maintained, was un-Christian as it would make a criminal of any candidate who wished to distribute charity. 'I wish to see more expense and merriment at elections... Some people are afraid to spend sixpence at elections; but for my part I like to see my constituents enjoy themselves; and I would never strive to curtail their innocent pleasures. It is an old established maxim "in vino veritas". Give a man some genial liquor to drink and he will open his heart to you.'

Sibthorp declared that he would persist in his custom of spending money for the comfort and entertainment of his fellow men no matter what busybodies were sent out from London to make 'a secret and scandalous enquiry into the private concerns not only of the constituency but also MPs, their character and conduct'. Needless to say, the secret ballot also excited his contempt: 'of all the dirty things in this world, of all the un-English disgraceful things, the ballot was the worst'.

For many years the most consistent of his campaigns was against those most unwelcome, new-fangled disruptions to the country – railways. He sympathised with the Duke of Wellington, who was reportedly suspicious of them because 'they encourage the lower classes to move about'. The colonel disliked them more because they were a dangerous innovation.

But he was at least consistent in his abomination of all transport improvements – on 3 June 1830 he had also opposed a Bill to construct a new Great North Road, cutting thirty miles off the journey from London to Edinburgh. Sibthorp said he knew the existing road well, travelling along it was easy and everywhere comfortable accommodations were to be had. He looked upon the scheme as 'a fancy measure of Mr Telford's, whom he took to be one of those visionary gentlemen who expected to feed upon the public'.

In tilting against railways Sibthorp achieved his apotheosis. In 1841 he declared, 'they are run by public frauds and private robbers whose nefarious schemes will collapse and all the old and happy mode of travelling on turnpike roads in chaises, carriages and stages will be restored'. In 1842, noting an increase in railway accidents, he hoped a bill would be introduced for the 'annihilation of railways'.

In 1844 he announced, 'I never travel by railroad; I hate the very name of the railroad – I hate it as I hate the devil.' Railways were a degrading form of transport and he later confided to the House his personal dismay at occasionally having to travel by the 'steam humbug'. He made it a point of honour never to travel by train except at election time to move from one to another of the many shires in which he held county votes. He ensured his lasting memorial in Lincoln by successfully opposing the routeing of the Great Northern Railway's main line to London through the city – a somewhat mixed blessing for his fellow citizens.

Sibthorp bore enormous burdens as he lived in an era of rapid change and it was his peculiar responsibility to resist the march of time at every step. He was an extremely busy Parliamentarian, constantly rising to speak on anything and everything, great or small.

He denounced the operators of London barrel organs for disturbing the peace, frightening horses and obstructing traffic. He denounced the filthy conditions of hansom cabs as likely to produce cholera but when a new and improved mode of transport, the omnibus, was introduced he denounced that too.

Omnibuses were overcrowded and their drivers' language was 'disgusting, threatening and alarming'. He denounced the Bill levying rates to build free libraries on grounds that 'he did not like reading at all and hated it when at Oxford.'

These frantic outpourings of reaction from the 1830s and 1840s were but a prelude to his most memorable campaigns after 1850. These last five years of his life were dominated by obscurantist xenophobia on a truly heroic and unprecedented scale. The outbreak of the Crimean War gladdened his heart and he confidently declared 'it would take ninety-nine foreigners to make one thorough good Englishman'.

He opposed Great Britain's joining the continental electric telegraph convention because 'by this scheme the Government is only encouraging the intrigues of the foreigner and rendering this country subservient to him'. He was, of course, also against telegraphs on principle, even without the reprehensible foreign dimension.

He proposed a tax on 'the lamentable influx of foreigners into this country', which was received with gales of laughter. 'He knew he had been often laughed at in the House and out of it – and he did not know but that he might be mobbed, but he would always declare that it was deplorable to see the sums of money that were carried out of England by foreign opera dancers and singers. Foreigners were encouraged too much in this country. They interfered with native talent. He was sorry to say that the higher classes encouraged all foreigners, whether of character or not – male and female.'

These eructations of bile culminated in the volcanic explosion of his fight against 'one of the greatest humbugs, one of the greatest frauds, one of the greatest absurdities ever known', than which 'a more wild-goose chase, a more undefined scheme, a more delusive or dangerous undertaking never had been attempted by any man.' He referred to the Great Exhibition of 1851 – the brainchild of that damned foreigner, Prince Albert.

Sibthorp's first skirmish came with the cutting down of some trees in Hyde Park on the site of the Crystal Palace, in which it was to be housed:

The Commissioners of Woods and Forests came like a thief in the night and cut down those trees. A gentleman who lives near the Park and pays £110 a year ground rent told me that he was admiring the trees one evening before he went to bed and when he got up in the morning to shave, they were gone.

Hyde Park is to be desecrated for the greatest trash, the greatest fraud, the greatest imposition ever attempted on the people of this country. The object is to introduce among us foreign stuff of every description – without regard to quality and quantity, to pave the way for the establishment of cheap and nasty trash and trumpery. It would be better for the promoters to encourage native industry, and support the industrious people of England, from whom they draw all they possess.

In July 1850 he was alarmed to learn that the previous day no fewer than 1,500 foreigners had landed in the country, 'many of whom, no doubt, had been surveying the ground where this Exhibition was to take place, and looking after matters with a view to their own interests'. When the Crystal Palace was built there would be an avalanche of fiendish foreigners 'talking all kinds of gibberish. Of course, the English people would not understand them, and they would get into all kinds of disturbances. Suppose a case: a foreigner called a cabman and told him to drive to a certain place; the cabman could not understand him and before he knew what he was about, he would have something like a stiletto in him.'

He thought that London should build a new jail for the hordes of felons who would be drawn to the capital. As well as foreign criminals, 'all the bad characters at present scattered over the country would be attracted to Hyde Park as a favourable field for their operations, and to keep them in check an immense body of police must be constantly on duty day and night. That being the case, I would advise persons living near the park to keep a sharp look-out after their silver forks and spoons and servant maids.'

Warming to his theme, he pondered also the moral threat to the honest country folk who came to view the great demon. 'The poor labourers were to come up to London helter-skelter, where they would suddenly find themselves amidst the temptations of a great metropolis. What would become of the chastity and modesty of those who might become the unsuspecting victims of those temptations? Their property, their wives and families would be at the mercy of pickpockets and whoremongers from every part of the earth.'

Finally, working himself into a paroxysm of anxiety, he heralded the certainty of foreign spies taking advantage of this heaven-sent opportunity: 'Her Majesty's Government and, I grieve to say, many of our gentry are "hail, fellow! well met" with every foreign ragamuffin. Nothing would suit the Government but that those amicable strangers should be allowed to pry into our dockyards and inspect the Tower and our arsenals. The whole nakedness of the country will be laid open to them. The only fit punishment for so treasonous a Government is to ship the whole lot to Botany Bay.'

Despite these jeremiads, Sibthorp generated little support and the Crystal Palace was opened by the Queen on 1 May 1851. On the same evening he fired another salvo in the Commons. He refused to visit it himself: 'My duty to God ["Oh! Oh!"] Yes, I repeat, neither my duty to my God nor to my country would suffer me to visit that showy bauble. I consider it my paramount duty as a good Christian and a good subject to absent myself from the Crystal Palace. I deeply regret to hear that the head of the Protestant church of this Realm should have been there invoking the blessing, the assistance of him who suffered for the sins of mankind.'

A thousand guineas would not induce him to look at Crystal Palace, the very sight of which 'almost sickens me'. He wished once again that the whole place could be destroyed. He had himself once vainly invoked the Almighty to have a trial run for the Apocalypse in Hyde Park whilst it was being constructed: 'Would to God that a heavy hailstorm or a visitation of lightning would put a stop to the further progress of that work.'

Balked of this ambition, Sibthorp continued to rail vehemently against the Exhibition long after it opened. On one occasion he brought an illustration of the 'foreign trash and trumpery' to the House of Commons and held up an engraved decanter which cost sixpence. 'How is a man in this country who is accustomed to eat roast beef and drink strong ale, after the manner of a Christian, to compete with those nasty foreigners who live on brown bread and sour krout and who manufacture decanters at sixpence a piece?'

Cantankerous to the last, the colonel rose for the final time in the House of Commons on 2 May 1855 to press for an inquiry into the expenses of his old enemy, Lord John Russell, for a mission to Vienna. He hinted at misappropriation of funds and looked upon it as an 'underhand, low piece of business' but would 'leave the public to draw their own conclusions'. He suffered a stroke shortly after and died in December, mourned as a picturesque and comic figure, but also as 'the finest recorded caricature of the conservative instinct'.

3RD MARQUESS OF SALISBURY

MP FOR STAMFORD 1853–68, PEER 1868–1903;
PRIME MINISTER 1885–6, 1886–92, 1895–1902

'A great master of gibes, flouts and jeers.'

Even by the standards of 150 years ago, Salisbury's opinions bordered on the eccentric. He was a passionate hater of democracy and believed it to be 'a dangerous and irrational creed by which two day-labourers shall outvote Baron Rothschild'.

He sat in the House of Commons from 1853 to 1868 but never had to face a contested election himself. His constituency, Stamford, was a small borough dominated by the influence of his cousin, the Marquess of Exeter. However, never having personally to engage in the rough and tumble of electioneering did not mitigate his profound distaste for

> the days and weeks of screwed-up smiles and laboured courtesy, the mock geniality, the hearty shake of the filthy hand, the chuckling reply that must be made to the coarse joke, the loathsome, choking compliment that must be paid to the grimy wife and sluttish daughter, the indispensable flattery of the vilest religious prejudices, the wholesale deglutition of hypocritical pledges...

He had another decidedly odd characteristic, for one who eventually got to the top of 'the greasy pole'. From the very outset of his Parliamentary career he abused the leader of his own party with the same unbridled vigour as he abused the voters upon whom his Parliamentary position theoretically depended. Two months after he first took his seat he wrote in an article, 'there is no escape from taxes, toothache or the statesmanship of Mr Disraeli'. Disraeli was then leader of the Tories and Salisbury's father was a member of the same Cabinet. But the son would not be deflected by the embarrassment caused to his father or leader.

Disraeli described him as 'not a man who measures his words' but 'a great master of gibes, flouts and jeers'. He lambasted some pedantic manoeuvre of Gladstone's as 'more worthy of an attorney than a statesman'. Gladstone was offended and demanded an apology. The next day it was given, but in unexpected terms. He said he realised his words had been too strong but 'I am only doing justice to my own feelings when I avow that I did a great injustice to the attorneys'!'

Salisbury had the supreme eccentricity for a politician of being wholly indifferent to the pursuit of political power. In modern parlance he would be described as 'laid-back'. In the middle of his maiden speech he paused, unable to suppress a yawn. When he had reached the pinnacle of his profession, as leader of his party he remained detached. On the first two occasions he was offered the Premiership he tried to turn it down. One can begin to understand why his son telegraphed him at the end of his first period as Prime Minister with the message: 'I hear you are turned out. Many congratulations!'

His eccentricity was immediately apparent from the way he dressed. A keen amateur botanist, as a youth he would spend all day roaming the countryside hunting for plants. He dressed so scruffily that he was once arrested on suspicion of being a poacher's boy. He carried this trait with him all his life. When Prime Minister in 1886 he was refused entry to the casino at Monte Carlo because he was thought to be a tramp. Why he was trying to get in in the first place remains a mystery.

Salisbury was also a keen amateur scientist and became a Fellow of the Royal Society. Hatfield was the second country house in England to have electric light, which he installed in

1881. The need for fuses was not then understood and the wiring frequently burst into flames when circuits became overloaded. Salisbury took these startling events in his stride – the family were instructed to toss cushions at the fire until it was extinguished. He was also one of the first to install the telephone, with wires trailing loose throughout the house. Unwary visitors jumped everywhere as he tested it with a repeated 'Hey diddle diddle, the cat and the fiddle, the cow jumped over the moon.'

At the age of seventy he was moved to try to reduce his considerable bulk by going for a spin around St James's Park on a tricycle. For this purpose he adopted a shabby black cloak and wide-brimmed felt hat. However, as he was too infirm to start the machine rolling without assistance, he was accompanied by a groom or grandchild whose job it was to start him off with a push. Then, if the machine lost impetus, their task was to revive it by pushing him as fast as possible. Needless to say, there was no noticeable effect on the PM's weight.

In physical comforts he generally preferred the practical to the conventional. At the end of his life he forgot to take with him to church the skull cap he habitually wore to keep his head warm. He solved the problem by taking off a grey woollen glove and perching it on top of his head for the rest of the service.

Lady Salisbury wrote that his dress once 'nearly caused the death from consternation' of the Prince of Wales, later Edward VII and a notorious stickler for 'correct' dress. In contrast to Edward's preternatural sensitivity to the slightest sartorial solecism, Salisbury was both absent-minded and completely indifferent to his appearance. A combination of these traits had caused him to put on the trousers of one uniform with the tunic of another. When this was pointed out to him he apologised to the Prince in a masterpiece of irony: 'It was a dark morning and I am afraid, Sir, that my mind must have been occupied by some subject of less importance.'

In later life physical failings, particularly short-sightedness, accentuated his eccentricities. He had difficulty recognising even close relations if he encountered them in unexpected situations. Standing by the throne at a court ceremony and seeing a young

The 3rd Marquess of Salisbury, Spy, *20 December 1900.*

man smiling at him, he asked his neighbour 'Who is that?' – only to be told, 'That is Lord Cranborne, your eldest son, my Lord!'

At a dinner party he asked his neighbour who was the gentleman seated across the table from him. It was W. H. Smith, his closest Cabinet colleague. Salisbury explained his failure to recognise him on grounds that, as he always sat next to him in Cabinet he was used to seeing him in profile rather than full-face!

HORATIO BOTTOMLEY

GLADSTONIAN LIBERAL CANDIDATE
FOR HORNSEY 1887; LIBERAL MP FOR
HACKNEY SOUTH 1906–12; INDEPENDENT MP
FOR HACKNEY SOUTH 1918–22

'Ah, Bottomley. Sewing?' 'No. Reaping!'

Horatio Bottomley's phenomenal success was a testament to enduring human gullibility. He swindled gigantic fortunes from millions of willing dupes. But he was also elected three times a Member of Parliament whilst he was doing it. A gifted performer on the platform, in filigrees of words he charmed votes as well as banknotes out of people who should have known better.

Bottomley spoke at the Oxford Union in 1920 and Beverley Nichols left this description of him:

> A grotesque figure, one would have said at first sight. Short and uncommonly broad, he looked almost gigantic in a thick fur coat. Lack-lustre eyes, heavily pouched, glared from a square and sallow face. He seemed to have a certain resentment against the world at large. It was not till he began to talk that the colour mottled his cheeks and the heavy lines on his face were lightened.

He went down well with the undergraduates and won his debate by hundreds of votes, but not all were taken in by his verbal pyrotechnics: Some called him 'Hotairio' Bottomley.

His beginnings were hard and unprepossessing. He was born in the East End in 1860, the son of a tailor's foreman and orphaned at the age of five. He was then sent to a typically grim Victorian orphanage, from which he ran away at fourteen, becoming first an errand boy at a firm of solicitors and later a shorthand writer in the High Court.

The knowledge he gained in these formative years stood him in good stead as he spent a large part of his life defending himself in trials for fraud and dishonesty. He learned both the art of the swindler, which got him into trouble, and the art of the lawyer, which often got him out of it. In fact he learned both together, as his preceptor was the swindling managing clerk of the solicitors' firm who, for years, levied and collected a wholly fictitious 'County Rate' on many firms in the City of London. He even had the gall to rent offices, from which the usual demand notes and final notices were issued.

The success of this barefaced fraud mightily impressed young Bottomley. Shortly afterwards he began his first business venture, the *Hackney Hansard*, publishing full reports of local debating societies which were modelled on the House of Commons and called 'Local Parliaments'. Astonishingly, there was a ready market for such a publication.

Bottomley soon graduated to more grandiose projects and began to display a genius for sucking money out of people's wallets. Fired by business success, he hankered after politics too and, in 1887, stood as Liberal candidate in the Hornsey by-election. He fought a lively campaign against the Tory, H. C. Stephens (of Stephens Ink) whom, most remarkably, he persuaded to lend him the money to fight his campaign. It was never repaid.

Encouraged by a modest success in reducing the Tory majority, Bottomley moved next door to fight North Islington. He nursed the constituency in an old-fashioned way – setting up soup kitchens, entertaining and giving lavish parties for children and old people every Christmas. But, unfortunately, in 1891 his political career came to a dead stop when he was forced into his first bankruptcy.

Encouraged by the success of the Hansard Company, he branched out into other publications and set up companies to acquire foreign printing and publishing businesses. These followed a pattern which Bottomley used ever after to enrich himself and impoverish his investors. The Anglo-Austrian Union was set up to acquire companies in Austria, with a paid-up capital of £93,000 – a considerable sum, considering that £1 in 1890 would be worth £100 today. At the board meetings, however, no accounts were presented or reports read. The company never acquired any assets other than the shareholders' funds, but Bottomley nevertheless euphorically declared a dividend of 8 per cent on the Preference shares and 15 per cent on the Ordinary shares.

The euphoria evaporated as quickly as the shareholders' money and a committee of shareholders was appointed to inquire into the company's affairs. A simple and instructive statement of accounts emerged:

RECEIPTS	EXPENDITURE	
Shares and debentures £93,022	Cash –	
	to Mr Bottomley	£88,500
	Debenture Interest	1,024
	Dividend Preference	690
	Ordinary	1,456
	Directors' Fees	1,116
	Stamp Duty and	
	Bank Charges	58
	Balance at Bank	26

The committee succinctly reported: 'The company has acquired no business in Vienna or elsewhere, has no property whatever, and its whole capital appears to be lost. There are not sufficient funds to pay the expenses of printing this Report.'

In tandem with the Anglo-Austrian Union was the Hansard Union, whose initial capital was no less than £1 million. The Debenture Corporation had underwritten £250,000 and, when its interest payments failed to appear, it put in a receiver. On 1 May 1891, Bottomley filed for bankruptcy.

This led to the first of Bottomley's many brushes with the law. He was charged with fraud as £600,000 was unaccounted for out of the £1 million. It seemed an open-and-shut case and was heard at the Old Bailey before Mr Justice Hawkins, renowned as a hanging judge.

Bottomley demonstrated for the first time the forensic skill and wit which baffled counsel pitted against him and later drew crowds to all his cases as though they were West End productions. The prosecution was led by a heavyweight team – the Attorney-General (Sir Charles Russell), assisted by the Solicitor-General (Sir John Rigby), and three other counsel destined for legal eminence. Bottomley defended himself.

In his opening speech Bottomley worked to get the judge on side. Referring to the extensive indictment, he observed that 'although not of advanced years' (he was only thirty-three) he 'had apparently found time to commit twenty-one pages of crime'. Hawkins genially interposed, 'That is nothing. I remember an indictment with ninety-nine counts,' to which Bottomley responded silkily, 'That, my Lord, must have been for some older criminal.'

Bottomley dragged the case out so long that Russell had to give up in the middle, leaving it to Rigby to lead for the Crown. This was a disaster as, although a great Chancery lawyer, he had no experience of dealing with juries. Hawkins took a malicious delight in showing up his limitations, even to the extent of passing a note down from the Bench to another counsel during Rigby's over-lengthy closing speech:

PATIENCE COMPETITION

| FIRST PRIZE: | Henry Hawkins. |
| HONOURABLE MENTION: | Job. |

Bottomley was an orator of genius, to which gift he allied the quickest of wits and a razor-sharp facility in cross-examination. Aided by his happy relations with the judge, he had the jury in the palm of his hand. After a three-month trial it took them only twenty-five minutes to acquit, despite the apparently over-whelming likelihood of a conviction at the start.

Hawkins was so impressed he urged him to take up the law. But Bottomley had other ideas which did, it is true, generate an enormous quantity of work for lawyers over the next quarter of a century – exploring the ramifications of his financial bubbles.

For a free rein in business he had first to dispose of his bankruptcy proceedings. Not that bankrutcy was ever allowed to cramp his style. It was in this period that he purchased the lease of his palatial flat off Pall Mall and built a private racecourse for the horses which he had never ceased to own.

He was also an inveterate distributor of largesse wherever he went. His secretary, Houston, reported that he never spent less than £25 on a journey from London to Manchester. His spending was of such an order that he was always short of ready cash. There was one train attendant who constantly changed cheques for him. One day, Houston informed him that the man had been sent to prison. 'Ah, we shall miss him, Houston,' he said. 'You had better send his wife some money.' 'But he is in prison for bigamy,' Houston replied. 'What a hero! Ah well! send both his wives some money then.'

Buoyed up by his forensic success, Bottomley produced an audacious scheme to persuade his creditors to take shares in some Western Australian gold-mining companies in settlement of his debts. These companies were then successively 'reconstructed' into new companies with enlarged capital and blessed with optimistic names such as the Nil Desperandum Gold Mining Company Ltd. Every year one or more went into voluntary liquidation and soon reappeared in a slightly different guise under yet another name.

The technique was simple. Reconstruction would be agreed to at a meeting packed with Bottomley supporters. The public shareholders would then receive a letter announcing that the new company's board had voted to double the holdings of every shareholder in the old company at half his original cost. On receipt of a cheque for only £50, shares originally costing £100 in the old company would be transformed into a new holding worth £200 in the reconstructed company. Astonishingly, money poured in and the bankruptcy proceedings were dismissed.

With the impudence and effrontery which became his trademark, Bottomley published a letter to his Trustee in Bankruptcy:

Dear Sirs,
I have much pleasure in certifying that you have been of very great assistance to me in connection with my affairs, and I shall certainly advise all my friends, as they become bankrupt, to avail themselves of your services.

Yours faithfully,
HORATIO BOTTOMLEY

Fuelled by this success, over the next ten years Bottomley launched nearly fifty companies with a nominal capital of some £25 million. There were two great mysteries to all this. First, and obviously, how could such a vast number of people have been gulled so willingly by frauds so flagrant? And perhaps just as mysteriously, how did Bottomley manage to dissipate so quickly sums so colossal?

Some money was returned to investors in the form of handsome initial dividends; these were always paid entirely out of capital. Then, large sums were paid to the stage army of poodle directors and other first-class passengers on the Bottomley gravy-train. Women, racehorses and champagne absorbed vastly greater amounts. But, when all is said and done, there is a physical limit to such routine dissipation. Bottomley, however, was a spendthrift genius who infallibly discovered the reciprocal of the formula hunted by medieval alchemists – he perfected a method of converting gold into lead.

For a time his exploits were lauded as financial wizardry. In 1897, still only thirty-seven, his photograph appeared in a *Financial Times* series called 'Men of Millions', which estimated he had made £3 million in promoting companies. However, the obverse of this soon became apparent for, in the five years from 1901 to 1905 alone, sixty-seven bankruptcy petitions and writs were issued against him.

No obstacle seemed to bar his path, however. Bottomley succeeded by a superabundance of charm, which made people almost positively want to lose their money to him. His shamelessness was so complete that it compelled seduction and he was able to turn even the most irate victim around. On one

occasion he was visited at his sumptuous flat off Pall Mall by a
disgruntled shareholder, who launched into a withering diatribe
against his financial morals. Bottomley listened demurely and
then, having made no attempt to justify himself, merely turned
his back, parted the tails of his frock coat and bent over – making
his bottom a target for the complainant's boot!

On another occasion Bottomley was presented with one of
his office-boys, who had been caught red-handed stealing
some stamps. The office manager wanted him sacked on the
spot for dishonesty. But Bottomley took pity on the boy and
did not even admonish him. Instead, dismissing the theft, he
airily told the manager: 'You'd better give him another chance.
We've all got to start in a small way.'

As an unashamed populist, snake-oil salesman and demagogue
it was natural that Bottomley should be determined to get into the
House of Commons, in spite of his increasingly dubious
reputation. Narrowly defeated at Hackney South in the 'Khaki'
election of 1900, he eventually achieved his goal there as part of
the Liberal landslide in 1906.

His campaign methods looked back to an earlier era. He threw
lavish parties for the electors – appearing as a particularly open-
handed Santa at Christmas time. He employed paid cheerleaders
to appear every time he entered a pub, bazaar or even just when
he got out of his car. An opponent who called a meeting to
expose Bottomley's dubious morality was forced to cancel it
when it was swamped by crowds of menacing Bottomley
supporters.

During the election itself Bottomley's campaigners went on
the offensive. The sitting MP put up posters with the slogan,
'Vote for Robertson and Reputation' – an obvious allusion to the
cloud over Bottomley's. Overnight, Bottomley had exact copies
printed and posted over the originals – but with the slogan
changed to 'Vote for Robertson and Repetition'. Robertson then
tried another poster, reading: 'Vote for Robertson, your old and
tried Member'. In a very short time, with the aid of a slip printed
in the same style and colour, Bottomley had altered it to 'Vote
for Robertson, your old and tired Member'.

Bottomley lunched in Hackney pubs, paying corkage on the bottles of champagne he took in with him. If the selected pub had inadequate facilities for eating he would have the lunch sent in too. It would be announced in advance that he intended to lunch or dine at a certain pub and this was the signal for crowds of the faithful to gather to cheer his entry and exit – and to cheer themselves at his expense in between. These tactics proved briliantly successful. Having lost by 4,714 to 4,376 in 1900, he turned the tables in 1906 and was returned in triumph by 6,736 votes to 3,257.

Bottomley believed firmly that the end justified the means. To win was the only consideration. When the January 1910 election campaign was at its most passionate, Bottomley's Tory opponent announced that Austen Chamberlain was coming to speak on his behalf in the largest hall in Hackney. Bottomley set to work immediately to make the meeting a failure.

He found fifty men and gave them three shillings each. He then sent them all off to have their boots heavily soled and heeled and liberally weighted with iron tips and hobnails. On the day of the meeting they assembled for inspection and received instructions to take up positions in various seats well to the front of the hall.

Chamberlain was given a patient hearing. But as soon as Bottomley's opponent rose to speak, one of the heavily shod gentlemen rose with him and clattered towards the door by the most roundabout route. The audience cried 'Silence.' In response, he retraced his steps and explained loudly that he was going as quietly as he could. Then he walked about, arguing as long as possible.

As soon as he vanished through the door, a second performer rose and repeated the same clattering and arguing. And so it went on until all fifty had disappeared. By that time both candidate and audience had lost their enthusiasm and the meeting closed without a word more being heard. Next day, Bottomley pressed the same men into his service with sandwich-boards – getting full value from the shoe leather and iron he had paid for.

'Chutzpah' is a word that might have been invented specially for Bottomley. At a meeting at the Albert Hall in the 1918 election, he inveighed against the announcement that the new House of Commons would not be summoned until after the Peace Treaty had been signed: 'That will not do for the Member for South Hackney,' as he portentously declared himself, although several days were yet to elapse before polling day. 'Unless Mr Lloyd George – who I am not certain is coming back – calls Parliament together a few days after December 14th 1918, I shall take a taxi-cab to Buckingham Palace and have a few words with His Majesty.'

It was characteristic audacity for Bottomley to suggest that he had the confidence of the King, but the crowning folly of the statement was that, although Polling Day was on 14 December, it was legally impossible to count the votes until the 28th, to allow for the Forces' votes to be brought from overseas!

In 1919 Lord Rothermere persuaded Bottomley to speak on behalf of his 21-year-old son, Esmond, a candidate in the Thanet by-election. He agreed with alacrity and began his speech at a great meeting in Margate: 'Ladies and Gentlemen, in the course of another few weeks His Majesty will send for me and ask me to form my first Business Government, and I am going to send for young Esmond to join my Cabinet. I have been watching young Harmsworth for a long time and am here tonight to ask you to give him your votes and so save me the job of finding him a seat elsewhere.'

Bottomley had, in fact, met him for the first time only a few days before! Such preposterous pronouncements would have been ridiculed if uttered by anyone else. But Bottomley was cheered to the echo and Esmond duly became the baby of the House of Commons.

The sequel is also instructive. Shortly afterwards, the young man whom Bottomley wanted in his Cabinet was campaigning for the Anti-Waste candidate in a by-election in Westminster. Bottomley appeared, supporting the opposing candidate, and issued a crude cartoon depicting Harmsworth as a baby in a pram, being pushed by two nurses – one his father (Lord Rothermere) and the other his uncle (Lord Northcliffe).

Bottomley was the supreme propagandist. As a journalist and speaker he had few equals. In 1906 he founded *John Bull*, an early prototype of today's 'red-top tabloid' journalism – a scandal-sheet specialising in inaccurate political predictions and putting strong emphasis on sport. It was first, foremost and forever British – soaked in strident nationalism and aimed at the bluff, beer-drinking, British workman, who was fond of the wife and kids but ready at any moment to go on a spree with 'the boys'. It was the ideal vehicle for 'man of the people' Bottomley.

Although *John Bull* was a financial success, its profits disappeared without trace into the vast morass of Bottomley's other murky financial dealings. In 1907 his Joint Stock Trust went into liquidation and the receivers spent over eighteen months trying to unravel the accounts, a task made more difficult because the most important books were 'missing'. Eventually he was charged with conspiracy to defraud, by having sold ten million duplicate shares.

In spite of having the best legal brains pitted against him, Bottomley's skill and wit in court triumphed again. He was acquitted. Alas! this was but a brief respite, as writs of all kinds shortly showered over him and, by 1912, he was bankrupt once more with a huge deficiency of assets. This also meant leaving the House of Commons and he applied for the Chiltern Hundreds.

Despite bankruptcy he had, through a variety of expedients, managed to retain control of his most important assets. In particular *John Bull* remained as a megaphone through which he could self-righteously trumpet the Bottomley cause and top up his income by fraudulent competitions and sweepstakes.

The outbreak of war in 1914 was, for him, a windfall stroke of luck for money-making and also provided unparalleled opportunities for indulging the worst kind of chauvinist journalistic populism. He vilified the Kaiser as 'The Potty Potentate of Potsdam' and called for 'No Mercy for the Butcher of Berlin'. A 'well-known physician' wrote an article headlined 'The Kaiser Certified Insane' and *John Bull* reproduced a spoof order for his reception in a lunatic asylum.

Anyone with a foreign name was considered fair game. An inoffensive man called Gottschalk, who had lived in England for thirty years, was pilloried as 'Foreign Foe in a British Tramway Office'. Henry Webb, a Government whip, was attacked for employing a German butler and his wife, who were 'probably spies': a former cook had seen the butler cleaning a revolver in the pantry. Weekly lists were published of Germans who were surreptitiously changing their names from Knopp to Knox and Baumann to Beaumont.

As the flames of anti-German paranoia grew, fanned by Bottomley, he became still more flamboyant. Anticipating the formation of his own Government, he announced: 'Under the Business Government every editor who either knowingly or recklessly publishes false news will be shot.' He urged vendettas against all Germans, whether naturalised or not: 'You cannot naturalise an unnatural beast – a human abortion – a hellish fiend. But you CAN exterminate it.'

All German property should be confiscated and all Germans locked up. Their children must be deprived of education. Those who had been naturalised should be made to wear a distinctive badge and be indoors by dark – which induces a particular shudder in view of events to come much later. After the war they must continue to be ostracised: 'If by chance you should discover one day in a restaurant that you are being served by a German waiter, you will throw the soup in his foul face; if you find yourself sitting at the side of a German clerk you will spill the inkpot over his vile head.'

Bottomley also displayed platform skills that more than matched his propaganda genius on the printed page and which were also turned to profitable account. Many politicians have a golden tongue, but few could match Bottomley's facility for scraping the gold off the tongue and into the pocket.

Six weeks after the 1914 war began Bottomley made a recruiting speech at the London Opera House. Two hours before the meeting several thousand people milled outside the theatre and, by eight o'clock, the number had grown to 25,000, of whom only 5,000 could be admitted. Other gatherings followed, all triumphant and culminating in a Grand Patriotic Rally which filled the Albert Hall. The impresario, C.B. Cochran, engaged him to prop up an ailing revue by appearing for a quarter of an hour at the end of the first act. He was paid £100 a time. Ticket prices were substantially raised, but weekly receipts rose nevertheless by £1,100.

Despite the stirring patriotic themes, Bottomley was quite unsentimental about his performances, seeing himself principally as an entertainer. The business aspect always dominated and he invariably insisted on money down before making the speech. Once offered £50, he insisted he had been promised guineas. 'No, pounds,' said the proprietor. 'It must be guineas,' Bottomley insisted. 'The opposition show will give me fifty guineas.' 'But you don't want to go there, Mr Bottomley. It's a low down place.' 'I can't help that,' he replied. 'I am an oratorical courtesan. I sell myself to the man with the most money.'

From 1915 to 1917 he addressed twenty recruiting meetings (which he did gratis) and delivered more than 340 patriotic war lectures (from which he made over £22,000). He demanded anything between 65 and 85 per cent of the gross takings from a meeting, with the proprietors of the hall paying for advertising, music, lighting and hall.

He took an obsessive interest in the size of the 'gate' and always spent the time when the chairman was introducing him counting up the numbers occupying the 4s, 3s, 2s, and 1s seats. He always calculated roughly the size of his prospective fee before starting to speak. Extraordinarily, he varied his text according to the amount of money to be made. His series of stock perorations graduated in degrees of eloquence and loftiness of thought solely according to the size of the receipts.

These 'patriotic' meetings became the means of Bottomley's rehabilitation. They made him, through the power of his oratory, an influential figure who could reach out to the masses in a way which almost no other political leader could rival. It was now a practical possibility to resume a political career which had, only a short time before, seemed irreparably shattered. But first he had to discharge his bankruptcy. That required money – and lots of it.

In 1913 he had realised that large sums of money could be made out of lotteries and sweepstakes. However, they could not be conducted legally in England, so he set up a gambling-by-post operation based in Switzerland. By this means Bottomley's ship came home – in a country hundreds of miles from the sea!

The draw in his first sweepstake, on the 1913 Derby, was claimed to be of scrupulous fairness. Suspicion is aroused by the fact that three of the winners were old friends of Bottomley's and two of them ex-convicts. But the point is of no great importance as the total prize money was only £15,000 and the cash received amounted to no less than £270,000. One and a quarter million people subscribed.

Tickets were sold at ten for a pound. However, to squeeze the lemon dry just before the closing date, Bottomley reduced the price to five shillings for three. He intended to keep every penny of these extra takings for himself. The envelopes accompanying the application forms for reduced-price tickets were a different colour from the rest, so they could be extracted from the mailsacks without difficulty and put on one side in Bottomley's Swiss hotel suite, to which they were directed. Soon the envelope-openers stood knee-deep in waste paper as cheques, postal orders, banknotes, gold and silver were removed by Bottomley. He estimated his share of the profits at £150,000.

He held a number of swindles of this kind throughout the war years. Draws took place at regular intervals but, as the published list of prizewinners contained simply a mass of numbers, no one could check who had won. The winner every time, of course, was Bottomley. One example suffices to illustrate the technique. A sum of £7,000 entered as prize-money in the accounts was shown as having been drawn out in cash. There was no evidence to show who had won the prize, but an examination of Bottomley's own account revealed a credit of the same amount soon after!

At the time of the 1915 Derby sweepstake Bottomley was addressing a series of meetings on the Clyde, urging munitions workers to put their backs into the war effort. Afterwards, he contacted all the leading employers in the area and offered, if they gave him the addresses of all their workers, to send them all at his own expense a printed copy of his speech. Thousands of addresses were supplied but, instead of a copy of the speech, each one was sent an invitation to participate in the 1915 Derby sweepstake.

The Government floated a Victory Loan, in which the smallest bonds were worth a nominal £5 and issued at a price of £4 5s. They were to be redeemed in annual instalments in a draw made by the Bank of England. Bottomley had the brilliant idea of inviting smaller subscriptions to a Victory Bond Club run by himself. Each 15s 6d subscription would buy a £1 share in a £5 bond. Additionally there would be a lottery for the interest and, as a further inducement and unlike the Government scheme, repayment of the capital on demand at any time. This gave the man in the street the chance to join in a great patriotic enterprise from which he would otherwise be excluded, but with the possibility of a successful gamble thrown in.

He advertised the scheme widely and 300,000 people handed over their money to him. In less than two months, £467,000 was subscribed, from which bonds to the value of £500,000 were bought. He received subscriptions to the tune of nearly £900,000 and in 1918 paid off all his old creditors. Relieved from his bankruptcy, he was re-elected at South Hackney, this time as an Independent, with a huge majority.

Unfortunately, the organisation of the Victory Bond scheme was absolute chaos. Victims of his earlier schemes who complained were ignored if they complained only once. But if persistent they were fobbed off with certificates in the next Bottomley swindle. Thus the Victory Bond scheme was insolvent from the start. But forgery was rife also. The bonds were not personalised to the subscriber, so the pledge of repayment on demand resulted in large sums being 'returned' to individuals who had subcribed nothing in the first place.

No attempt was made to check the receipts against the issue of certificates. An envelope was torn open, the money tossed onto a pile and the letter, without any endorsement of the amount that had accompanied it, was put on one side to be dealt with later.

Mistakes could not be checked or rectified. Certificates were sent out before cheques cleared and, if they were dishonoured, there was no means of checking either the number of certificates issued or to what address they had been sent. All the while Bottomley was raiding the receipts to pay earlier debts and finance new hare-brained schemes. Financial doom inevitably careered towards him at the speed of an express train.

By October 1919 at least one fifth of the capital subscribed had passed into Bottomley's pocket. Part of this he 'invested' in taking trainloads of constituents for outings in Epping Forest – a facility he offered also to prospective members of his Parliamentary Group.

At 10s per 1,000 he purchased a million names and addresses of subscribers to the Golden Ballot and then set a large staff to work amalgamating them with the names of those who had participated in his own schemes. This expenditure was treated as though it was part of the Victory Bond Club although, in fact, it was a preparation for future schemes. In this way he acquired 1,750,000 envelopes already addressed to those likely to prove willing victims in the future.

When one scheme had had its day and money was no longer flowing in sufficiently to pay those demanding their money back, the solution was simple – start up a new scheme and develop a fresh cash flow. Such was the gullibility of millions of his dupes, they were prepared to exchange their worthless certificates in the old scheme for worthless certificates in the new and subscribe more to boot.

The Victory Bond Club was succeeded by the Thrift Bond Prize Club, which ostensibly gambled in French Credit National bonds. The more brazen the proposal, the more success it appeared to have. Thus, if a man had £10 in the Victory Bond Club, he was invited to send another £5, for which he would receive a Credit National bond with a face value of £15. The fact that £15 bonds could be purchased in the market at that time for £9 was not mentioned.

Many victims deposited their Victory Bond Club certificates and additional cash at Bottomley's offices, without even receiving an acknowledgement. In so doing they surrendered every scrap of evidence that they had subscribed to the Victory Bond Club. Fifty thousand subscribed £15 to the French Bond scheme. Bottomley received £750,000 for bonds which would cost him at the most £500,000 to buy. On a straight deal alone, he would have made £250,000, less expenses, and further profits were made through syndicate operations on the rate of exchange. Not content with this, Bottomley offered a 'second brew' – a further bond at the reduced price of £12 – pointing out the advantages of two French bonds with a face value of £40 for the trifling expenditure of £27.

Bottomley visited Paris twice a week, each time returning with suitcases full of cash. The merry-go-round of wild and senseless spending soon began to seem like something from a Mad Hatter's tea party. He bought the German battleship *Deutschland* as a publicity stunt and two obscure newspapers which required constant feeding with more cash. He bought shares in racecourses, theatrical enterprises, thousands of bottles of champagne and even, absurdly, debentures in a temperance hotel in Worthing!

A man who, according to Bottomley, had responsibility for paying prizewinners in the Club's draw, was handed £9,500 from the Victory Bond Club. There was no evidence there ever had been a draw and the man's principal employment was to place Bottomley's bets with the bookies! By the time the Receiver stepped in, in October 1921, the rake's progress had run its course and all that remained in the coffers was the sum of £22 9s 7d.

When re-elected to Parliament in 1918 Bottomley had founded the Independent Parliamentary Group, which became a political force in its own right. Lloyd George's Government was an uneasy coalition of Liberals and Conservatives and no sizeable opposition party had emerged at the 1918 election. The Liberals split into three groups, united in the mutual detestation of their respective leaders. The Tories, for their part, disliked serving under Lloyd George. Bottomley, therefore, designed his Group skilfully to attract malcontents from both major parties and, by placing an emphasis on 'improving the lot of the working man', weaned votes away from Labour.

Its programme was populist to the core – war reparations to be strictly enforced, British supremacy to be maintained 'unfettered by Leagues of Nations', exclusion of undesirable aliens, strict economy, 'keeping faith with ex-servicemen', reform of the House of Lords. But what the policy most strongly advocated was 'the introduction of Business principles into Government – including the issue of Premium Bonds'!

Bottomley and a sidekick, both elected in 1918, were soon joined by three others in subsequent by-election successes. But the shades quickly darkened after a disgruntled former associate, Reuben Bigland, published and widely distributed a libellous pamphlet exposing some of Bottomley's most shameless frauds. Bottomley sued for criminal libel. Bigland's evidence incriminated himself, but he was bent on revenge at any price. Bottomley lost disastrously and was charged with fraudulent conversion in the Victory Bond scheme. Convicted on twenty-three counts out of twenty-four, he was sentenced to seven years' penal servitude and, after a failed appeal, expelled from the House of Commons in August 1922.

He was confident as ever of rehabilitation, but this was the end of his eccentric career in politics, business and the press. Had his schemes and behaviour been less reckless, he could have retained a vast fortune and in the confused political climate of the 1920s made himself into a real power-broker. But he always flew not just too near the sun, he propelled himself into it.

Catastrophe was always inevitable. Serving his sentence in Wormwood Scrubs, Bottomley was put to making mailbags. A prison visitor engaged him in polite conversation: 'Ah, Bottomley. Sewing?' His powers of repartee had survived his traumas and his lightning reply was the measure of the man: 'No. Reaping!'

LORD HUGH CECIL, BARON QUICKSWOOD

MP FOR GREENWICH 1895–1906, OXFORD UNIVERSITY 1910–37; PEER 1941–56

'I was astonished at the obsoleteness of his opinions, the subtlety of his arguments and the cast-iron rigidity of his mind.'

Fifth son of the 3rd Marquess of Salisbury, Lord Hugh was known in the family as 'Linky' – because his appearance was so odd that he reminded them of the 'Missing Link', the hypothetical connection between the human race and the apes. He was tall, pale, bony and slight – he weighed only seven stone at eighteen, hardly varying from this weight throughout his life.

A lifelong bachelor, he lived at Hatfield until he left home for the first time at the age of sixty-seven. This was to return to Eton, which he had left in the early 1880s, having been removed back to Hatfield after only a few months on account of his delicateness.

His nephew, Lord David Cecil, described him as

> not a man of action, with neither taste nor talent for practical affairs. He was interested less in getting things done than in discovering what he thought. Furthermore his thoughts were usually eccentric and controversial, and were made more so because he liked to follow them uncompromisingly to their logical conclusions whatever

practical difficulties those might raise, and also to express them in their most extreme and paradoxical form.

Algernon Cecil, a hirsute cousin, was disconcerted to be asked: 'Algernon, why have you grown that absurd beard?' In extenuation he replied, 'Our Lord grew a beard.' But Linky trumped this ace with his rejoinder: 'Our Lord was not a gentleman.'

The great political controversies at the turn of the nineteenth century included Free Trade v Tariff Reform, Irish Home Rule and Social Insurance etc. But these were of secondary importance to Linky, whose greatest Parliamentary crusade was implacable opposition to an obscure measure, the Deceased Wife's Sister Bill. By a canon of 1604 it was forbidden for a man to marry his deceased wife's sister. Lord Hugh denounced such a marriage in the most violent terms – 'an act of sexual vice' and 'as immoral as concubinage or bigamy'.

For many years he frustrated all attempts at this harmless reform. In 1902, a Bill seemed certain to be carried by a substantial majority, so he organised a small group of diehards and friends (including the young Winston Churchill) to dawdle through the Division Lobby so slowly that the count of votes could not be taken until the debate had exceeded its allotted time and the measure was lost.

He carried his intransigence on this question to preposterous extremes. His brother Robert built a small country house in the Weald of Sussex but, horror of horrors! Lord Hugh discovered that their next-door neighbour had married his deceased wife's sister! He urged Robert to show them not the slightest friendship or cordiality and when the neighbour's carriage broke down one day on a road nearby he swept by in his own carriage without offering an iota of assistance. The neighbour, however, exacted revenge for this ungracious attitude by planting along the boundary of his estate a line of trees which gradually cut off the Cecils' view of the South Downs.

Linky had odd views also about the countryside. He complained that the Sussex water had an excess of iron, which infallibly produced acute indigestion, and that the forest was infested with poisonous snakes. He gave this practical advice: 'Do not sit in your garden unless on a very high chair. I have been told that snakes are afraid of the human voice, so you must talk aloud all the time – reciting poetry perhaps.'

He thought it unseemly that Neville Chamberlain, a Unitarian Prime Minister, should advise the Crown on the appointment of bishops. He told the Church Assembly that, in another age, Chamberlain would not be exercising authority in Downing Street but be burnt at the stake at Smithfield for heresy!

In 1936 he was appointed Provost of Eton, an office similar to that of Dean of a cathedral. Kenneth Rose wrote of him 'He had long believed that controversy, particularly when acrimonious, was one of the pleasures of a civilised life. Eton brought him many rewarding opportunities for the practice of his art and the exercise of a life-long contempt for schoolmasters.'

Sir Osbert Sitwell wrote to him on his appointment: 'To think of you as provost almost reconciles me to Eton, which I so hated.' Sitwell had always proclaimed in his *Who's Who* entry: 'Educated: during the holidays from Eton.'

As Provost, although not in holy orders himself, he exercised authority over the College chapel and its services. He took great trouble over the selection of visiting preachers and extended his truculence in theological controversy into this new sphere. Hensley Henson, Bishop of Durham, wrote 'after an evening of deep disagreement' with Linky: 'I was astonished at the obsoleteness of his opinions, the subtlety of his arguments and the cast-iron rigidity of his mind. He is a medievalist in the methods of his reasoning, the strength of his prejudices and the obscurantism of his outlook.'

The Second World War was deprecated as a disruption of his otherwise orderly life. He continued to dine in knee-breeches and silk stockings and expected his guests to maintain the same standards. He objected to air-raid precautions as smacking of hysteria. He wrote to *The Times* in September 1939 to say that it was wrong to encourage people to think too much of their own safety. 'Indeed, would it matter very much to the event of war if a theatre full of people were bombed?'

Elliott, the headmaster, was concerned to protect the safety of the boys. Linky took a more robust view, opposing his proposal to build air-raid shelters as a needless extravagance and reminded him that, under the statutes of Eton, the head was responsible only for 'the studies and discipline of the school' – from which a right to protect the boys from stray bombs could not possibly be inferred. Elliott disagreed: 'How can I possibly either teach or discipline the boys if they are dead?' So acrimonious was this dispute that Provost and headmaster ended up scarcely on speaking terms and the matter had to be resolved by the governing body, who unanimously and pusillanimously voted for the shelters.

Linky was asked early in the war what he would do if a bomb did fall on the school. He replied with some sangfroid, 'I should ring for Tucker' (his butler). In December 1940 two stray bombs did fall on Eton, one of which ploughed through the head-master's schoolroom but failed to explode and buried itself in the ground. Linky did ring for Tucker, who handed him a particularly shabby old hat which would not matter if it got dirty. 'No, no, Tucker,' the Provost exclaimed. 'My best hat to see the ruins.' Upon arrival at the site he proceeded to poke the bomb crater vigorously with his umbrella, shrieking 'It's a dud. It's a dud.' Shortly afterwards it exploded.

In 1941 Linky was made a peer by Winston Churchill, whose best man he had been in 1908. This brought to eleven the number of Cecils in the Upper House – three sons of the 3rd Marquess, Salisbury, Cecil of Chelwood and Quickswood; a son-in-law, Selborne; two grandsons, Cranborne and Wolmer, each called up in a lesser title of his father during his lifetime; a nephew, Balfour; two great-nephews, Rockley and Rayleigh. There were also two members of the other branch of the Cecils, Exeter and Amherst of Hackney.

Churchill's letter offering the honour deserves wider circulation:

My dear Linky,
I hope you will give me the pleasure of submitting your name to the King for a Barony. It would be good to have

you in the House of Lords, to repel the onset of the Adolf Hitler schools, to sustain the aristocratic morale, and to chide the Bishops when they err; and now that I read in the newspapers that the Eton flogging-block is destroyed by enemy action, you may have more leisure and strength.

Lord Hugh Cecil – 'Linky'.

SIR HUGH RANKIN BT.

1899–1988

'The only baronet in the United Kingdom who is living on National Assistance.'

Sir Hugh Rankin, 3rd Baronet, never attained or even sought high political office. In 1949–50 he reached his peak, being elected firstly, to Perth District Council then, secondly, a councillor for the borough of Rattray and Blairgowrie and finally, a county councillor for Perthshire.

These successive successes were surprising. Perthshire was one of the most solidly Conservative areas of Scotland, whereas Rankin stoutly declared: 'I am a blood-red militant Communist in every possible way. ABSOLUTELY BLOOD-RED.'

Born in the middle of the Tunisian desert in 1899, he was the elder son of Sir Reginald Rankin, a big-game hunter who had hunted for the extinct giant sloth in Chile and shot the largest snow leopard on record in India.

Sir Hugh, unlike so many today, was not a career politician. In fact, he had several careers. Having run away from school at Harrow, he became a riveter's mate in a Belfast shipyard. Then he joined the Army, serving as a trooper in the 1st Royal Dragoon Guards in the Sinn Fein campaign from 1920 to 1922 ('oldest surviving member', as he pointed out in *Who's Who* in 1988). Shot by a sniper and invalided out, he later observed laconically that all along he had been 'fighting on the wrong side, I'm afraid'.

From 1929 to 1931 he was a 'whole-time "piece-work" sheep shearer in W. Australia, covering area between Bunbury and Broome' (about 1,800 miles apart). In 1938, having returned to England he became a 'representative on committee of British sheep breeders in London appointed to petition Government re sheep industry' and in 1962 was 'runner-up All Britain Sheep Judging Competition (6,000 entrants)'.

He also had deeply spiritual inclinations, but declared he had 'always hated and loathed the Christian religion'. Travelling in the Middle East he was converted to Islam by the 5th Lord Headley, a Muslim peer whom he succeeded in 1935 as President of the British Muslim Society. However, his patience with this body was quickly exhausted: 'They were very rude . . . and knew nothing of law and order or methods of procedure. I was disgusted with the whole lot of them.' He resigned after a fracas, decided to form his own new, non-sectarian Muslim Association and, in 1937, was the British representative to the first all-Muslim conference at Geneva.

He joined the RASC as 2nd lieutenant in 1940, at the age of forty-one, and served as a captain in India until 1945. However, he later 'realised what an awful fool I had been to fight for Britain. If a revolution comes – and come it must after the next world war – I'll do my damnedest to see it succeeds.' In India he also had a blinding revelation: 'The Muslim religion is a fighting one, so I dropped it and became a Buddhist.' In 1944 he became a 'practising Non-Theistic Theravada Buddhist and performed the Holy Buddhist pilgrimage, the 2nd Britisher to do so', becoming also Vice-President of the World Buddhist Association.

In 1959 he declared it was 'no news' that Abominable Snowmen existed: 'It is part of our known belief that five Bodhisattvas ["Perfected Men"] control the destiny of this world. They meet together once a year in a cave in the Himalayas to make their decisions. One of them lives permanently on the higher Himalayas. One of them lives in the Scottish Cairngorms.' He said that he and his wife had clearly seen the Scottish Bodhisattva in the Larig Ghru Pass.

A man of varied interests besides politics, he listed his recreations as follows:

Study of domestic animals; golf (holds an amateur record amongst golfers of Great Britain in having played on 382 separate courses of UK and Eire), shooting, coarse fishing, hunting, motoring, cycling on mountain tracks to tops of British mountains (President Rough Stuff Cycling Association 1956); study of ancient trackways; bowls; tennis; archaeology (wife and himself are only persons who have crawled under dwarf fir forest for last half mile of most northerly known section of any Roman road in Europe, terminating opposite end of Kirriemuir Golf Course).

To his other distinctions he added the impressive titles of Hereditary Piper of the Clan Maclaine, *News of the World* Knight of the Road (for courtesy in motor driving) and Broadsword Champion of the British Army, 1921.

In 1932 he adopted by deed poll the additional surname of Stewart. However, he changed both his mind and his name again in 1946, discontinuing the surname by deed poll. At the same time, for completeness, he changed his Christian name from Hubert to Hugh.

In 1965 he claimed to be 'the only baronet in the United Kingdom who is living on National Assistance' and that his title had always been a hindrance. He was, however, prepared to turn his hand to anything: 'Anything except being a butler. I hate snobbishness.'

In a highly entertaining entry in *Who's Who* he detailed his political odyssey:

Joined Labour Party 1939 and holds extreme political views; has been a Dominion Home Ruler for Scotland, member of Scottish National Party; joined Scottish Communist Party 1945, resigned 1980; Welsh Republican Nationalist and Welsh speaker; now left-side Labour; also zealous SNP who desires an independent Red Republic of all Scotland, except Orkneys and Shetlands.

What a pity he was only a baronet, as he would have made a splendid deputy to the leader of the Communist peers, Lord Milford.

EARL WINTERTON

CONSERVATIVE MP FOR HORSHAM 1904–51

'Arsenic and old lace.'

Lord Winterton was an Oxford undergraduate just a few weeks past his twenty-first birthday when first elected in a by-election at Horsham in 1904. As its youngest Member he was the 'Baby of the House'. When he retired in 1951 he was its 'Father' – a unique double distinction.

Whilst canvassing in the by-election Lord Winterton's mother frequently encountered a fierce controversy. The large influx of Jewish refugees fleeing from Russian pogroms had fuelled a populist movement to restrict immigration, the first steps towards which were taken the following year through the Aliens Act of 1905.

In one cottage she was told by the wife of an agricultural labourer that her husband would vote for her son against 'them foreigners'. Lady W. expressed surprise because there were few foreigners in rural Sussex in those days. She got the indignant reply: 'That's where you are wrong, my Lady. Why, there's foreigners from Surrey coming into this parish every day. We've 'ad pretty near enough of 'em.' So much for political education.

In 1904 his father was still alive, so Winterton was actually elected under the subsidiary or 'courtesy' title of Viscount Turnour. He did not succeed to the earldom until 1907. Shortly afterwards he met a constituent who apparently did not recognise him. The Member introduced himself: 'Hello. I'm Winterton,' he exclaimed. The constituent replied: 'How stupid of me. I thought you were that ass, Turnour.'

Winterton acquired a reputation for asperity and cantankerousness, which he rather enjoyed. During the Second World War he formed an alliance with Emanuel Shinwell, a fellow member of the Awkward Squad on the other side of the House. This unlikely alliance was popularly dubbed 'arsenic and old lace'. They combined to offer critical comment on the conduct of the war as they deemed necessary, ensuring that Parliament's rights were defended and that it did not wither into a 'negligible factor' in wartime.

Winterton was a tall, angular figure sporting a high-buttoned jacket and rather short, narrow, 'drain-pipe' trousers. Arms tightly folded, long legs entwined like bindweed, he was always ready to uncoil like a spring to raise points of order or expatiate on some matter 'of the gravest constitutional importance'. He seemed always on the point of boiling over at some injustice to a fellow citizen or affront to the dignity of the House. His lean torso would sway backwards and forwards on the bench, choler would mantle his face and he would rub his long hands so violently together that he must have generated no little heat. In fact, he once dislocated a thumb.

He was described by one political commentator as 'an irascible old gentleman who could be observed almost any day of the week, standing outside the House of Commons and tapping his cane impatiently on his thin legs because the policeman was not holding up the traffic smartly enough for him.'

In this spirit, in the Commons in 1944, he denounced 'the Forces' favourite', Vera Lynn, and other 'radio crooners' as a threat to morale, saying: 'They resemble no known American accent and remind one of the caterwauling of an inebriated cockatoo. I cannot believe that all this wailing about lost babies can possibly have a good effect on troops who are about to engage in a very serious pursuit in which their lives will be endangered.'

He frequently contributed eccentric letters to the *Daily Telegraph*. Typical of them is the following:

Sir,

In recent years it has been the custom in railway dining cars and in certain restaurants, though not where the head waiter or maitre d'hotel knows his business, for the steward, waiter or waitress to say when serving the customer: 'Thank you' or 'Thank you very much' or 'excuse me'.

These terms are completely meaningless. The person serving has nothing for which to thank the person whom he or she is serving, nor is there any reason to excuse himself or herself for carrying out a plain duty.

The object cannot be to remind the customer to thank the person who is serving, because no one, unless very boorish and bad-mannered would fail to say 'thank you' after the dish has been served.

I have been sorely tempted more than once to make an equally irrelevant reply, such as 'Merry Christmas' or 'The same to you and many of them' but have hitherto refrained from doing so for fear of hurting the feelings of anyone concerned.

It is not, I think, priggish or pedantic to say that this is a deplorable example of the misuse of the English language and misunderstanding of the meaning of words which prevails despite three-quarters of a century of universal education.

'That ass, Turnour.'

TREBITSCH LINCOLN

LIBERAL MP FOR DARLINGTON 1910

'I shall always treat him with the respect due to an elected representative of the people – and, the reserve necessary in dealing with a liar.'

'The election of Trebitsch Lincoln to the House of Commons in January 1910 stands out as one of the oddest aberrations in British political history' was the verdict of his biographer, Bernard Wasserstein. Few MPs also see themselves as a religious Messiah.

Ignacz Trebitsch was born into a prosperous Orthodox Jewish household in Hungary in 1879. At the age of sixteen he decided to become an actor and enrolled in the Royal Hungarian Academy of Dramatic Art – an appropriate training for the real-life dramas and fantasies to come. Shortly afterwards, however, he fled the country on account of two charges of petty theft.

Attracted by the prospect of Queen Victoria's Diamond Jubilee celebrations, he came to England. Thereafter, he rarely stayed in one place for more than a few months – unless compelled by some external force, such as imprisonment or lack of a passport.

Down-and-out in the East End, he was taken in by the London Society for the Promotion of Christianity Amongst the Jews, a missionary society operating under the aegis of the Church of England. He returned to Hungary briefly, only to flee once more when accused for a third time of stealing a gold watch. This time he went to Hamburg, where he was taken in by the Irish Presbyterian mission and was eventually baptised a Christian by another Hungarian Jewish Irish Presbyterian. However, after thirteen days he tired of being an Irish Presbyterian and decided to become a Lutheran. He left this sect shortly afterwards, having developed a 'nervous headache'.

Returning to Hamburg, he reverted to Irish Presbyterianism and was packed off as a Christian missionary to convert the Jews of Canada. Alas, he quickly discovered that money was in short supply. To rectify this deficiency, he persuaded the Anglican Archbishop of Montreal to make a takeover bid for his Mission. So, having been in the course of three years an Orthodox Jew, a Presbyterian and a Lutheran, Trebitsch now became an Anglican.

Shortly afterwards, however, he decided to return to England, leaving behind a trail of dishonoured loans and unpaid bills. Astonishingly, he then persuaded the Archbishop of Canterbury, Randall Davidson, to appoint him curate of the parish of Appledore in Kent, with a promise of ordination as a Church of England priest on condition that he sit examinations. Sitting them was no problem but passing them was rather different and his results were dismal.

Fortunately, his father-in-law died at that point and left Mrs Trebitsch some money. Financial independence swept away Trebitsch's spiritual pretensions and he now devoted himself to temporal studies – international politics and economics. He also changed his name to the more English-sounding 'Lincoln' and looked around for a position which would bring him into contact with politicians.

Temperance and the evils of drink were major political controversies in 1905 and Lincoln applied for a job with a society engaged in temperance propaganda. He was unsuccessful in this but, by good fortune, he obtained an appointment to see Seebohm Rowntree, the York chocolate millionaire and philanthropist – also a Quaker, strong Liberal and social reformer. He must have been intrigued by the cosmopolitan Lincoln because, immediately after their meeting, Lincoln sent the following telegram to his wife: 'Am permanently engaged as secretary to

Mr Seebohm Rowntree to investigate different countries – Holland, Belgium, Germany, Denmark. Salary paid in advance. Leaving shortly.'

Rowntree was a pioneer of empirical social research and a valued adviser to Lloyd George, President of the Board of Trade 1905–8 and Chancellor of the Exchequer 1908–15. He opened up a new world for Lincoln, far away from stultifying suburban domesticity. In his new position, effectively Rowntree's policy analyst, he could thrust himself into the attentions of 'the great and the good', and even directly influence Government policy.

Astonishingly, Lincoln was chosen in 1909 as Liberal candidate for Darlington – astonishing, considering he was only twenty-nine, spoke English with a very strong Hungarian accent and was not even a British citizen. His naturalisation followed a month after being selected (although he later untruthfully backdated this to 1908 in his *Who's Who* entry).

His work for Rowntree required him to travel widely in Europe, where he needed access to unpublished Government documents on all manner of obscure topics, such as Belgian land-management. The advent of the new Liberal Government in 1905 had given Rowntree influence with senior Foreign Office Ministers, thus enabling him to obtain various impressive letters of credence for Lincoln.

Immediately after being selected for Darlington he set off for Hungary and the Balkans. Staying in first-class hotels at Rowntree's expense and armed with his Foreign Office credentials, doors were opened to him everywhere to hob-nob with high officials and Ministers. All this attention was flattering to his limitless vanity and the mode of tourism most congenial. In the course of it Lincoln also developed a taste for another kind of fantasy – impressing his hosts as an international financier and wheeler-dealer. He announced, quite untruthfully, that he had the backing of multi-millionaires like Sir Ernest Cassell (the Anglo-German financier and close friend of Edward VII) and the merchant banker, Samuel Montagu. In Hungary he even announced he was ready to invest up to £2 million on suitable business projects. In Belgrade also he claimed to be thinking of

Trebitsch Lincoln: 'Such a splendid man as me'.

setting up an Anglo-Serbian bank with capital of £400,000. Needless to say, having returned to England, nothing more was heard of these ficitious schemes.

Lincoln had assumed it would be several years before a General Election and that he could continue for some time to swan around Europe in this agreeable way. The 1906 Parliament might have lasted until perhaps 1913 but, when the Lords rejected Lloyd George's 'People's Budget' in 1909, the resulting furore revolutionised the political situation. Instead of waiting years, Lincoln now faced the prospect of an election within weeks. Remarkably, in January 1910, when the Conservatives made huge gains of seats at the expense of the Liberals, the exotic Lincoln bucked the trend and defeated Darlington's well-established and local Conservative MP by a bare majority of 29.

In their campaign, the Conservatives had appealed to one facet of the insular Englishman, by unashamedly attacking Lincoln as a foreigner. Lincoln responded by advising electors they had a choice – they could vote either for his opponent 'who fought against the people' or 'for such a splendid man as they have in me!'

Whereas Darlington Tories appealed to British xenophobia, Lincoln counter-attacked by appealing to an equally powerful English emotion – sentimentality towards dumb animals. He luridly exploited 'tariff reform', a major issue between the parties nationally, by issuing a dramatic warning: tariffs had raised the price of food in Germany to such an extent that working families had been driven to eating horses and pet dogs to avoid starvation. Under a Conservative Government, the people of Darlington would also be forced onto a diet of Labrador, Alsatian and no doubt, in extremis, Jack Russell and Chihuahua. Lincoln thus deflected the object of Darlington's xenophobia away from Hungary and onto Germany, a more familiar target and one easier to revile. It proved a most successful if unlikely tactic.

As his biographer has succinctly observed,

> Without much assistance from the local Liberal press, Trebitsch, a stranger to Darlington, a novice on the hustings, a man who had himself never voted in a British election, a candidate whose most distinctive campaign plank had been the complaint that German workers ate the flesh of dogs, had at the age of 30 succeeded where Disraeli and countless others had failed, in being elected to the House of Commons at the first attempt.'

It was a stupendous achievement.

In the euphoria of his unexpected election there was one ominous exception to the wave of congratulation. A British diplomat in Budapest who, having met him, suspected him of being an arrogant fraud, wrote to the Foreign Office, 'I do not congratulate the people of Darlington on their choice of an MP but if Mr T. Lincoln comes back here I shall always treat him with the respect due to an elected representative of the people – and the reserve necessary in dealing with a liar.'

MPs received no salary in 1910, but Lincoln took the view that he ought to increase his spending to match the rise in his status. Despite losing such secure income as he had, he spent recklessly and lavishly. Rowntree still subsidised him very generously but this was nowhere near sufficient to cover his extravagant tastes.

The Austro-Hungarian Government added to his problems. Lincoln had asked some irritating Parliamentary questions about the Austrian annexation of Bosnia-Herzegovina and, in retaliation, the Imperial Government informed the British Foreign Secretary of his early background as a petty thief.

He might have weathered this storm, but 1910 was a year of continual political crisis and another General Election took place in December. By then Lincoln was floundering in a sea of debt and the exposure of his shady past increased the pressure on him. The smash came in November 1910. Within barely a week of polling day he was obliged unwillingly to resign as Liberal candidate. This left H. Pike Pease, whom he had defeated in January, to regain his seat for the Conservatives on the back of what the new Liberal candidate described as the 'contumely and scandal' surrounding his predecessor.

Lincoln was forced into bankruptcy, paying his creditors a mere five shillings in the pound. After this watershed, his life took even more bizarre turns. He operated on the irrational maxim that, if you spent irresponsibly enough, you must generate sufficient income to pay for it all. So, notwithstanding his own insolvency, he tried his hand at speculation in oilfield development companies in the Balkans – leading to predictable failure in each case.

The outbreak of war in 1914 had given him a potential break by providing him with work at the GPO Mount Pleasant sorting office, censoring mail to Hungary. Unfortunately, this did not last long. Not content merely to read people's letters, he insisted on writing his own comments on them, a practice which led to dismissal.

Financial desperation now impelled him in the direction of bare-faced fraud. He applied to John Goldstein, a financier, for a loan of £1,000, which was agreed subject to finding a guarantor. This was no problem for Lincoln, who immediately suggested Rowntree, giving his address as the National Liberal Club. Goldstein wrote to him there and received a reply to all intents signed by Rowntree confirming the guarantee, on which basis Lincoln was advanced £750. However, it seems that Lincoln had merely gone to the Club, plucked the letter addressed to Rowntree from the table where members' letters were left for collection and fraudulently penned the appropriate reply.

Inevitably this idiotic deception was unmasked and reported to Scotland Yard. Coincidentally, in the very same week he was found guilty of fraud in Romania and sentenced in absentia to seven months' imprisonment and a fine of £2,000. As a desperate measure he embarked on a new career move – the former journalist, ex-missionary, unfrocked parson, failed politician and bankrupt businessman decided to become an international spy!

The British War Office refused the offer of his services as a double agent, so he decided to try the other side. He caught a ferry to Holland, which was neutral in the First World War, and arranged to meet a German diplomat. German Intelligence was delighted to acquire the services of an ex-MP and sent him back to London. Here he tried to double-cross the Germans but the Admiralty threatened instead to report him to the police. But, before he could be arrested, he decamped post-haste for New York.

Here he wrote two sensational articles for an American newspaper *The World*, headed 'Revelations of Mr Lincoln, former Member of Parliament, who became a German spy'. He moved into an apartment with his brother, who quickly decided he could take no more and escaped into the US Army. This proved an unhappy decision, as his brother, now an object of suspicion on account of Lincoln, was put under surveillance too. He was spotted in an act of sodomy with a fellow GI and sent to Alcatraz.

The British Government, meanwhile, had taken a dim view of Lincoln's articles. For a former British MP to announce publicly he had spied for Germany was a humiliation for Britain in the battle for US public opinion. Britain applied for Lincoln's extradition on charges of fraud. He was arrested but managed to escape before he could be deported and held a sensational press conference whilst on the run. Recaptured eventually in a mammoth police exercise in New York, he was sentenced on his return to Britain to three years in prison, where he became a neighbour to Sir Roger Casement, who was later executed for high treason.

In 1919 Lincoln was freed – but ordered to be deported. However, the Foreign Office was fearful 'he might easily become a sort of Lenin of Central Europe' in the chaos following the collapse of the old imperial regimes. Just at that moment, Hungary was under the control of Bela Kun's short-lived Soviet Republic, so Lincoln's deportation was put on hold. Then, when the Kun regime was ousted shortly afterwards, Lincoln was unceremoniously bundled out of the country – the only ex-MP ever to be deported.

Unknown to the authorities, his political enthusiasms had moved somewhat to the right since 1910 and his next move was to Berlin to agitate for the restoration of the Hohenzollern monarchy. He failed in an attempt to contact the exiled Kaiser, but did sail to the remote Friesian island where the ex-Crown Prince was detained.

When the 'Kapp Putsch' took place in 1920, Lincoln allied himself to the Freikorps (a right-wing private army) and tried to seize control of Berlin as a precursor to the violent overthrow of the Republic and repudiation of the Treaty of Versailles. The Government took fright and fled from Berlin to Dresden, leaving a vacuum in the capital. The following day two brigades marched in without opposition, to be met by Kapp, clad in morning coat, top hat and spats. As a central figure in the putsch, Lincoln became for a few days a member of what passed, in the postwar breakdown of authority, for the German Government. He was placed in charge of foreign press relations and greatly relished his absolute power to censor the British press which had so reviled him in the past. Revenge was sweet, for however short a time.

After a mere five days the putsch collapsed and the *Daily Telegraph* rounded on Lincoln:

> There is something almost Olympian about this man's scoundrelism. He has been handicapped by nature with a face in every feature of which deceit, dishonesty and brutality are written for all to see, yet he has been a clergyman of the Church of England, a Liberal member of the British Parliament and adviser on foreign affairs of the German usurper who put himself forward as the champion of purity and truth. More than that, as an Hungarian Jew he got into the confidence of a clique consisting exclusively of the most virulent anti-Semites of the most violent type.

It was quite astonishing that Lincoln could have been accepted by such types and it has even been claimed that he met Hitler at this time. It is possible but, if so, he must have thought the future Führer so insignificant compared with his own world-historical importance that it never occurred to him to mention the fact – something which would have been entirely in keeping with Lincoln's egocentric character, of course.

On the run again after the failed insurrection, Lincoln fled next to Eastern Europe to embroil himself in nationalist movements in various countries. In the course of this he succeeded in selling to the Czech Government a suitcase full of papers, many of which he had stolen from his most recent allies in Germany. He alleged that they provided evidence of a vast conspiracy by counter-revolutionary associations in Central Europe. Although this was pooh-poohed by British diplomats, the Czechs took it seriously. *The Times* published a three-part series of articles in a very prominent position on its editorial page under the headline 'European Plot Divulged'. The following day *Le Matin* in Paris did the same. Over the next week the story was taken up around the world and Lincoln became a by-word for international political intrigue and sinister influence.

Then in 1922, for reasons which remain obscure, he fled to China. Typically, he reached the Orient in the most roundabout way. Having been deported from Austria, he sailed for the United States and entered on a false passport. He was later apprehended and was deported from there too, but he was allowed to make his own arrangements for departure, travelled across the continent to California and sailed from there to Japan and then to China.

He knew no Chinese but shortly afterwards he popped up as an adviser to various warlords in Szechwan, in Central China, doing his best to damage British trading interests there. He remained in China for the rest of his life, apart from sporadic wanderings as far afield as Europe, India and California. He was banned by the Government from entering British territory anywhere in the world but this posed little problem. When necessary, he simply forged the passports required and, at one time, carried as many as seven.

In 1925 in Tientsin he converted to theosophy, a creed invented in New York in 1875 by a Mrs Blavatsky. As a religion it drew on Buddhist writings, Egyptian hieroglyphics and the Kabbalah for its 'science of ancient and proved Magic'. Soon afterwards, however, he was reported as staying in the guise of an Austrian under an assumed name in a small Buddhist monastery in Ceylon. He had already abandoned one more religious creed for yet another. Or, as he put it, he had 'decided to walk out of a lunatic asylum – the world'.

At this time he appears to have been obsessed with the idea of living in Tibet. His aim, on the one hand, was to pursue a serene and contemplative existence and, on the other, to devote himself as an act of revenge to stirring up religious ferment in Central Asia in order to undermine British imperial rule.

In 1931 he was ordained a Buddhist monk, known as the 'Venerable Chao Kung' and based himself in Shanghai. He abandoned western garb and surrounded himself with a gaggle of sycophantic followers, appointing himself as their 'abbot'. Over these dupes he established a hellish regime, as recalled by one: 'One meal per day, about 16 hours of work out of 24, rarely being permitted to speak aloud and being tyrannically dominated all the while by the Abbot, were not conducive to happiness. After having seen Chao Kung in an embarrassing position with one of the younger nuns, I decided the time was ripe for me to leave.'

When the Japanese invaded China he became an outspoken supporter of Japan. In 1941 he approached Nazi German emissaries in Shanghai and declared that, if only he could meet Hitler alone, three Tibetan wise men would emerge from the wall and save Germany. The SS ideologists, following Himmler's example, peculiarly prone to believe all manner of crackpot mystic nonsense, took this at face value. No such meeting occurred but, when Rudolf Hess landed in Scotland later that year, he was found to have in his possession two phials of 'sacred liquid' provided by a Tibetan Grand Lama!

As the Japanese entered Shanghai he was accused by the Germans of arms dealing and disowned. By 1943 most of his family in Hungary had been wiped out by the Nazis and he wrote a public letter to Hitler denouncing his Final Solution. He was arrested by the Japanese and died after only two days in a Shanghai hospital, supposedly poisoned by Nazi agents.

It had been a full life – Hungarian fraudster, Jewish apostate, Anglican curate, German revolutionary, American journalist, Chinese Buddhist abbot, Japanese apologist – and British MP.

LORD WILLIAM CECIL

BISHOP OF EXETER 1916–36

'Without a ticket, how on earth shall I know
where I'm going?'

Second son of the Prime Minister, the 3rd Marquess of Salisbury, he was known to family and friends as 'Fish' (because he was a queer fish). He married Lady Florence Bootle-Wilbraham, fondly known as 'Fluffy', and sat in the House of Lords for twenty years as Bishop of Exeter.

Appropriately to his calling he was 'other-worldly' and the kindest of Christian souls. He was addicted to parish visiting but was a social cripple, with no small talk. In polite company he tended to withdraw into himself, whilst simultaneously affecting to listen to his garrulous hostess by regularly nodding appreciatively in apparent agreement with whatever was being said.

In such circumstances it was up to Fluffy, the more socially versatile, to keep the conversation alive. On one occasion, however, the Bishop's performance was more than usually cataleptic and even Fluffy was moved eventually to disengage.

'Well!' she said to their visitee, 'we must be going now. We only looked in to say how do you do.' Suddenly, at the sound of these words, Fish's trance was broken. Hearing only the final words of her salutation, he jumped up and thrust out his hand. 'How do you do,' he said, obediently following his wife out of the door and vigorously wiping his feet on the mat as he went – all the time blissfully unaware that he was on the way out rather than in!

On trips abroad with his seven children he exhibited a considerable eccentricity. At home he would have no connection with domestic finance, apart from occasionally signing a cheque. But abroad it was different. He had so often been pickpocketed he decided to protect himself by wearing a money belt with little pockets all around. But, unfortunately, he tended to put it on upside-down, with the result once that he not only lost all his money but also the family return ticket home.

He loved the warmth of the sun and made many trips to the south of France, often by bicycle – always wearing yellow glasses, a broad-brimmed hat and a brown silk suit. He later decided that red was a protective against the sun's strong ultraviolet rays so all the girls were put into red frocks and the boys into red shirts.

Being extremely absent-minded, he repeatedly failed to remember to bring back his pyjamas after preaching in some far-flung part of the country. Eventually exasperated, Fluffy laid down the law sufficiently bluntly to force the issue to the forefront of his mind. On his next return home she opened his case and was delighted to find the pyjamas – but less pleased to discover also the sheets of the bed in which he had slept the previous night.

When promoted to become Bishop of Exeter he declined to use the Bishop's Palace except for an office and preferred to live in a much smaller house just outside the city, travelling in by bicycle. He chose one with straight handlebars so as to avoid interlocking it with other machines and painted it orange for instant recognition. But even then he would still frequently mistake someone else's more anonymous bike for his own. On one occasion he eventually realised, but not until halfway home, that he was riding not his own bright orange contraption but a woman's machine painted black. He swiftly pedalled back to Exeter, apologised to its anxious owner and, raising his hat, promptly remounted the same bicycle and rode away!

Trains were even more fraught with difficulty. He was once unable to find his ticket when confronted by the ticket inspector. The kindly official reassured him: 'Don't worry, my Lord. We all know who you are.' The Bishop, however, replied in some consternation, 'That's all very well for you. But without a ticket, how on earth shall I know where I'm going?'

He also had a passion for inventing scientific domestic improvements. Deciding that hot-water bottles were old hat, he thought it a better idea to warm the beds by the more up-to-date means of electricity. He encased a naked electric light bulb inside two old fencing masks and fastened them together with old bits of wire. This device he then plugged into the mains and thrust between the sheets for just long enough to avoid setting them on fire.

He also devised a new central-heating system, which involved placing radiators under the armchairs. When his nephew Lord David Cecil objected, 'But you will not be able to move the chairs; it does not sound a very comfortable plan,' Fish's eyes began to twinkle: 'My dear boy,' he said, 'when one is putting in a heating system, comfort must go to the wall.'

SIR JOHN WARDLAW-MILNE

CONSERVATIVE MP FOR KIDDERMINSTER 1922–45

'He is, in fact, rather an ass.'

Wardlaw-Milne would be remembered by few today had he not made the strangest proposal of the Second World War.

Harold Nicolson described him in his diaries as 'an imposing man with a calm manner which gives the impression of solidity,' but rather spoiled the effect by continuing, 'He is in fact rather an ass and the position he has acquired as one of the leaders of the back-benches has caused his head to swell badly.'

In 1942 Wardlaw-Milne moved a motion of no confidence in Churchill. At one of the darkest times of the war, just after the fall of Tobruk, this was a sensational and dramatic action. It was avidly seized upon abroad to exaggerate the degree of political crisis.

The dividing line between heroism and lunacy is notoriously thin. It was certainly brave of Wardlaw-Milne and his supporters to assert the right of Parliament to call the nation's war leader to account. But rocking the boat provoked inevitable accusations of disloyalty, sabotage and succouring the enemy. Wardlaw-Milne's criticism was serious. He made a good case. Churchill was interfering too much in the daily conduct of the war by combining the office of Prime Minister with that of Minister of Defence. Coordination of the war effort should be in the hands of a senior serving officer as Commander-in-Chief, who could give his undivided attention to military matters.

But then almost immediately Milne shot himself in the foot. Without warning, he made the ludicrous proposal that the man for the job was – His Royal Highness the Duke of Gloucester, known familiarly as 'Clapper', on account of his habit of clapping his hands to attract the attention of servants.

'Chips' Channon noted in his diary: 'The House roared with disrespectful laughter and Winston's face lit up as if a lamp had been lit within him and he smiled genially. He knew now that he was saved and poor Wardlaw-Milne never quite regained the hearing of the House.'

A. P. Herbert listened to the speech and was reminded of a remark of his father's: 'Sir, your last observation is like the thirteenth stroke of a crazy clock which not only is itself discredited but casts a shade of doubt over all previous assertions.'

Michael Foot described the scene in his biography of Aneurin Bevan:

At first there was a gasp, followed by a noise which that assembly has not heard before or since, a loud, long, excruciating cacophony, half-groan, half-guffaw. The House of Commons can be the rudest place in the world. Sir John's gaffe, wrote Churchill, 'proved injurious to his case, as it was deemed a proposal to involve the Royal Family in grievous controversial responsibilities'. This matchless meiosis may be taken as the final proof of Churchill's romantic loyalty to the throne. The House had other thoughts. It dearly loved dukes, but it could not see Royal Gloucester as Britain's answer to Rommel. Sir John never recovered.

CAPTAIN ARCHIBALD RAMSAY

CONSERVATIVE MP FOR PEEBLES & SOUTHERN
1931–45

'My view is not pro-Hitler... [but] pro-British.'

Ramsay was arrested in May 1940 and interned in Brixton prison under section 18b of the Defence of the Realm Regulations, remaining in captivity until 1944 – the only MP to suffer this indignity. The Home Secretary gave as the official reason his 'views and activities prejudicial to the public safety or defence of the Realm. He was preaching anti-war propaganda and anti-Semitism at a time when Great Britain was nearing a crisis, and this could have a detrimental effect on the morale of the nation.'

Educated at Eton and Sandhurst, Ramsay fought gallantly in the First World War, was severely wounded and invalided out of the Army. He was elected to Parliament in 1931 and, for six or seven years, pursued an unremarkable backbench career. He was a strong Christian and an even stronger anti-Communist, combining these two strands in support of General Franco in the Spanish Civil War. Then, in 1938, he had a blinding revelation which transformed him from worthy backbench nonentity into a crank and a crackpot.

He suddenly 'became aware that Bolshevism was a Jewish conspiracy'. Inspired to further research, he concluded that the invisible hand of Jewry had directed most of the revolutionary movements in history, including the Roundheads and Oliver Cromwell, the French and Russian Revolutions, and the Spanish Republic.

In 1939 he founded the Right Club 'to oppose and expose the activities of organised Jewry, in the light of the evidence which came into my possession in 1938. Our hope was to avert war, which we considered to be mainly the work of Jewish intrigue centred in New York.' 'The Protocols of the Elders of Zion' supposedly set out their plan for world domination.

The plot was thickened with lavish helpings of another paranoid theory – that international Freemasonry was also in league with the Jewish conspiracy. Ramsay was much influenced in his views by a book written by another rabid eccentric, Mrs Nesta H. Webster's *World Revolution: The Plot Against Civilisation*, which revealed that the protocols were 'the revised programme of illuminised Freemasonry formulated by a Jewish lodge of the Order'.

According to this theory, instructions had been given to the Jewish people by a shadowy group of 'Elders', whom King Solomon had originally appointed as a secret committee and which had remained continuously in existence from ancient times, new members being co-opted as necessary to continue the line. The 'instructions' contained extremely detailed plans for the complete disruption of Christian civilisation and its replacement by a new world State ruled by Jews and Freemasons!

In 1941 Ramsay's constituency complained that it had been deprived of representation on account of his incarceration and he was later pressed to resign as a result of revelations in a libel action he had initiated against the *New York Times*. Although he denied being a fifth columnist or wanting a German victory in the war, he did admit distributing various extreme and offensive anti-Semitic pamphlets and verses. 'My view is not pro-Hitler and not defeatist. I am anti-Jewish and pro-British.'

He was accused of passing information to the German legation in Dublin, which he denied. He was also falsely accused of having agreed to become Gauleiter of Scotland in the event of a successful Nazi invasion. Ramsay sued successfully for libel, but the judge awarded him 'contemptuous damages' of only a farthing. In spite of pressure from his constituency he still refused to resign and even continued to table written

Parliamentary questions to Ministers from his cell in Brixton prison.

Astonishingly, even after Germany had surrendered and the horrors of the Holocaust had been revealed, Ramsay still continued to disseminate his barmy opinions. His last Parliamentary action, in June 1945, was to table an Early Day Motion calling for the reimposition of the Statute of Jewry of 1290!

> This House realises that the protection afforded to His Majesty's liege subjects from arrest and punishment without trial and from Jewish extortion and exploitation by the provisions of Magna Carta signed at Runnymede in 1215, confirmed and elaborated by the Statute of Jewry passed in 1290 under Edward I, rightly acknowledged as one of the greatest law-givers of this realm, was mistakenly and harmfully impaired by the repeal of the Statute of Jewry in 1846, the ninth year of Queen Victoria's reign; that the repeal of this Act released the very evils which Magna Carta and the Statute of Jewry recognised and against which they were specifically directed; that these evils have from that moment reappeared in ever-growing proportions; that they have now become a grievous menace to His Majesty's liege subjects throughout the realm and are in turn evoking a rising tide of public feeling against the Jewish nation; that the Statute of Jewry provided for protection from violence for all Jews who obeyed its provisions; and this House therefore calls upon His Majesty's Government to reintroduce the Statute of Jewry and enforce its provisions.

In answer to protests that such a motion should appear on the Order Paper, the Speaker explained that he was the protector of minority opinions in the House, whether he agreed with them or not. Within weeks the 1945 General Election swept Ramsay away. He died in 1955, unsurprisingly having taken no further part in politics.

DAME IRENE WARD

MP FOR WALLSEND 1931–45,
TYNEMOUTH 1950–74; PEER 1974–80

'What absolute bosh you are talking!' (To Adolf Hitler)

Irene Ward was possibly the most formidable woman ever to occupy the Conservative back benches. Six feet tall, seventeen stone and always bristling with one of her fearsome hats. When seated in the Commons Chamber she gave the impression of a First World War Dreadnought riding at anchor at Scapa Flow. When on action stations she combined long strides with one of the loudest voices in Parliament and was utterly impervious to all attacks. She was a much-loved Parliamentary character in both the Commons and Lords for fifty years.

Born long before women were given the vote – exactly when remained a mystery as she never revealed her age to reference books – she was first elected in 1931, defeating Britain's first woman Cabinet Minister, Margaret Bondfield, to become one of only thirteen women MPs.

The first constituency she assaulted was Morpeth, in the north-east coalfield, in 1924. She lost then and once again in 1929, but was successful at Wallsend in 1931, holding it until the Labour landslide of 1945. She then switched to the next-door seat of Tynemouth in 1951 and held that until she retired in 1974. She went into dry dock (certainly not mothballs) in the House of Lords as Baroness Ward of North Tyneside and died in 1980.

An early newspaper report described her as having 'an adventurous disposition. A while ago she heard that efforts were to be made to raise the wreck of a famous vessel laden with gold from the depths of the sea. She was so intrigued that she wanted to be allowed to go down with one of the divers and, in order to become efficient in diving, she visited a diving apparatus firm, donned a diving suit and practised in their tank.'

She quickly made her mark as a major House of Commons 'character', a fearless defender of her constituency and every individual constituent. In the darkest days of the Second World War there was a serious shortage of blue serge, used for making naval uniforms. A choice had to be made. Should the limited supplies be earmarked for the men at sea on battle stations or for the WRNS serving ashore? The Admiralty decided the fighting men must take priority.

Dame Irene disapproved and rose in her place to question the First Lord of the Admiralty himself. This, in itself, was an awesome sight – although a woman, she was a first-rate man o' war. The Minister gave his anodyne explanation, which provoked her to rise again and fire a broadside: 'Is the Minister seriously telling me that the skirts of the Wrens must be held up until the needs of the men have been satisfied?' The House collapsed with mirth, greatly enhanced by the obvious innocence with which the question was asked.

In her day Dame Irene was famed for her eccentric protests – long before the student protests of the late 1960s made sit-ins fashionable. In a stuffier age her methods of drawing attention to grievances were very unconventional. In 1960 she invaded the Government front bench in the Commons and, depositing her ironclad handbag on the seat adjoining the Prime Minister's, she refused to budge all through Question Time in order to draw attention to the plight of service widows on low pensions. She sat serenely and impassively, surmounted by an enormous fur hat, monopolising the attentions of the Press Gallery whilst Harold Macmillan struggled to answer questions from the Dispatch Box, affecting not to notice the indomitable Dame's unmistakable and mountainous presence.

Her appetite was whetted by the success of this ploy in grabbing the headlines. There were plenty of other causes dear to her heart which might benefit from similar publicity. She gained a reputation as a geriatric delinquent and was once suspended from the House for blocking a Commons vote.

It all began quietly enough. Dame Irene, the political equivalent of Margaret Rutherford, silently steamed over the horizon into the Chamber wearing an impressive hat and a white gardenia. She manoeuvred herself into position and stood stolidly in front of the table which divides the two front benches and bears the mace. There she stayed, impervious to entreaties, blocking the floor with her bulk, refusing to sit down and shouting protests at the Speaker, preventing the House from proceeding with a division.

Eventually, patience exhausted, the Speaker 'named' Dame Irene. MPs are normally referred to by their constituencies as 'the hon. Member for...' but, in cases of very bad behaviour, the Speaker mentions the Member by name, which leads to his or her suspension from the House. This is usually accompanied by wild scenes of confusion and schoolboy mirth.

To the delight of tourists in the Gallery, the Serjeant at Arms then moves forward to escort the miscreant Member from the Chamber, if necessary at the point of the sword. The Serjeant at that time was the equally redoubtable Rear Admiral Sir Alexander Gordon-Lennox, red-jowled and well-upholstered, resplendent in velvet knee-breeches, black silk stockings and silver-buckled shoes. The admiral manoeuvred forward with trepidation, his sword clanking from his waist. His previous naval training had not prepared him for capturing a 'woman o' war'.

Dame Irene, quivering with anger, waited until he berthed alongside her. He tapped her arm. She bowed to the Speaker, turned and bowed to the Tories and, stately as a galleon, glided majestically towards the door. She brought the roof down by asking the Serjeant in a plainly audible stage whisper, 'Will you take my right arm or my left?' as they swept out through a storm of cheers and laughter. By reducing the proceedings to farce Dame Irene was actually making a serious point – that the Government was curtailing discussion of the Budget and acting dictatorially.

She stood out in the greyness of what was then almost exclusively a male club. There was no more magnificent sight than Dame Irene, in the words of one commentator, 'rising flower-bedecked like Venus from a sea of handbags and papers to pose a question'.

Fiercely loyal to her own constituency she was no respecter of authority. Complaining that her question about a shortage of hospital beds in her area had not been answered, the Speaker informed her it had been answered minutes earlier with a broadly similar one about Cardiff. That was not good enough for Dame Irene, who bellowed from her seat: 'The Minister is a dictator. I do not like dictators. Why should Newcastle be done out of a reply. It is absolute nonsense.' The Minister sat silent while battle raged between Dame Irene and the Speaker, who tried to placate her with precedents: 'I think it was in 1693 this House first resolved that Members who are not speaking should keep quiet.' Dame Irene retorted, 'I was not born in 1693.'

She always managed to have the last word, as in this exchange with the Secretary of State for War in 1943. Dame Irene: 'Why are soldiers not allowed to use free travel vouchers to visit Luxor [near Cairo] like members of the RAF?' Sir James Grigg, 'You are misinformed. Free vouchers are granted to the nearest leave centre, as in the RAF.' Dame Irene protested: 'That was not so when I was there.' Sir James: 'This isn't the first time I have had a dispute with you on a question of fact.' Dame Irene shot back: 'And it isn't the first time that I am right and you are wrong.'

She relished controversy and would tackle anyone without a qualm. She took part in a Parliamentary delegation to Nazi Germany in 1936 and attended a diplomatic tea party at Ribbentrop's villa. Suddenly there was a pause in the polite chatter, and Dame Irene's stentorian voice could be plainly heard telling someone: 'What absolute bosh you are talking!' The object of her plain speaking was none other than the Führer, Adolf Hitler, himself.

A. P. HERBERT

MP FOR OXFORD UNIVERSITY 1935–50

'Oxford University is now represented by a boat-builder and a buffoon.'

For more than a decade A. P. Herbert (better known as APH) observed the very unmusical comedy of the House of Commons from the inside and in 1946 wrote the libretto of a musical comedy about it. In *Big Ben!* Lord Lavender sings:

> While the Commons must bray like an ass every day
> To appease their electoral hordes,
> We don't say a thing till we've something to say –
> There's a lot to be said for the Lords.'

By this reckoning APH MP's natural habitat was certainly not the Commons but the Lords.

He was an anomalous Member for an anomalous constituency. Until 1950 the House of Commons agreeably contained eleven university seats: Oxford and Cambridge each sent two 'burgesses' to Westminster; all other English universities combined also sent two; Scotland three; Wales and Queen's Belfast, one each – all elected by their respective graduates.

Unlike other MPs they were not elected by a 'first past the post' system but by the single transferable vote (STV) – the complications of which virtually require a degree in mathematics to understand. The count under STV in an election for two Members is rather like musical chairs without the music. Every so often a chair is removed until only two candidates can be seated and those are the winners. The more candidates the more potential confusion. Disconcertingly, under STV a candidate coming bottom of the poll on the first count can still win if he is everybody's second choice.

To discover the winner you go through a series of steps. For two seats you divide the number of votes cast by three to find the 'quota' and anyone securing more than that number is elected on the first count. If only one candidate's votes exceed the quota, his 'surplus votes' are then redistributed among the rest. If that fails to bring another candidate over the quota, the bottom candidate is eliminated and his votes redistributed among the remainder. If that still fails to do the trick, you carry on eliminating candidates and redistributing their votes till someone does reach the quota.

The university seats often returned independent MPs, eccentric characters who could never have been elected for a normal constituency, where it was necessary to jump through party hoops. In fact, A. P. Herbert was not a politician at all, but a professional humorist, a regular contributor to *Punch*, light versifier, playwright and lyricist.

For many years Oxford University's two MPs had been Lord Hugh Cecil and Prof. Sir Charles Oman – both distinguished and independently minded but who took the Conservative whip. In 1935 Oman announced his retirement and Prof. C. R. M. Cruttwell, another Conservative don, was nominated as Cecil's running-mate. In a considerable upset, he was beaten by APH.

How did he manage to defeat the Oxford political establishment? Formidable difficulties had to be overcome at short notice. Virtually all the voters were widely dispersed in far-flung rectories and the like. Also, canvassing, poster displays and public meetings were 'not the done thing'. So the only way of influencing them was to circulate a manifesto. APH's was original, both in style and substance. Under 'Capitalism and the Socialist' he wrote: 'My reason, such as it is, rebels when I am asked to believe that, after thousands of years of a not wholly fruitless civilisation, not merely a new but the best and only way of managing this complicated world has been revealed to my old football-captain, Sir Stafford Cripps.' Under 'Agriculture' he was startlingly honest: 'I know nothing about agriculture.'

More subtly, he also deployed cunning flattery by deliberately inflating the status of the recipients on the envelopes – BAs became MAs, colonels and captains became brigadiers and admirals, mere reverends were translated to canonries and archdeaconries, and even knighthoods were bestowed on some with names made more euphonious by adding the prefix 'Sir'.

To everyone's astonishment (not least his own) he triumphed, whereas poor Cruttwell suffered the indignity of losing his deposit. With some trepidation, APH then wrote to his fellow burgess, Lord Hugh, to congratulate him upon his re-election. This elicited the following reply, typical of his bleak candour:

Dear Herbert,

Thank you for your very kind congratulations. I wish I could reciprocate them, but sincerity obliges me to say that I deeply and keenly regret, on public grounds, your election to the University seat.

APH's parliamentary campaigns involved crusading against Britain's then highly restrictive laws on divorce and uncivilised pub opening hours. In his book *Independent Member*, Herbert describes his eccentric introduction to a political career: 'My first official contact with the British Parliament was at Bow Street Police Court where, on 17 May 1934, I laid an information against the Kitchen Committee of the House of Commons for selling 'liquor' without a licence.'

The House of Commons, as part of a royal palace, always assumed it was exempt from the licensing laws and its bars have always stayed open day and night to solace its Members so long as the House is sitting. Elsewhere in Britain in 1934, bars were permitted to open for only a few hours around lunchtime and for about five hours in the evening. Herbert wisely thought the best way to force the Commons to abolish these absurd and puritanical restrictions was to apply their rigours to the MPs themselves in their own lair.

A letter to Sir John Ganzoni MP, Chairman of the House of Commons Kitchen Committee, inviting him to bring the Commons' refreshment arrangements within the law to avoid the painful necessity for legal action, elicited only an acknowledgement. As APH wrote: 'The House of Commons, like a gigantic "bottle-party", sat dumb and defiant, challenging the accusers to come on. So we went on.'

He then appeared before the Chief Metropolitan Magistrate at Bow Street, Sir Rollo Graham-Campbell, and asked for criminal prosecutions to be instituted against all the MPs who were members of the Commons Kitchen Committee. Unfortunately, Sir Rollo decided that Parliamentary privilege protected the legislators and refused to issue the summonses. However, APH would not accept his judgment as 'closing time' on the matter. He appealed the decision to the High Court and appeared in due course before the Lord Chief Justice, Lord Hewart, Mr Justice Avory and Mr Justice Swift.

Justice Swift, alas, proved a misnomer. APH did not get justice, swift or otherwise. Lord Hewart dismissed his appeal, quoting Lord Denman in 1839: 'All the privileges that can be required for the energetic discharge of the duties inherent in the House of Commons' high trust as the grand inquest of the nation are conceded without a murmur or doubt.'

A vital question occurred to APH – was it really the case that 'the energetic discharge of Parliament's duties' required uncontrolled access to booze?' But no questions were possible and all he could do was find a pub in which to drown his sorrows. But there was one snag – they were all closed in the middle of the afternoon. However, if only he had waited a year to bring his case, he would have found the perfect solution to the problem – retire to the Smoking Room of the House of Commons (to which he had just been elected) and enjoy the very privileges he had been so vigorously assailing.

Episodes such as this often triggered Gilbertian theatrical ideas in his fertile brain. His revue *Big Ben!*, for example, included scenes from the Terrace and the Smoking Room as well as a full-dress Second Reading debate in the Chamber on an

Alcohol Prohibition Bill, conducted entirely in song. One real Parliamentary exchange which found its way into the original libretto was a set-to between Jack Jones (Labour MP for Silvertown), a vocal advocate of the virtues of beer-drinking, and the teetotaller, Nancy Astor. She was waxing in lurid detail on the damage alcohol was supposed to do to men's stomachs when Jones, the proud possessor of an impressively prolapsed corporation, interposed, 'I heard what the noble Lady had to say about our stomachs. I tell the noble Lady that I'll lay my stomach against hers any day.' This exchange was printed in *Hansard* and provoked much merriment at the time. However, it failed to pass the Lord Chamberlain, then the guardian of the nation's morals in the theatre, and had to be excised from the show.

APH had a genius for finding comic potential in the most commonplace and unlikely material. It might, for example, tax even the most innovative and inventive humorist to insert humour into the writing of a cheque. But APH managed it. One of his eccentricities was to write cheques on anything unusual which came to hand, eschewing the printed forms provided by the bank. This practice began as a joke at a Savage Club lunch with the illustrator George Stampa in 1927. APH owed Stampa £1 and paid by taking a table napkin and drawing a cheque on it. Stampa then added a flourish in the form of caricatures of those who sat around the table. He then duly presented it at his bank, the Golders Green branch of the Westminster Bank, where this unusual cheque was cleared in the usual way.

Emboldened by this success, APH then decided to test the patience of banks in multifarious ways. A cheque written on a champagne bottle didn't bounce. How would a cheque written on an egg fare? Would it be scrambled in the clearing system? National & Grindlays Bank proved they could take a yolk and it was duly honoured.

APH's eccentricity was commemorated by *Punch* on the sixtieth anniversary of his first contribution. On a warm August day in 1970 outside Barclays Bank in the shadow of St Paul's Cathedral, the editor solemnly presented him with a cheque for £5 – written in large letters on the left flank of a cow. APH duly took it into the bank and gave literal meaning for the first time to the term 'cash cow'. Barclays played ball but drily announced that they hoped 'not to see the practice extended'. It is not known whether the bank milked the customer with clearing charges for hay and the services of a milkmaid.

APH also wrote the only known cheque in verse. Enraged to receive an £85 surtax demand from the Inland Revenue he took a piece of his own 12 Hammersmith Terrace writing paper, duly stamped it (in those days each cheque bore 2d Stamp Duty) and crossed it 'Inland Revenue A/C', to be presented for clearance at National & Grindlays Bank, Parliament Street. The words in capitals were typed in red:

Dear Bankers, PAY the undermentioned hounds
The shameful sum of FIVE-AND-EIGHTY POUNDS
By 'hounds', of course, by custom, one refers
To SPECIAL INCOME TAX COMMISSIONERS:
And these progenitors of woe and worry
You'll find at LYNWOOD ROAD, THAMES DITTON,
   SURREY.

This is the second lot of tax, you know,
On money that I earned two years ago.
(The shark, they say, by no means Nature's knight,
Will rest contented with a single bite:
The barracuda who's a fish more fell
Comes back and takes the other leg as well.)
Two years ago. But things have changed since then.
My earnings dwindle; and the kindly State
Gives me a tiny pension – with my mate.
You'd think the State would generously roar
'At least he shan't pay SURTAX any more'.
Instead, by this un-Christian attack
They get two-thirds of my poor pension back.

Oh very well. No doubt it's for the best;
At all events, pray do as I request;
And let the good old custom be enforced
Don't cash this cheque, unless it is endorsed.

To his astonishment, after the poetic cheque had been cashed he received a reply from the Office for the Special Commissioners for Income Tax:

Ref: S.T.H. 31097/40

Dear Sir,

It is with pleasure that I thank
You for your letter and the order to your bank
To pay the sum of five and eighty pounds
To those here whom you designate as hounds.
Their appetite is satisfied. In fact,
You paid too much and I am forced to act,
Though such a course is easy, it would seem.
Your liability for later years
Is giving your accountants many tears:
And till such time as they and we can come
To amicable settlement on the sum
That represents your tax bill to the State
I'll leave the overpayment to its fate.
I do not think this step will make you frown:
The sum involved is only half-a-crown.

Yours faithfully,
A. L. Grove.

Even APH had to admit at this point that he had been beaten at his own game. He replied:

Your ref. S.T.H. 31097/40

I thank you, Sir, but am afraid
Of such a rival in my trade:
One never should encourage those –
In future I shall pay in prose.

APH became famous for introducing eccentric Bills in the House – including a 'Public Refreshment Bill', designed to remove the licensing laws' anomalies in an ingenious way. It had only one clause:

The laws of England concerning the provision of public refreshment, including the sale or supply of wine, beer, spirits and the like, shall be made, mutatis mutandis, the same as the laws of France.

The Bill had a First Reading and was printed but, alas! the Government did not allow it to go any further.

APH must have been a terrible trial to the bores and literal-minded pedants in whom the Commons always abounds. He simply refused to conform. One magnificent example of eccentricity deserves repetition at length – the Bill which he drafted in verse:

THE SPRING (ARRANGEMENTS) BILL

> Whereas in every lawn and bed
> the plucky crocus lifts his head,
> and to and fro sweet song-birds go,
> the names of which we do not know:
>
> Whereas the woods no more are dumb,
> the Boat Race and the Budget come,
> the Briton swells his manly chest,
> his mate, as eager, scrubs the nest,
> and Spring, with light but lavish hand,
> is spreading madness o'er the land:
>
> It is expedient – but in rhyme –
> to legislate for such a time:
> Be it enacted, therefore, by our King
> with Lords and Commons in a fairy ring,
> assembled joyously at Westminster
> (or any other place that they prefer):

PROVISION FOR A SEASON CALLED SPRING

1. (i) It shall be lawful everywhere for citizens to walk on air, to hang their hats upon the trees and wander hatless if they please: and notwithstanding any cracked provision in a

previous Act, to give a constable a kiss is not felonious after this.

(ii) All citizens who choose to ride on taxi-tops and not inside: and those who do not use their votes because they're busy painting boats: and any miscreant who hums, instead of doing dismal sums: whoever does a silly thing need only answer ''Tis the Spring': and this shall be a good defence in any court with any sense:

Provided that in late July, this Act, of course, does not apply.

Financial Provisions

2. If any person feels he must get out of London now or bust, because the Spring is in his bones, but he must work for Mr Jones, it shall be lawful for the same to give the Treasury his name, and say 'Upon sufficient grounds I want about a hundred pounds': and there shall not be any fuss concerning sums expended thus.

Repeal of Redundant Statutes

3. Subsection (i) of section Four of any Act that seems a bore, and all the Acts concerning beer, and every Act that is not clear (always excepting Schedule A), shall be repealed and thrown away.

House of Commons – Reform of Procedure – Music etc

4. (i) There shall be banks of maidenhair arranged about the Speaker's chair: and roses white and roses red shall hang above the Speaker's head: like some tremendous window-box, the Galleries be gay with phlox: and goldfish, lovely but aloof, shall swim above the glassy roof.

(ii) From now until the First of June all speeches shall be sung (in tune). The Speaker shall determine what hon. Members are in tune or not.

(iii) When in Committee of Supply the House may hum (but not too high). The Clerk-Assistant-at-the-Table shall choose the key (if he is able).

(iv) A band shall nearly always play (not on the first Allotted Day) behind the Speaker's Chair at three and on the Terrace after tea.

Saving for Committees

5. On any day in May or June Committees shall adjourn quite soon: Provided, if the cuckoo call, Committees shall not sit at all.

Sittings of the Upper House

6. The House of Lords shall never sit on sunny days till after Whit: and they shall rise, if they have met, when it is foggy, fine or wet.

Termination of Official Report

7. (i) Except as hereinafter hinted, Hansard shall not again be printed, and save as in this Act is learned, all previous Hansards shall be burned.

(ii) It is a pity, history teaches, to make reports of people's speeches, and afterwards to be unkind, simply because they change their mind. It is a most disgusting thing to make such comments in the Spring: so, as from when this Act is passed, that day's Report shall be the last.

(iii) And, as respects exceptions, see Subheading (a) of Schedule B.

Powers and Duties of Departments

8. (i) The Secretary of State for Home Affairs shall now proceed to Rome, to Moscow, Washington, Cathay, or anywhere that's far away, and not return to English skies until the Speaker certifies that Spring has ceased to be a fact under the Moss (Collection) Act.

(ii) Meanwhile o'er all his grim domain a lovely golden girl shall reign: and this delicious creature shall give cosmic parties in the Mall (paying the bills, if she is dunned, from the Consolidated Fund). The Civil Service, hand in hand, shall dance in masses down the Strand: and all the Cabinet shall wear wild dandelions in their hair.

(iii) It shall be deemed that everyone has come into the world for fun. This shall be printed on the wall of every office in Whitehall.

Penalties for Certain Expressions

9. (i) No kind of crisis shall excuse a man exploring avenues: no lesser doom does he deserve when he is straining every nerve: and special punishment is earned by those who leave no stone unturned.

(ii) The penalty for each offence shall be elastic but immense.

(iii) A pension shall reward the man who modestly does all he can.

Interpretation

10. (i) The greatest care has been employed to make this measure null and void: not one expression in this Act means anything it says in fact.

(ii) Examples we decline to give: the lawyers, after all, must live.

Application

11. This Act applies and shall be good where anybody thinks it should:

Provided that, if strong objection should be expressed to any Section, that Section shall not have effect except for those who don't object.

Schedule B (a)

Any speech, motion, question, amendment or interruption by APH.

For over fourteen years APH was a constructive as well as an original MP and showed his form, if not from day one, at least from day two – when he made his maiden speech. New MPs are often advised to get some feel for the House before plunging in, and some do not survive the experience. As Lord North's son, Frederick, recalled,

I brought out two or three sentences, when a mist seemed to rise before my eyes. I then lost my recollection and could see nothing but the Speaker's wig, which swelled and swelled till it covered the whole House. I then sank back on my seat and never attempted another speech, but quickly accepted the Chiltern Hundreds, assured that Parliament was not my vocation.

APH was spurred into action by Baldwin's announcement on the first day of the new Parliament that no Private Members' Bills could be introduced before Christmas and the Government were going to take all the time of the House which would be freed. As an 'independent' Member APH was naturally outraged by this piece of whips' jiggery-pokery as he had his own Bill to reform the marriage laws ready to go. After an inspired speech, virtually extempore from scribbled notes on the back of an old Bill, and in which, with the confidence of an old hand, he effectively silenced some derisive sedentary interventions, he had the further temerity to divide the House. He lost by 232 votes to five.

Winston Churchill sought him out afterwards and complimented him on his composure and aplomb. 'Call that a maiden speech? It was a brazen hussy of a speech. Never did such a painted lady of a speech parade itself before a modest Parliament.'

He brought many recondite talents to the Commons. For example, as a novice Parliamentarian studying the Order Paper one day, he counted nineteen redundant full stops on one page alone. The King's Printer must have been reproducing millions of such solecisms daily in the many thousands of other Government publications for which he was responsible, so APH complained to him about the pointless waste of effort and ink involved. The latter-day Caxton, brought up with a start by APH's learned intervention, put a stop to all unnecessary stops forthwith.

APH was not to everyone's taste. When Lord Hugh Cecil retired in 1937 Sir Arthur Salter, whose family owned an Oxford boat business, was elected to succeed him and one Oxonian bishop was overheard in the Athenaeum lamenting with disgust that 'Oxford University is now represented by a boat-builder and a buffoon.'

But APH had many serious achievements to his credit as a private Member, including important liberalisations in the erstwhile puritanically restrictive divorce, entertainment, betting and drink laws – which was no mean feat for an MP, twenty-five per cent of whose constituents were clergymen! It was a tragedy that the abolition of the university seats in 1950 deprived Parliament of his wit and humanity.

12TH DUKE OF BEDFORD

PEER 1940–53

*'If every man went to work he would need to work only
ten seconds a day to produce the total requirements
of the country.'*

The 12th Duke of Bedford was the eccentric son of an eccentric
father. The 11th Duke served as ADC to the Viceroy of India,
Lord Dufferin, and after the First World War almost completely
retired from the world to his ancestral home at Woburn Abbey.
There he devoted himself exclusively to estate management and
his superb collection of rare animals and birds.

He was evidently not the life and soul of the party, even a
political one. According to his grandson, the 13th Duke, 'He had
a disconcerting way of deadening every social gambit. It was
either "indeed" or "quite" or just silence, rather like playing
tennis and having the other person hitting the ball into the net the
whole time.' He seldom visited London more than twice a year,
for meetings of the Zoological Society over which he presided,
yet he still maintained two fully staffed houses in Belgrave
Square. There were also four cars and full-time chauffeurs based
in London.

The rare guest who travelled from the metropolis to Woburn
was driven as far as Hendon in one car and accompanied by
another carrying the luggage. At Hendon two cars from Woburn
would be waiting, to which both passengers and bags would be
transferred for the remainder of the journey.

At Woburn the Duke managed, in a manner typical of many Victorian aristocrats, to combine profligacy and discomfort. The vast house had no central heating except in some corridors, but seventy wood fires were kept burning continually in the rooms throughout the winter. There were over fifty indoor servants and every guest had his own footman, standing sentinel behind his chair at meals. Nobody bothered to look to see if there was anything to sit on before sitting down; it was unthinkable that one's designated flunkey would not be there to slide a timely chair under the upper-class bottom.

In a textbook illustration of the gulf in attitude separating aristocracy and plutocracy, the Duke lived an isolated life of frugal, almost Spartan simplicity – despite possessing an income of well over £200,000 a year. He insisted on wearing old clothes, ate simple food and slept in a brass bed with a hard mattress.

During World War I the old Duke quarelled with his son, who was a pacifist, and they did not speak, or communicate with each other at all, for twenty years. The 13th Duke did not even know of his grandfather's existence or that he was the eventual heir to the dukedom until he was sixteen years old, when a servant accidentally let it out.

The young boy, in fact, occasioned a fleeting *rapprochement* between his father and grandfather. The only point on which they apparently agreed was that the boy was likely to prove unsatisfactory so they joined together to alter the entail on the Bedford estates and appointed trustees for his lifetime. Yet another bond developed later still, when father and grandfather united once more to disapprove of the boy's first marriage.

The old Duke, who died in 1940, had rarely visited the House of Lords and played no part in politics. The 12th Duke, however, was a political eccentric. His son described him as 'only interested in animals and birds and fishing and shooting, and religious and social movements which he picked up and then dropped'.

His pacifism was well known and had created great controversy in the First World War. He chose to become a conscientious objector, despite this being quite unnecessary as his eyesight was so poor that he was classified as medically unfit to fight anyway. However, he declared himself on a point of principle and spent most of the war years washing dishes in a YMCA in Portsmouth.

He became a diligent lay preacher in the Church of England but, disenchanted with the 'smug religiosity' it retained from the Victorian age, he eventually withdrew and denounced it as a 'warmongering church'.

His religious enthusiasms then transferred to the 'Oxford Group', also known as 'Moral Rearmament'. This craze particularly attracted credulous members of the upper and middle classes, who organised house parties to induce a feel-good factor by public confession of sins and absolution obtained by mutual hand-wringing and back-slapping. The inventor of the idea was an American, Dr Frank Buchman, who became rich. He was described by Malcolm Muggeridge as looking 'like a successful businessman of the Rotarian sort and when in London stays at Brown's hotel'. When taxed with his expensive lifestyle Dr Buchman retorted without embarrassment that God was a millionaire, so he felt no necessity to economise.

Bedford was also a sucker for another quack theory imported from across the Atlantic: Social Credit, the invention of a Canadian engineer, Major Douglas, to explain the Depression in the 1930s. The theory held that not all costs incurred in production give rise to equivalent purchasing power, so creating a persistent deflationary effect. The Major proposed to cure this by the simple expedient of the State periodically expanding credit to keep pace with expanding productive capacity i.e. printing more money and handing it out! The theory was later embraced by Prime Ministers Harold Macmillan, Harold Wilson and Edward Heath with predictably inflationary results.

Bedford became a painfully sincere propagandist for both these utopian fads, in which the contrary demands of flesh and spirit seemed to be so agreeably reconciled without any real sacrifice – except, of course, that which percolated into the predictably healthy bank accounts of the founders.

In 1929 he had surprised many friends by appearing on Socialist platforms and in 1936 made a speech in which he advocated that 'if every man in the country went to work he would need to work only ten seconds each day in order to produce the total requirements of the country'. His other alternatives were to put every citizen to work for four or five hours a day and produce with the aid of machinery enormous quantities of goods, throw the surplus into the sea at intervals and set to work making more. Failing that, one could go on with the present system, getting steadily worse; or destroy machinery and go back to handicrafts; or destroy money and go back to barter.

Before the outbreak of war he enthusiastically promoted conscientious objection again. In March 1938 he had written that Hitler was ambitious, as the Anschluss showed, 'but there is very little evidence that he would engage in aggressive war with neighbours of a non-German origin who did not treat him unfairly and none at all that he would have the German nation behind him if he attempted a venture of such a kind'. As strong was his pacifism in impelling him publicly to do and say anything he could to prevent war with Hitler, so also was his belief that rearmament was preventing monetary reform, which was absolutely vital to the future well-being of mankind.

Needless to say, he never belonged to a conventional political party but, in 1939, was induced to become chairman of the 'British People's Party' (BPP). The leading lights in this outfit were radical ex-members of Mosley's British Union of Fascists (BUF) who had come from the far Left. John Beckett, the leader, had previously been Labour MP for Gateshead (1924–9) and Peckham (1929–31). He had gained notoriety by seizing the Speaker's mace and threatening to carry it out of the House. After he lost his seat he became Director of Publicity for the BUF and editor of *Blackshirt*.

The BPP's optimistic aims included 'abolition of a financial system based on usury, abolition of all land speculation, protection of the small shopkeeper and abolition of all class differences'. But basically it was against war. It failed to secure any public support and, shortly after the outbreak of war, Beckett was imprisoned under Regulation 18B as a fellow-traveller. An attempt to revive the BPP after 1945 was a dismal failure.

In 1940 Bedford caused considerable outrage by taking a leading part in a plan to stop the war through negotiations with the German Minister in Dublin. He published a pamphlet setting out the 'terms' he claimed to have agreed but his statements were disowned by the Germans and became the subject of heated protests in Parliament. Lord Mansfield lamented the Duke's 'woolly humanitarianism'. But Viscount Simon, the Lord Chancellor, denounced his views as 'utterly irresponsible and completely pestilential'.

He had initially been given official permission to go to Dublin to further his peace propaganda, but the Home Secretary refused him a second bite of the cherry. The Duke then declared he was prepared to risk imprisonment or internment to pursue his obsessions. There was much public resentment at his posturings and, in protest, the statue of the 5th Duke in Russell Square was disfigured with a daub in yellow paint: 'Grandfather of a quisling'.

He succeeded to the dukedom in 1940 and throughout the war continued to voice his heretical views, which were frequently criticised in both the Commons and Lords. In 1944 Lord Simon said acidly after one of his speeches in the Lords, 'The mildly philosophical air with which he puts forward his observations conceals a capacity to support any yarn which supports his jaundiced views.'

Having been accused of Fascism during the war, after it he was accused of being a Communist. In one of his last speeches in the Lords he spoke in support of Dr Hewlett Johnson, the controversial 'red dean' of Canterbury, a silly and unworldly utopian apologist for the Soviet Union in the 1940s and 1950s.

Bedford tried unsuccessfully to force his various eccentric theories on his son, whom he refused to send to school – perhaps following the example of the 12th Duke who had put in his *Who's Who* entry, 'Education: Collection of pictures at Woburn Abbey.' After a series of tutors, the adolescent heir to the dukedom was settled by his father in a lodging-house for students on the Bedford estate in Bloomsbury with an allowance of £98 a year. He urged him to qualify for entrance to Cambridge, offering to pay crammer's fees and 'an adequate allowance'. However, the young man sensibly spent the first £25 instalment on a skiing holiday and soon tired of the crammer!

A prominent naturalist and a particularly ardent ornithologist, the Duke spoke authoritatively on these subjects and acquired many rare specimens. In 1935, after securing permissions from various governments, he travelled halfway round the world and collected 3,000 beautiful birds. But it was typical of his character to have pangs of conscience; he liberated most of them in the South Seas on his way home. The rest he brought to England for breeding purposes, providing them with as much liberty as possible.

The Duke was prone to strange experiments with food, including one which involved cooking the velvet from the horns of his deer. It did not catch on. For several years also, in an endeavour to refute the theory that birds or animals of brilliant colours or forbidding appearance were inedible, he used to cook greenfinches, tawny owls, cormorants and other birds. In 1949 he advocated the production of African antelopes for food.

He also developed a homing strain of budgerigars and wrote a piece in *Country Life* on the topic, accompanied by a photograph of himself surrounded by his flock. He was especially attracted to the study of parrots, pheasants, fish, deer and bison (American and European), all of which he kept at Woburn. Birds were ultimately the death of him. He was accidentally shot by a gun with which he intended to shoot a hawk which was threatening his budgerigars.

He was an obstinate heretic in politics and theology and was looked upon by the conventional-minded as a crank. He could not be constrained within a normal party framework and he often acted in a manner which lacked discretion. He was successively accused of being a Communist and a Fascist and wandered from cause to cause, always favouring the least popular. He was the rarest bird in his aviary, a man of paradox – a pacifist who objected to using arms against the Germans who were bombing babies in London at the time, and yet thought nothing of shooting a hawk which threatened a budgerigar; a vastly rich man who, whilst maintaining his huge estates, expounded the doctrine of 'Sell all thou hast and give to the poor.' Lord Salisbury summed him up succinctly: 'He dearly loves to be in a minority of one.'

LT. COL. A. D. WINTLE

LIBERAL CANDIDATE FOR LAMBETH NORWOOD
1945

'I am never bored when I am present.'

The term 'an officer and a gentleman' might have been coined for Wintle. Punctilious and disciplined in all things, dress was a matter of unchanging daily drill – each morning he screwed his monocle in his eye (rimless, of course, with no namby-pamby artificial aids like galleries and ribbons to keep it in place) where it unfailingly remained until he went to sleep at night, whether the day had been spent under fire in battle or jumping hedges on the hunting field.

Similarly, in civilian life, Wintle's psyche was epitomised by the umbrella. Whilst it was essential for the English gentleman to carry one ('No gentleman leaves the house without one'), it was, of course, entirely forbidden in any circumstances to unfurl it. Wintle did, in fact, unfurl his once – but only to insert a note announcing 'This umbrella has been stolen from Col. A. D. Wintle'.

The umbrella had a seminal influence upon Wintle's development as an eccentric and illustrates his unshakeable belief in the innate superiority of the Englishman over all foreigners. As he succinctly put it: 'There are two classes of insular Englishmen – those who think that no foreigner is as good as an Englishman, through sheer ignorance; and those like me who know it from experience.'

When he was a small boy Wintle's aunt gave him an umbrella, purchased at the Army & Navy Stores. It made him feel he had taken an important step on the road to becoming a complete English gentleman. He could hardly bear to be parted from it and would go at odd intervals of the day to admire it in the hall-stand. For years, he even took it to bed with him.

But the umbrella was not a mere artefact. It had an almost sacerdotal significance, as he explained:

> The umbrella, I felt even then, represents an important difference between the Frenchman and the Englishman. The Frenchman knows he is intelligent, knows he understands things. So, on getting up in the morning, he consults his thermometer, his barometer and his hygrometer. He then works out a calculation to see if he should expect rain and if he should take his umbrella with him. But, as all calculations are notorious for tending to go wrong, invariably when he has decided it will be dry and he does not require his parapluie, down comes the rain and he is soaked through.
>
> The Englishman, on the other hand, is too stupid to understand all these barometers and things. But he ALWAYS takes his umbrella with him, anyway, for the good and simple reason that no gentleman ever leaves the house without it.
>
> There is, of course, also the fact that no true gentleman ever unfurls his umbrella... which means that the Englishman also gets wet. But the reasons – and the thinking – are different and that is why it is so mavellous to be an English gentleman... which I'm sure I have known since I was born at the age of nought.

Wintle's belief in the inherent superiority of the English appears to have been a genetic inheritance. He records a 'delightful English aunt' whose attitude to languages was that 'to learn them was totally unnecessary if you were English and, in any event, would only encourage foreigners to be impertinent to their betters'.

Wintle's opinions were certainly not those of an ignorant bigot. He was, on the contrary, a highly intelligent and learned bigot. He spoke perfect unaccented French and German, the legacy of having lived across the Channel with his parents as a young boy.

He spoke as he found:

To be English means that you belong to Volume I in the World Pedigree Library. There is no better listing. The French are to be found in Volume V or VI. Before 1914 I generally accepted that the Germans were all in Volume II. This meant that the Kaiser was on page 1 of Volume II, which was pretty good for him but not as good as the last page in Volume I, in which one might find the most awful types of ruffians – who nevertheless were English. I have long since downgraded the Germans to just one book above the French, although it's a toss-up really. Let's have as little as possible to do with both.

His views on the French were particularly jaundiced:

Darwin talked of Africa holding the Missing Link, poor innocent. No doubt he sought it among the apes whereas it is evident for all to see around the Champs-Elysées any Sunday afternoon. There, by the thousands, are typical French families taking their walks at a creep of 1 m.p.h. There is father with a greasy bowler and a couple of fly-buttons showing. Mother evinces coquetry with a fashionable hat, but offsets it by black carpet-slippers which are kinder to her bunions. These she will discuss at the slightest provocation. About twenty paces ahead is the eldest daughter with her fiancé, both hoping that nobody will connect them with the unsavoury progenitors behind. Flitting like a fly between the two groups – or rather like an ill-trained poodle – is a horrible youth, leaping on heaps of rubble, climbing lamp-posts, throwing stones and hurling insults.

Not only is none of them house-trained but they are not street-trained either. Occasionally the father or the fiancé will pause to micturate against some convenient tree while their companions stand beside them continuing the conversation. And over all there are the pungent smells of stale garlic, sweat, dust and ill-kept wounds.

Wintle had 'a good war' twice. In the Kaiser's war he ran over an unxploded bomb at the Third Battle of Ypres and lost an eye, several fingers on his left hand, half a thumb on his right and a knee bone. He was hospitalised but swiftly tired of that and discharged himself to go back to the Front, where he captured thirty-five prisoners single-handed.

Wintle was extremely annoyed that the war ended when it did. The politicians had been too soft in granting an armistice – enabling the Huns to preserve their strength for the build-up to what he called 'Act Two'. When the Treaty of Versailles was signed he wrote in his diary:

June 19th: Great War Peace signed at last.
June 20th: I declare private war on Germany.

In the Second World War he was in the thick of it again but in a more unconventional role. He started off in an unpromising way by being court-martialled. Predictably, he considered that the brass hats and politicians were not prosecuting the war effectively enough, so he decided to take charge himself. In June 1940 he impersonated the Air Ministry's Director of Intelligence, Air Commodore Boyle, and commandeered an RAF plane to fly to France to prevent the French Air Force falling into the hands of the Boche.

Unfortunately, Wintle's commanding manner had spurred the officer in charge of getting the plane ready to such efficiency that he finished in double-quick time and rang the Air Ministry with some pride to say so. They, of course, knew nothing about it and, as a result, Wintle was stopped and threatened by Boyle with a court-martial for taking the law into his own hands.

At this mindless obstructionism, Wintle saw red and shouted, 'While you sit there blood is flowing in France, not ink.' He then drew his revolver and waved the muzzle under Boyle's nose like a wagging finger. 'You and your kind ought to be shot,' he yelled, naming a number of senior officers who deserved it as much as he did. Wintle then broke the revolver, spilling out the bullets to show he had not been bluffing, leaving Boyle shaking with fright.

The following morning he was arrested and put in the Tower of London. The timid young escort officer lost the rail warrant for the journey before they got to the station. Wintle snapped with exasperation at his incompetence, 'For heaven's sake stop fumbling. Wait here by the baggage while I go and get another warrant.' He obeyed meekly whilst the prisoner disappeared out of sight. Wintle found the Rail Transport Office, asked for a warrant and, as there was no other officer present, signed it himself. He must be the only prisoner in the Tower who had to sign his own warrant to get there!

After he had passed a few weeks in the Tower the War Office, sensing they had bitten off more than they could chew, had the charges reduced and Wintle was let off with a severe reprimand. This bothered him not one bit and made him a hero with all ranks who shared his contempt for incompetent chairborne warriors.

Brought up in France and Germany and speaking perfect French and German, he was a natural for unconventional warfare behind enemy lines. In 1941 he went to occupied France as an undercover agent. Sadly he was betrayed, captured and imprisoned in a Napoleonic fortress near Toulon. Needless to say, Wintle immediately set out to prove the natural superiority of the Englishman.

'I decided to make my jailers as uncomfortable as possible. I decided on a hunger strike. My guards, in their shoddy uniforms, unshaven, with filthy boots were unworthy of custody over a British officer. I knew the Geneva Convention and my rights. I demanded to see the Fort Commandant. He appeared, wiping the food from his mouth with a filthy napkin. I told him, in pretty concise terms what I thought of him, of his job, of France, of Frenchmen in general and in particular. I announced that I refused to eat till I had a guard and a commandant worthy of my rank and nation.

He retaliated by providing me with jail swill for food, removing my little radio set and stopping my snuff and tobacco allowances.

Nevertheless I kept up my propaganda, my taunting and my hunger-strike; there was little else that I could do. Then, one night, they tortured me with a magnificent dinner. Though ravenously hungry by this time – having gone for thirteen days without food – I still meant business. They even brought the chef to hear my compliments, but they were half an hour late. I informed them that when I was not hunger-striking I dined at 7 not at 7.30 and stressed that unpunctuality was yet another undesirable characteristic of Vichy Frenchmen. Like whipped curs, they withdrew.

After the banquet-spurning, astonishing things began to happen. Guards and jailers took to shaving. They cleaned their boots and their buttons. But I would still inspect them as they entered my cell and comment on their incompetence. Then I began to eat again for the principal reason that I was planning my next escape.

Wintle's mind was perhaps concentrated also by discovering that the Germans had ordered that he be shot as a spy. Many years later Wintle was the subject of the TV programme *This is Your Life*. To his astonishment, the BBC had tracked down that fort commandant whom he had abused and humiliated. Monsieur Molia recounted how he was moved

entirely because of Col. Wintle's dauntless example and his tirade of abuse and challenge, to defect from Vichy. I took 280 men from the prison garrison – most of whom had also been inspired by the Colonel or shamed by him – and joined the Resistance. Many of my men were later killed fighting the Germans but we harried and did down the enemy for years as Colonel Wintle would have wanted us to do.

Wintle's name is also still revered by members of the legal profession. Indeed, walking through the Aldwych recently, shortly after my victory over Mohamed Fayed in the Court of Appeal, I bumped into an old Cambridge friend of mine, now a senior member of the Bar. He suggested that, if Fayed got leave to appeal further, to the House of Lords, I should represent myself – just as Col. Wintle did successfully in the famous case of Wintle v Nye.

Wintle's sister, Marjorie, was for many years companion to an elderly and eccentric aunt living in Hove. Aunt Kitty was very possessive and prevented Marjorie from either marrying or taking up a career. Wintle naturally worried about how Marjorie would support herself if left on her own. He raised the matter with Kitty, who dyspeptically assured Wintle his sister would be well provided for in her will.

In due course Kitty became heavily dependent upon her family solicitor, Frederick Nye – who, in addition to looking after her business affairs, even carried out simple domestic tasks like ordering coal and finding tradesmen when needed. Unfortunately, this proved to be a disastrous mistake.

As Wintle later wrote: 'My father impressed upon me from earliest infancy that the greatest circumspection should be observed in all one's dealings with solicitors. Nor have I ever had cause to have second thoughts in the matter.'

When Kitty died in 1947, after a long illness, Nye made the arrangements for the funeral. He took the Hove house-keys, which Marjorie had had for years, and went on his way. It then emerged that the rather simple aunt had made an extremely complex will and codicil some years before, both of which had been witnessed by two of Nye's clerks.

Marjorie, who had selflessly cared for her aunt for twenty-five years, was left an annuity of £40; a small income which Wintle's 87-year-old mother had been receiving was stopped. But Nye, whom Kitty had disliked was, astonishingly, left the bulk of the estate of £115,000 (over £2 million at today's values).

Wintle was sure Kitty had had no idea of the size of her estate or what she was doing in signing the will. He wrote to Nye time after time without response and was repulsed from his door when he tried to beard him in his office. Frustrated beyond measure, Wintle then adopted the tactic of writing libellous letters about Nye to all and sundry – Nye's neighbours, the Law Society, newspapers, MPs, the police. But Nye took no action, either to vindicate himself or stop the letters.

Wintle consulted lawyers, the Law Society, the Solicitor General and Scotland Yard. Nothing could be done. Whilst it was clear Nye's conduct was not that of a gentleman, he had done nothing illegal. An eccentric old lady may write an eccentric will. It could be contested, but only by relatives of the whole blood. Unfortunately, Wintle and Marjorie's father had been only a half-brother to Kitty – they shared a father but not a mother.

Balked at every turn, Wintle refused to give up. He resolved to teach Nye a lesson, and would use means which, as a former cavalry officer, he understood perfectly – a sound thrashing with a horsewhip. This would have to be done in the proper manner and on the proper part of the anatomy, of course. Furthermore, the event would be photographed, so that there was a record of a job done with style.

Marjorie, however, counselled caution. A private-enterprise flogging would more likely excite hostility not sympathy. There was already, even in those days, some outcry by 'do-gooders and other uninformed liberals against the excellent discipline of corporal punishment'. A different plot was hatched.

Wintle borrowed a friend's flat in Hove and telephoned Nye. Adopting a fruity accent and a fictitious title (the Earl of Norbury), he invited Nye to visit him to help carry out a shady property deal for cash. The bait was eagerly swallowed and Nye said he would be around by taxi immediately.

Whilst waiting for him to arrive, Wintle prepared a dunce's hat made of paper and left the door open. Nye arrived and, in response to a cheerful disembodied greeting from the noble 'Earl', ventured into the hall. Wintle then rushed round behind him and pushed him into the sitting-room.

'Now will you please take your trousers off?' The shady solicitor trembled but obeyed. Wintle rammed the dunce's hat on

Nye's head, photographed the ridiculous sight both front and rear and then pushed him trouserless into the street. He set off for London and exhibited the trousers in the trophy room of the Cavalry Club. The next step was to telephone the police, the press and Nye's partner, then go home to wait for the balloon to go up.

The police duly arrived with a warrant for Wintle's arrest. He was delighted, imagining that he would be able to raise the question of the will at his trial, if only in mitigation of his sentence for the assault. Unfortunately, Mr Justice Byrne, at Lewes Assizes, would have none of it and sent Wintle down for six months.

'Colonel Bogey' as he was called by the newspapers, arrived at Wormwood Scrubs caparisoned in Savile Row suit, buttonhole of red carnation and black, gold and blue striped Royal Military Academy, Woolwich tie. A crowd of wellwishers was outside to cheer him in.

It is difficult to imagine what the average old lag made of this strange inmate. When eventually transferred to an open prison in Kent, Wintle was issued with a sou'wester for outdoor work. But he quickly found an indoor use for this: 'An Englishman must keep up appearances in all circumstances and always I have maintained my hair with cream. On earnings of only tenpence a week it was difficult to get enough of the necessary. So I always wore my sou'wester when I took a shower to protect the last vestiges of haircream from being washed away.'

He found 'being behind bars was rather similar to army life, but much less efficent'. But he was soon out and ready to return to the fray. His trial and incarceration were not in vain. The vast publicity which the debagging of Nye had generated led to a mountain of mail from all over the world. Among the wellwishers were several full cousins of Kitty's, hitherto undiscovered. They could legally contest the will. One of them nominally assigned his interest to Wintle, thus enabling him to take direct legal action against Nye.

He immediately 'leaped into the saddle, calling up numerous costly outriders in the shape of solicitors, barristers and the like.' To finance the battle, he sold everything he had collected over the years, including many prized possessions, and mortgaged his house. 'Alas, my outriders proved to be less reliable companions. In the manner of dismounted Portuguese refugees, they all spilled at the first ditch – the Probate Division of the High Court.'

The case lasted almost a week and Wintle comprehensively lost. The judge was even moved to remark: 'Colonel Wintle has dragged Mr Nye into court to expose him. He ought to pay for his pleasure.' This was a setback but Wintle was not downhearted. 'I repaired to a local hostelry and gave myself a good talking-to. If a cavalry officer falls on his backside he immediately remounts and goes on again.'

He concluded that his mistake had been to have any truck with lawyers. Now that he had no money, he would go it alone 'on the basis of the old cavalry motto: Always keep trotting and, when in doubt, gallop.' He appealed to the Court of Appeal. The case turned on whether the judge below had misdirected the jury. One of the three bewigged and black-robed Lord Justices, 'in an opinion of luminous lucidity' agreed with him. But the other two old fools insisted that Kitty's will should stand, so Wintle was unhorsed again.

His amanuensis, ex-Trooper Mays, commiserated that he had lost. Wintle's response was explosive: 'Lost, sir! Oh no, sir! We've been out of the saddle twice, but we have just remounted. The winning post is at the end of the course and no one has reached that yet.' Wintle petitioned the House of Lords, the highest court in the land – selling one of his last remaining valuables, an antique coffee pot, to pay the registration fee.

In those pre-computer and -photocopier days litigants had to produce a printed case for each of the five Lords of Appeal, including all the documents relied on. Wintle was now a pauper and could not afford printing, so he laboriously typed out separate copies of his 253-page, single-spaced submission for himself, all the judges and Nye's legal team. There was one silver lining to the cloud of refusal of legal aid – as an English pauper he was entitled to the return of his registration fee from the House of Lords!

For three days Wintle laid out his case, to be followed by m'learned friends for Nye. The Lord Chancellor, Viscount Simonds, congratulated Wintle on the clarity of his exposition and observed 'Colonel Wintle, it is quite clear that no one in any of the courts below has understood the will and its complications.' Wintle clinched his argument with the response, 'Would it be presumptuous, my Lord, to suggest that the somewhat simple Miss Kitty Wells may not have understood it either?'

The culmination of his ten-year legal battle was a unanimous decision for Wintle – the first time that a layman had achieved such a result in the highest court, the House of Lords. The will was set aside and Nye had to pay all Wintle's costs, not just in the Lords but also the courts below.

It was a sensational victory. Among the many letters and telegrams of congratulation was one which came with a jeroboam of champagne from the members of Lincoln's Inn who, 'dining in the presence of HRH the Princess Margaret, have drunk a toast in your honour and to your success.' Wintle said generously, 'Maybe lawyers aren't all such a bad lot, after all!'

Wintle had demobilised himself in 1945. Realising he would get no further promotion because of his unconventional actions and lack of respect for superior officers, he decided to get out of the Army by the quickest possible route – standing for election to Parliament.

He was chosen (as one of the least likely Liberal candidates) to fight Lambeth Norwood in the imminent General Election. His platform was simple and robust: 'The last person who went into the House with any good intentions was Guy Fawkes. It's time they had another, like me, with explosive ideas.' Tragically, Norwood felt that five years of wartime explosions was quite enough and opted for a quiet life instead. Wintle clocked up only 3,944 votes and, failing to get one eighth of the votes cast, lost his deposit. Alas for England!

Sadly, unlike in war and the courts, Wintle failed to display his customary dogged determination in pursuit of Parliamentary ambitions. However, I have a feeling that, if he had been elected, the pantomime procedures of the House of Commons would have exasperated him so much he might well have been tempted to fulfil his manifesto commitment to the letter. And where Guy Fawkes failed, he would undoubtedly have succeeded.

LT. COL. SIR WALTER BROMLEY-DAVENPORT

MP FOR KNUTSFORD 1945–70

'Don't let the NHS get me!'

Walter Bromley-Davenport was my predecessor but two as MP for Knutsford and, although the constituency boundaries changed significantly between his day and mine, he regarded me as his spiritual successor.

Soon after I was selected as the Conservative candidate for Tatton in early 1983 I was summoned to his vast 'Jacobethan' pile, Capesthorne Hall, to be inspected over lunch. Everything we ate had been shot, fished or picked on his own estates – including the smoked salmon, which had been caught on his own salmon river in Norway.

I shall never forget my first sight of him. We arrived at the Hall, pulled the ancient bell and, after what seemed an eternity, heard bolts and bars being drawn back with wheezes, thuds and groans. The butler greeted us and conducted us to the library, down a maze of passages. When the door was opened, we could barely discern the former Member through clouds of thick, black smoke billowing from the open fire.

Suddenly, through the fog, loomed Walter's stocky figure, both arms outstretched with two glasses in one and a bottle of champagne in the other. With a hearty cry of 'Get this giggle-water down you!' he thrust the lot into my unprepared hands. We literally got on like a house on fire – which is precisely what was

178

producing the smoke. Walter, however, was more concerned with thirst extinguishers than fire extinguishers.

Walter Bromley-Davenport was almost the last of a now vanished Parliamentary breed – an hereditary Knight of the Shire. One of his ancestors had been Lord Chancellor under Elizabeth I and another was Speaker of the House of Commons during the reign of Queen Anne. His grandfather, father and uncle had also represented Cheshire constituencies for seventy years between 1806 and 1906.

He liked to convey the impression of a buffoon. The thickset frame, plastered-down hair, centre parting and stentorian voice supplied verisimilitude to what was, in fact, a self-perpetuated caricature. He had no pretensions to intellectualism – which befitted a former welterweight boxing champion of the British Army.

Julian Critchley, who survived five years in the House with him from 1959 to 1964, wrote in his obituary notice: 'He was a great Parliamentary character. Noisy, opinionated and robust of opinion, he was a low comedian every bit as much at home on the boards of his great house, where amateur theatricals were the order of the day, as he was in the Commons.'

His favourite trick was to disconcert Labour MPs at the start of their speeches by bellowing across the Chamber: 'Take your hands out of your pockets!' This would sometimes work, even if the victim was holding notes at the time! He was reputed to have the loudest voice in the House and, at meetings where there was too much noise, he would bellow in military style: 'Quiet! You young officers.'

It was not just 'other ranks' on the opposite side of the House over whom he asserted his voluble authority. An amusing incident occurred in 1955, when Lt. Col. Walter Bromley-Davenport rose and began to ask a question at exactly the same moment as his hon. and gallant Friend Brigadier Otho Prior-Palmer, MP for Worthing. 'Sit down!' thundered the Colonel, which the Brigadier immediately did with all the smartness of a private on parade. Points were then raised with the Speaker as to whether it was in order for a mere lieutenant-colonel to bark orders at a brigadier and, indeed, whether it was in order for the brigadier to obey them. A deadpan Mr Speaker Morrison replied laconically, 'We know no military ranks in this House. All men are equal here.'

Walter often put his powerful voice to good effect. During the Second World War he joined a crowded train at Crewe only to find all the seats were taken. Totally unperturbed, he marched up the train bellowing 'All change at Platform Four.' This had the desired effect – enabling Walter to find a seat with ease.

Like many MPs of his class and background until the 1970s, he had no ambition to be a Minister. But he did put his military and pugilistic experience at his party's disposal as an Opposition Whip from 1948 to 1951. Sadly, however, this stint on the front bench was short and came to a sudden but celebrated conclusion.

In the 1950–51 Parliament the Labour Government had an overall majority of only eight. On every major division, therefore, there was a good chance it could be defeated if the troops were organised. The Tories embarked upon a war of attrition – wearing down an increasingly exhausted Labour Party by endless three-line whips and all-night sittings with as many surprise votes as possible. To be effective, this tactic required Tory MPs to be disciplined in their attendance, often well into the small hours. The whips' task, and an essential one, was to spot the backsliders and stop them slinking off home early.

When things were hotting up, the order would be given: 'All doors!' One whip was then posted at each exit from the Members' Lobby and any Tory MP trying to pass through would be told to wait until the vote had taken place. Walter's bulldog frame and manner made him perfect for the task of dealing with even the most determined homing bird.

One night he was stationed near the door to the staircase leading down to the Members' Entrance and espied a man in evening dress rushing across the Lobby. He shouted to him to stop and go back. This had no effect. He tried to intercept the man as he got to the door and was brushed aside.

Not to be outdone, Walter fired off a mild expletive and delivered a well-aimed kick to the miscreant's backside, causing him to tumble head over heels down the staircase, landing in a dishevelled and bruised heap at the bottom. Mission accomplished!

Unfortunately, however, his aim was better than his eyesight. The groaning victim proved not to be a Tory MP at all, but the Belgian Ambassador. The ensuing diplomatic incident ensured Walter's swift return to the back benches, where he remained happily and noisily ever after.

His contributions to debate tended to take the form of loud expostulations from a sedentary position, rather than studied eloquence in a speech. A typical intervention of his during Prime Minister's Question Time occurred in December 1968. Harold Wilson was being questioned about visits abroad when Walter rose to ask him: 'Could the Prime Minister make any proposed visit of indefinite duration, when everyone will benefit except his host?' Wilson replied amiably, 'The hon. Gentleman will be aware that I get this question regularly from himself and others at this time of year, but even so it doesn't stop me from wishing him a very happy Christmas.'

Whilst Walter was vigorously partisan, relations with his political opponents were always good-natured. Labour MPs ritually cupped their ears when he rose to speak and shouted 'Speak up!' or 'What's he saying?' The joke never palled. The House likes its humour simple and indulges its characters.

Outside the House his jokes did not always succeed so well. At a meeting during the 1955 General Election he was reported as saying that 'there is a hard core of Socialist voters who are spurred on by envy, greed, malice and hate. If you took a gorilla, stuck a banana in each hand and made it their candidate, they would elect it rather than give their vote to the Conservatives.'

Reynolds News, a Labour Sunday newspaper now long defunct, printed a photograph of Walter's face in distinctively truculent grimace. Above it screamed the headline: 'VOTE FOR A GORILLA'.

The newspaper was annoyed that Walter's insult had been ignored by the 'Tory press', unlike the wall-to-wall vilification which Aneurin Bevan had received for declaring that Tories were 'lower than vermin' – a remark which led to his being kicked down the steps of White's (described by a clubland historian as 'that most gruesome collection of old Tories') by an uncontrollably irate member who had spotted the champagne Socialist leaving after a decidedly feudal lunch.

Bevan was never one to allow left-wing views to bar the enjoyment of 'right-wing' pleasures. Paul Johnson, then editor of the *New Statesman*, found himself seated next to Bevan at a grand dinner thrown by some Press Baron. Johnson, a Socialist in denial of his solid middle-class public school background, felt uncomfortable with the lavishness of the occasion. Bevan, the product of a miner's cottage and having no class antecedents to live down, revelled in every sybaritic pleasure.

At the side of each plate sat an enormous hand-rolled Havana cigar. Johnson ostentatiously announced that, as a Socialist, he could not betray the workers by so much as touching such a symbol of the hated capitalist oppressor class. Bevan had no such inhibitions and puffed away merrily whilst expertly cradling the accompanying magnificent cognac. After Johnson's high-minded homily, Bevan's high-pitched Welsh lilt rose to a squeak in a mixture of amusement and contempt: 'Oh! You're one of those are you? Well, give it here then.' At that he stretched right across, grabbed the cigar and stuffed it into his top pocket for later enjoyment.

In 1955, although re-elected for Knutsford with one of the largest majorities in the House, he was unable to take his seat because the Lord Chancellor's office had not received the writ testifying to his return. The Returning Officer had not sent it back by registered post and, as a result, it lay undiscovered for some days in a sack of unopened mail. Without the official notice declaring he had been elected it was impossible for Walter to enter the Chamber.

Much mirth was caused by this novelty, not least because he was the most persistent critic of the Post Office in the House. Further amusement ensued, considering the decibel count of his voice, when he told the House he had telephoned the Postmaster-General's office about it, but the line was so bad that they could not hear each other speak. Finally, his voice rising to a throaty climax which a Wellington Barracks drill sergeant might envy, he declared, 'All this justifies my actions since 1945 in trying to get the Postmaster-General's Department to WAKE UP.' At this staccato bark several Members, lulled to a doze by earlier soporific exchanges, woke up with a sudden start.

Walter was knighted in 1961. The following year he survived a serious attack by a mad axeman with a grudge against hereditary titles which Walter, not being, alas, a baronet, did not possess. Rescued by his butler, he still had the presence of mind, though badly wounded, to boom a last instruction: 'Don't let the NHS get me!'

Fortunately, he survived the assassination attempt long enough for me to invite him to address my eve-of-poll meeting in Knutsford in the 1987 General Election. He was delighted to be asked, as he felt that my two immediate predecessors as MP had rather ignored his skills on the hustings. His rumbustious tub-thumping speech concentrated on universal themes like the Evils of Socialism and the Great Simplicities of Conservatism. It was a great theatrical success.

My attention was drawn to a dog-eared pile of yellowing papers – his speech notes. I asked him afterwards when he had written his speech. 'In June 1945. When I came back from the war!' He had delivered exactly the same speech at his own eve-of-poll meeting in Knutsford in the General Election forty-two years before. No one had noticed.

In the 1979 election he telephoned my immediate predecessor, Jock Bruce-Gardyne MP (an extremely distinguished economic journalist), with some words of advice. He bellowed down the blower: 'Listen here, Bruce-Gardyne, there's something you should know about. It's called the PSBR. That's the Public Sector Borrowing Requirement. Hang on a minute. I've got a fellow here who knows all about it.' Footsteps clumped heavily away from the receiver and then returned again. 'Pity,' he roared. 'Fellow's gone to sleep.' With that the phone was slammed down again and Jock never did find out about the PSBR – at least not from Walter.

One of his obituarists wrote of him: 'One hardly recalls the Bromley-Davenport speeches. If collected they would fill the tiniest of shelves.' When he did open his mouth he was often most effective when he did not say anything at all. Few Members could match the eloquence of a Bromley-Davenport yawn – which, like his voice, was also reputed to be the loudest in the House.

In 1967 he interrupted a speech by Michael Stewart, then First Secretary of State, with a yawn like a hippopotamus. This led to the following exchange:

Mr Stewart: 'I am sorry the hon. Gentleman is so tired.'
Sir Walter: 'Not tired; bored!' (Laughter).
Mr Stewart: 'At least the hon. Gentleman has come to hear me, which is more than he did for his rt. hon. Friend the Member for Mitcham' (Robert Carr, the Shadow First Secretary).
Sir Walter: 'The rt. hon. Gentleman is well known as one of the biggest bores in the House. I have been patient and good mannered in listening to him. I apologise that I could not conceal my boredom. As I can no longer conceal it I will leave the Chamber.'

At that point Walter stumped deliberately but theatrically out, having completely wrecked Stewart's speech.

His experience in amateur theatricals at home in his own theatre at Capesthorne gave him his masterly sense of timing and repartee. A not unfriendly obituary in the *Guardian* concluded: 'He was not so much a performer, more a personality. Nobody would look to him for quiet scrutiny, liberal thinking or deep and patient analysis of the flow of events. But the House likes its characters and Bromley-Davenport gave a good deal of simple if hardly quiet pleasure.'

LORD PAGET
OF NORTHAMPTON QC

LABOUR MP FOR NORTHAMPTON 1945–74;
PEER 1974–8

'When self-indulgence has reduced a man to the shape of Lord Hailsham, sexual continence involves no more than a sense of the ridiculous.'

Son of a Tory MP, rich, red-faced, gravel-voiced, educated at Eton and Cambridge, Master of Foxhounds, voluntary defender of Field Marshal von Manstein at the Nuremberg War Crimes Tribunal, Treasurer of the British–South Africa Parliamentary Group in the apartheid era, apologist for Ian Smith's white Rhodesian regime. These distinctions, and many more, made eccentric qualifications for Paget's thirty years as a Labour MP.

Foxhunting was the great passion of his life and he occasionally cut an astonishing figure in a House of Commons division by turning up to vote still clad in his hunting pink and riding breeches. He was a popular Master of the Pytchley, one of the smartest hunts, despite holding political opinions which the most charitable in the hunting fraternity would have ascribed to eccentricity.

Paget had a strongly developed sense of right and wrong. He instinctively supported the underdog and regarded public opinion with contempt if it offended his sense of justice, pursuing his instincts regardless of any adverse impact on his prospects of political advancement. That quirk was sufficient to mark him out as an eccentric, even in his day, when the House of Commons had not yet been degraded into a mass of monochrome ciphers programmed to respond supinely to whatever order is transmitted remotely by electronic pagers.

Hence, he volunteered to defend without fee Field Marshal von Manstein against war crimes charges at Nuremberg in 1949, despite the public obloquy this invited. But Paget believed that a serving officer in the field was not to be compared with Nazi war criminals and he was outraged that public prejudice had made it impossible for von Manstein to obtain proper facilities for his defence. Paget was not the kind to look away from individual injustice, unlike so many in the current House of Commons who are prepared actually to perpetrate it for temporary party political advantage.

Paget was frequently at odds with the more simple-minded in all parties. Nauseated during the Profumo crisis by the avalanche of Pecksniffian cant from supposedly practising Christians, he publicly defended Profumo as a gallant officer, whatever his other failings. Lord Hailsham appointed himself chief pharisee and worked himself up on television into a paroxysm of righteous indignation, at one point calling Profumo a liar nine times in seventy words. Paget publicly attacked Hailsham as 'an unctuous beast giving a virtuoso performance in the art of kicking a fallen friend in the guts'.

The Labour Party was at the time stirring the pot hoping to make maximum political capital from the blazoning of seedy details of sexual trivia. Hypocritically, it pretended to be not sexually censorious but concerned instead about a non-existent security risk from the simultaneous affair with the Russian naval attaché on the part of Profumo's mistress, Christine Keeler. Paget responded tartly to his own party: 'A Minister is said to be acquainted with an extremely pretty girl. As far as I am concerned, I should have thought that was a matter for congratulation rather than inquiry.'

He shared the sentiments of Macaulay that 'we know of no spectacle so ridiculous as the British public in one of its periodical fits of morality'. In the Commons debate after Profumo's resignation Paget spoke for no more than five minutes, but took the prize for the most savagely caustic attack of all – directed not at Profumo but Hailsham: 'When self-indulgence has reduced a man to the shape of Lord Hailsham, sexual continence involves no more than a sense of the ridiculous.'

It was poetic justice also that Profumo's chief persecutor in the Labour Party, the odious Col. George Wigg MP, was himself ultimately prosecuted as a kerb-crawling client of street prostitutes!

Poetic justice also awaited – even more painfully – one of the chief pharisees on the Tory back benches. John Cordle MP had unctuously complained, 'that it was an affront to the Christian conscience of the nation at a time when standards in public life need to be maintained at the highest level' that the Queen was to grant Profumo the traditional audience for a Secretary of State to deliver up his seals of office in person. A spiteful hue and cry was set up in the press and Parliament over this, forcing Profumo to 'ask to be excused' and spare the Queen any embarrassment of meeting him.

The Queen, however, knew her Christian duty, and wrote a letter warmly thanking him for his service to his country. Fifteen years later Cordle, the self-appointed 'Christian conscience of the nation', was forced to resign from the Commons himself after being embroiled in the Poulson scandal of local authority corruption.

Paget could have become an MP in his final year at Cambridge. The Tory candidature at Market Harborough became vacant in the 1929 General Election and it was his for the asking. He could thus have followed the last five generations of his forebears as a Tory MP. There was, however, one difficulty – he had been converted to Socialism and, like many of his class at Cambridge between the wars, had even dallied with Communism. His father accepted this news with equanimity but suggested that, in that case, he had better start earning his living. He was called to the Bar and practised with some success.

Despite his decision in 1929, he did resolve to enter the Commons – but only as a Labour MP, standing unsuccessfully for Northampton in 1935 and ultimately getting elected in 1945.

He was a decidedly idiosyncratic Socialist, vocally and unrepentantly rejecting some of the most cherished shibboleths of the Labour Party of his day.

He attacked his own party leader, Harold Wilson, with contemptuous zeal as 'a conman...all the troubles of the Government can be summed up in one word – Wilson'. He was almost the sole supporter on the Labour benches of Ian Smith's white-minority Government in Rhodesia and resigned the whip over the imposition of sanctions after UDI in 1965. Despite being opposed to capital punishment, he advocated executing one IRA internee in reprisal each time an innocent person was killed by an IRA bomb and he declared in a debate on the 1964 Obscene Publications Bill that there was no greater source of brutality, sadism and murder than the Bible. In another eccentric sally for a Labour MP, he called for the restoration of National Service. He also had no sympathy for the soft 1960s approach to crime then so prevalent on the Left and took a robust attitude, rejecting as tosh sociological excuses for hooligans and muggers. In 1987, he supported a butterfly collector who was being prosecuted for fighting off a drunken attacker on the London Underground with a few slashes from his swordstick.

Alone in the Labour Party in the 1980s, he belonged to the British–South Africa Parliamentary Group, much to the fury of Labour MPs because, without his membership, the Group would have lost its all-Party status and the right to use the facilities of the Palace of Westminster. Paget was an eccentric of the best kind, standing aloof from political correctness, however unpopular it might make him or however much ridicule he invited.

GEORGE BROWN

LABOUR MP FOR BELPER 1945–70; PEER 1970–85

'He always found it hard to resist a camera, a microphone,
a quarrel, a drink or a pretty woman.'
(Peter Paterson: Tired and Emotional)

No one has ever been met who behaves like Mr Brown...
he is impossible: he is too much; one would not invite him
to cucumber sandwiches with one's maiden aunt – but he is
a remarkable man with some of the qualities and all the
courage of a great statesman.

So said a *Times* leader in 1967. The happy consequence was that
several maiden aunts wrote in to say that, actually, they would be
delighted to share cucumber sandwiches with Mr Brown.

George Brown became an MP aged 30 in 1945, a PPS three
days later and a Minister at 33. He was a pillar of the trade-union
movement and, prior to his election had been a fur salesman and
a Transport Union official. Conscious of lacking a university
education, he was always suspicious of middle-class Labour
intellectuals like Richard Crossman, whom he thought looked
down their noses at him. A huge inferiority complex, inspired by
resentment at the class system, produced chips on both his
shoulders and many explosive and entertaining encounters
during an eccentric political career which, amazingly, took him
to the brink of the premiership.

189

He also fancied himself as a charmer and a ladies' man and behaved accordingly. He kissed everybody. The wife of one senior civil servant was much put out when he did not kiss her. 'He kisses everybody,' she complained. 'What's the matter with me?' A foreign ambassador's wife responded to a salacious suggestion at dinner by saying, 'Pas avant la soupe, Mr Brown.'

Never overawed by the presence of royalty, he once knelt to kiss Princess Margaret's hand at a reception, in an absurd but chivalrous gesture. However, the effect was slightly marred by his inability to get up again, which had both him and the Princess convulsed in giggles.

The personal characteristic for which he is most remembered was his drinking. When he became Foreign Secretary in 1966, the Foreign Office produced a 'Guide to Ambassadors and Embassy spokesmen when dealing with the foreign press.' This contained a list of words to explain the new Foreign Secretary's anticipated behaviour – 'tired, overwrought, expansive, over-worked, colourful, emotional,' with each helpfully translated into French, Italian, German and Russian. From this document *Private Eye* adopted a phrase which entered the language as a euphemism for drunkenness – 'tired and emotional.' It was in this state that Brown's eccentricities became most pronounced.

A typical example was his behaviour on the assassination of President Kennedy in 1963. He had met Kennedy on three occasions – for 45 minutes in June 1962, 55 minutes in June 1963 and for ten minutes on 24 October 1963. By any standard his acquaintanceship was slight to non-existent.

On the evening of 22 November he attended a National Day reception at the Lebanese embassy, followed by another reception and dinner at Shoreditch Town Hall. The news of Kennedy's death was brought to him with an invitation to appear on ITV's flagship current affairs programme *This Week*.

At the studio he first got into a fight with Eli Wallach, an American actor, whom he provoked into stripping off his jacket, and yelling, 'Come outside and I'll knock you off your can!' Eventually Brown was interviewed by Kenneth Harris, who angered him by his opening question, which hinted that Brown had overstated his closeness to Kennedy: 'I know you met President Kennedy once or twice. Did you get to know him as a man?'

Brown glared ferociously, 'Now, you're talking about a man who was a very great friend of mine. We understood what the world was about and what the division between East and West was about...' and so on. He made frequent references to 'Jack' and 'Jackie', implying close familiarity, with his voice slurring and arms windmilling around. His eyes welled with tears as he warmed to his theme: 'Jack Kennedy, who I liked, who I was very near to...One is terribly hurt by this loss...'

Richard Crossman wrote in his diary: 'At the first moment I saw that he was pissed and he was pretty awful. He jumped up and down and claimed a very intimate relationship with Kennedy.' The full story of Brown's altercations in the TV studio eventually found its way into the newspapers and led to an almighty row, not least because supporters of his rival for the leadership of the Labour Party, Harold Wilson, used it as a stick to beat him. The Labour Party was dedicated to the brotherhood of man but, for many of its leaders, brotherhood was only seen as a prerequisite for fratricide.

As Labour's Deputy Leader, Brown was assured of high office when Wilson became Prime Minister in 1964. His first two years, as First Secretary in charge of the new department of Economic Affairs, produced its crop of blunders and embarrassments but Brown really came into his own when he became Foreign Secretary in 1966. His very first day at the Foreign Office produced a real Whitehall farce. By tradition the FO lines its officials up at the imposing quadrangle entrance to the High Victorian *palazzo*, to greet and applaud its new political master into the building. Unfortunately, Brown was blissfully unaware of this and slipped unobserved up to his office through a back door, leaving the assembled proconsuls disappointed. Thus, before he could be officially welcomed into the Office, Brown had first to be winkled out of it. His Principal Private Secretary had to race upstairs to ask if he would mind retracing his steps, re-entering the building by the main entrance. This was but the first of the many misunderstandings and disasters which peppered his nineteen-month tenure of the office. Even before Brown arrived at the FO he had showed his form in an altercation with Lady Reilly, wife of the British Ambassador to France, at a dinner at the French Embassy in London. After she had failed to identify for him the French woman guest sitting on his other side, he shouted at her 'You are not fit to be an Ambassador's wife.' For good measure he repeated himself in a still louder voice, stunning all the other guests into embarrassed silence. Everyone then tried desperately to make polite conversation, but Brown persisted: 'You are not fit to be an Ambassador's wife,' by which time Lady Reilly was visibly on the edge of tears.

Always quick to detect a personal slight himself, even if only in his imagination, he was wholly unconcerned about his own offensiveness to others. Christopher Ewart-Biggs, later Ambassador to Dublin and assassinated by the IRA, was in 1966 a Counsellor at the FO. He was blind in one eye and wore a pair of spectacles with one black and one clear lens. No one had previously been bothered by this harmless eccentricity, but Brown took against him. He ordered Biggs to stop wearing them. 'If you've got something wrong with your eye, wear a patch. Wear sunglasses if you like, but you're not coming into this office with one plain and one dark lens so stop it now.'

Seated next to an elderly lady at another dinner party, he found she was the wife of an ambassador at an important diplomatic post. 'What kind of impression must such an old and unfashionable woman give of Britain?' He asked her directly, 'Why can't you look as attractive as the young woman sitting opposite?'

He was one of the most undiplomatic heads of the Diplomatic Service ever, but his gaffes served to amuse as often as to offend. In polite conversation with a Latin American ambassador, he discovered that he had eight children, which inspired the incredulous observation: 'Eight children? Why you can hardly have been out of bed at all.'

In November 1967 Brown distinguished himself by his extraordinary behaviour during the State Visit of President Sunay of Turkey. The President and Mrs Sunay were met at

Victoria Station by the Queen and Prince Philip, with the Prime Minister and the Home Secretary (Roy Jenkins) both in attendance kitted out in morning-dress tail coats and striped trousers. But no tail coat was ever made which could cope with the outsize chips on Brown's shoulders and he adamantly refused to conform to bourgeois tradition. He insisted on lining up in his ordinary lounge suit whilst all the rest were bedecked in their official finery.

A State Banquet was given by the Queen at Buckingham Palace that evening, and another given by the Turks the following day. In due course it was Brown's turn to entertain the President as Foreign Secretary, at a magnificent dinner and reception held at Hampton Court Palace, with after-dinner entertainment by the students of the Royal Ballet.

Brown arrived, hot-foot from a Soviet Embassy party to celebrate the fiftieth anniversary of the October Revolution. He had, no doubt, imbibed freely but nevertheless appeared to be perfectly sober. However, after downing three large gin and tonics in quick succession at Hampton Court, he became an entirely different character. Lord Mellish, as Minister of Works, had responsibility for organising the event and recalled that he 'began to behave like an absolute shit.' Mellish suspected the worst when Brown began his speech of welcome with elaborately embroidered compliments to the President on being married to 'the most beautiful woman in the world.' Although Madame Sunay did not have a handlebar moustache and a build like a heavyweight boxer, Brown's fulsome encomium was so obviously wide of the mark as to be risible. If the Turks had been as touchy as Brown, they might have thought he was taking the Mickey.

But worse was to follow. Espying Mellish, a tough ex-docker and devout Roman Catholic, in the audience, he started, for no apparent reason, to lash out at his church, claiming that the only true Catholicism was the High Church Anglicanism which he himself espoused. This then led him into a disquisition upon the details of a complicated and quasi-theological dispute between the Transport & General Workers' Union (of which both he and

Mellish had once been officials) and the Dockers' Union. Quite what President Sunay made of all this, every word of which was simultaneously translated for him, it is difficult to imagine.

Whilst this was going on, Sir Alec Douglas-Home (former Prime Minister and then the Shadow Foreign Secretary) whispered to Mellish 'My God! I hope he doesn't recognise me' and tried to remain as inconspicuous as possible by shrinking into the table. Relief was audible when the ballet began. But after a very short time Brown's patience ran out. He turned to an astonished President Sunay and said in a treacly but very audible slur, 'You don't want to listen to all this bullshit. Let's go and have a drink.'

Only days before, Brown had set the scene for this disaster at a dinner at the Savoy Hotel for American and British businessmen. On this occasion he had publicly accused his host, the Canadian–British newspaper magnate, Lord Thomson of Fleet (owner of *The Times* and *Sunday Times*), of being a cheat and breaking his word; a story sensational enough to cause the national newspapers that night to remake their front pages.

Brown's strange behaviour at this time was caused by the many bees buzzing around in his bonnet on the matter of the press. Principal amongst them was the sensational row which had developed after Lord Chalfont, his junior colleague as Minister for European Affairs at the Foreign Office, had mused in a press briefing about the possible adverse consequences for NATO should the Wilson Government's application to join the Common Market be rejected. Chalfont implied that, if Britain were rebuffed yet again, it might turn its back on Europe, quitting NATO and pulling back the British Army on the Rhine.

Brown was furious because the briefing was supposedly 'off the record' and it was a breach of confidence to report it. He tarred Lord Thomson, as a press baron, with this brush. Brown's mood was explosive and fuelled by a blazing row he had had about the Chalfont affair the previous evening with diplomatic correspondents attending a Foreign Office reception to mark the retirement of a senior official. The *Mirror* correspondent had walked out after Brown made some highly insulting remarks about his father, Cecil King, Mirror Group chairman and a leading long-term Labour supporter.

Brown was also fuming about a hugely successful investigation by the *Sunday Times'* Insight team. This had vastly increased the paper's circulation with an exposé of the bumbling ineptitude of the FO and the security services in the flight of the spy Kim Philby to Soviet Russia, following in the footsteps of his fellow traitors, Burgess and Maclean.

At the Savoy Hotel dinner, the assembled senior executives from American multinationals like Coca-Cola, Westinghouse and Philip Morris, and the accompanying contingent from Britain's 'Great and the Good' were looking forward to hearing Brown on 'Britain in a Changing World'. Lord Thomson, as chairman, was to introduce him. Although an extremely successful business tycoon, he was a bumbling speaker and looked unprepossessing in his extremely thick bottle glasses.

Thomson began with an excessively laboured story to the effect that Brown had been advised by his doctors that, if he wished to live to be 100, he should give up smoking, drinking and women. The point of the 'joke' was that, although Brown might not live to be 100, however short his allotted span, it would feel like l00 years.

The volatile Brown took umbrage. Rising to his feet with Foreign Office speech in hand, he focused first on the hapless Thomson: 'I think you made the most of your opportunity. The only thing I will say in response is that you are the only man I have ever known who actually cheated me.' Thomson tried in vain to intervene but Brown cut him off, 'I am not telling a joke. I am being absolutely serious. You actually once gave me your bond and broke it. My dear Roy, I think everyone here who has heard the jokes you have presumed to tell about me should know you broke your word.' The audience listened in uncomprehending and embarrassed silence at this unprovoked tirade.

Brown then continued with a barely coherent attack upon *The Times* and *The Sunday Times*, whose Editor-in-Chief,

Denis Hamilton, was sitting in front of him. 'Your papers are doing a very great disservice to the country. I don't want any misunderstanding. I am your guest. But I must make it quite clear: I think you are overdoing it, and it is about time you stopped. Some of us are concerned about the country. Some of us think it is about time we stopped giving the Russians a head start on what we are doing and – my dear Roy – I ask you and *The Sunday Times* to take this into account and, for God's sake, stop.'

At this point Brown looked around the room for other victims. Spotting Sir Maurice Bridgeman, Chairman of BPI and Sir Paul Chambers, Chairman of ICI, he went on 'I'm told Maurice Bridgeman gets £50,000 a year – and nobody has heard what Paul Chalmers...er, Chambers, gets, but whatever it is it's a jolly sight too much.'

At last Brown got on with his prepared speech. But, by this stage, no one cared about the FO's platitudes and, at the end, he was besieged by reporters interested only in the details of his astonishing attack on Thomson's honesty. Brown then took the opportunity to quarrel loudly with them for ten minutes, ending by announcing that the British press was 'the most prostituted in the world' and that he had decided to break off diplomatic relations with them. In the Babel of shouting Brown's voice could plainly be heard, shrieking 'Will you just shut up for a second? I am answering a bloody question. Can I just answer one question before I get a another? My speech runs to 64 pages (he exaggerated); just print that.'

After this extraordinary exhibition, for the next few days the papers were full of speculation about Brown's future. 'How much longer can Wilson stand it?' was the headline in the *Evening Standard*. Amazingly Wilson put up with it for four years altogether and refused to accept Brown's frequently repeated 'tired and emotional' attempts to resign. In 1998, under the thirty-year rule, the Public Record Office released Government documents for 1968. Included was a file from No. 10 entitled 'First Secretary (Resignations) File'. A thick wad of notes was compiled by the Prime Minister's Principal Private Secretary, Michael Halls.

One crisis had erupted over a meeting Wilson was due to have in Paris in June 1967 to discuss Britain's application to join the Common Market, which General de Gaulle was likely to veto. News broke that Mr Kosygin, the Soviet Prime Minister, was due to make an unexpected stopover in Paris on his way to a meeting at the UN and Wilson decided that the French might try to make capital out of this. He called a meeting at which he informed Brown he was sending Michael Palliser, an FO civil servant seconded to No. 10, to Paris as a liaison officer for the next few days.

Halls recorded Brown's reaction in an official note: 'At this point the Foreign Secretary, who was in an excitable state, who had evidently been drinking but was not drunk, exploded.' Wilson had to tell Brown 'that he had no intention of accepting orders from the Foreign Secretary in his own Cabinet Room.' Halls added, 'The Foreign Secretary became abusive and upbraided Michael Palliser (whom the PM then asked to leave).' Brown then 'demanded a shorthand writer so that he might dictate his letter of resignation. This was refused and he then tried to telephone his office to dictate his resignation in the form of a press handout. The phone-call was disconnected and the Foreign Secretary then left the room.')

Brown was persuaded by officials to return to the discussion. 'When he did so the PM remarked jokingly, and picking up an earlier thread of the argument, that now that the 16th resignation was out of the way, they could discuss the matter further when the occasion came for the 17th. At this stage the Foreign Secretary exploded and returned to the Foreign Office.'

Brown's turbulent conduct made him the most talked-about politician of his day. Reports of his latest adventures percolated daily through the Whitehall Private Office system. If no report arrived, officials worried that his behaviour had been so dreadful that no one dared mention it. One insider recalled: 'Usually we received word that he had insulted Jean Monnet, or been rude to this ambassador or that, or to Princess Margaret. People just expected George to behave badly and they were disappointed if he didn't; it must mean that there was something wrong with their party or that George didn't like them.'

Brown was a fervent pro-European and Internationalist but he often behaved with a contempt for foreigners which would not have disgraced Lord Palmerston. At another meeting in Paris, Brown launched into a highly offensive attack on Giscard d'Estaing, then the French Foreign Minister. When he had finished, Brown turned to a British diplomat and said, curtly, 'You translate that for this Frog.' Translation was unnecessary, however. Giscard had not only heard every word but, having perfect idiomatic English, had also understood it.

At the end of a day of talks with the Belgian Government, Brown was treated to a splendid banquet in Brussels. The Belgian Prime Minister, Foreign Minister, Defence Minister, Chiefs of Staff and many others turned out for the occasion and a boisterous but otherwise uneventful meal ensued. To the relief of his official minders, Brown behaved himself whilst at the table.

However, just as the party was breaking up he suddenly ran to the door and, waving his arms in the air, started shouting 'Wait! I have something to say!' An official then recalled, 'I thought, oh God, this is going to be terrible, and it was. We rushed over to him just as he was saying, "While you have all been wining and dining here this evening, who has been defending Europe? I'll tell you who has been defending Europe – the British Army. And where, may you ask, are the soldiers of the Belgian Army tonight? I'll tell you where the soldiers of the Belgian Army are. They're in the brothels of Brussels!"' Brown vas quickly grabbed and hustled away, whilst his hosts stood frozen to the spot in embarrassment.

Further trouble was to come, back at the British Embassy. Sir Roderick Barclay, the Ambassador, proposed sitting down to review the day's negotiations. Brown irascibly agreed, saying 'There's no fire in this room. I'm cold. I want a fire and I want a large whisky and soda.' When nothing happened about the fire, Brown demanded imperiously, 'Fire. I want a fire.'

The Ambassador was apologetic, 'I'm terribly sorry, Secretary of State, but it's getting on for midnight and all the servants have gone, so it would be rather difficult.'

Brown replied with staggering ill-grace, 'Where's your wife?'
He was told, 'She's in bed, as she normally is at this time.'
Brown was unmoved, 'Well, get her up, then.'

The unfortunate Lady Barclay was duly roused to come down
and lay the fire, a task somewhat unusual to one of her exalted
station.

The ultimate George Brown story, however, concerned a visit
made to South America shortly after his appointment. In
Uruguay, the Government pulled out all the stops to celebrate the
arrival of the British Foreign Secretary, in recognition of the
pivotal role Britain played in securing the country's
independence from Spain.

A glittering State Banquet and ball was held. The tables
glistened with polished silver and flawless crystal. Ruritanian
full-dress military uniforms dripped with gilt. The members of
the Corps Diplomatique were caparisoned in court dress with
orders and decorations. The cream of Montevideo society turned
out for the great occasion, the ladies swathed in magnificent
ballgowns made by top designers.

The new Foreign Secretary had been fully briefed on protocol
by British officials. He knew what was expected of him and
intended to play his part with gusto. Formal toasts at the end of
dinner would be swiftly followed by the band striking up to
herald the ball's opening dance, at which point Mr Brown would
invite the wife of the President to take the floor with him and
begin the dancing.

During dinner Brown enjoyed himself in his usual uninhibited
fashion. He was the picture of amiability as champagne, chablis,
claret, sauternes and port followed one another, along with the
accompanying dishes, down the International Statesman's throat.
By the end of dinner the names attaching to all the new faces
encountered that evening were becoming somewhat confused.
But one thing he knew. When the band struck up he had to ask
the stately lady in the magnificent red watered-silk ballgown to
take his arm for the first waltz.

When the band did play, the Foreign Secretary was taken by
surprise. He could not remember exchanging toasts with the

President. Perhaps in the conviviality and splendour of the evening they had been forgotten. But it would be undiplomatic to point out his hosts' mistake and he had better get on with the dancing.

He jumped to his feet, tottered around the table, placed his hand on the red silk-clad shoulder of his dancing partner and gestured towards the dance-floor. A horrified shake of the head told him his offer was being rebuffed. This was too much. The Uruguayans may have cocked up the toasts and insulted Her Majesty but he was blowed if he was going to allow himself to be insulted too. The President's wife was jolly well going to dance with him whether she liked it or not. At that he yanked the unwilling creature by the arm and away from the table.

By now, the genteel formality of the evening was descending into confusion and farce. For, three things had unfortunately contrived to go wrong. First the Foreign Secretary was drunk. Second, the music was not that for the first dance but the Uruguayan national anthem. And lastly, the lady in the watered-silk gown whom he had so vigorously propositioned, was not the President's wife but none other than His Eminence the Cardinal Archbishop of Montevideo.

LT. CDR. BILL BOAKS DSC

LEADER – LAND, SEA AND AIR, ROAD AND PUBLIC SAFETY, DEMOCRATIC MONARCHIST, WHITE RESIDENT AND WOMEN'S PARTY 1951–86

'If I had been selected I think I would have been the next Prime Minster.'

In his day, Boaks was unquestionably the most successful Parliamentary failure. Throughout the 1970s and 1980s no by-election was complete without his candidature for the Air, Road, Public Safety, Democratic Monarchist, White Resident Party.

As a prelude he spent thirty years in the Royal Navy, joining at sixteen as a 6d-a-day boy and rising to the rank of lieutenant-commander. He was awarded the DSC after his destroyer was sunk under him at Dunkirk and, as a gunnery officer on HMS *Rodney*, he also took part in the sinking of the *Bismarck* in 1941. Fortified by these experiences of ships sinking to the bottom, Boaks later adopted his political maxim: 'Always steer towards the gunfire.'

When he became a landlubber in 1951 he turned to road safety. Virtually his first act was to buy a 1935 Vauxhall 12, which he christened 'Josephine' and painted in black and white zebra stripes – creating what was almost certainly the world's first mobile zebra crossing. He then covered her with placards advising pedestrians: 'Don't rush to get across'. Concerned for the safety of illiterates also, he fitted four loudspeakers, through which he would shout as he drove along: 'I am stopping for pedestrians in my path.'

The car also proved invaluable in his political campaigns. His debut occurred at Walthamstow East in the 1951 General Election. There was, however, a slight accident to start with. He planned to stand against Mr Attlee (who was MP for neighbouring Walthamstow West) but failed to discover until after close of nominations that he had nominated himself for the wrong constituency. Nevertheless, displaying the dauntless spirit of Dunkirk, he amassed 174 votes for the one-man political party he founded for the occasion – ADMIRAL – (Association of Democratic Monarchists Independently Representing All Ladies). The mention of ladies was occasioned because he campaigned for equal pay as well as road safety. He painted 'She loves me, she loves me not' all over his car, found his love unrequited and lost his deposit.

In 1952 he added a naval dimension to Josephine, decking her out with a mast and mainsail to accompany the zebra stripes and placards which were festooned with slogans in favour of equal pay for women and higher family allowances for children. In this arresting vehicle Boaks was soon arrested. Unfortunately his public-spirited activities led to a fine of £5 3s. He had committed the heinous offence of 'using a vehicle wholly or mainly for advertising purposes within a 3 mile radius of the statue of King Charles I at Charing Cross'. The police also maintained that Boaks was a blatant distraction and danger to other motorists – which was rather a blow as his protest was about dangerous drivers.

He contended he was using the car mainly not to advertise but to deliver letters and denied it was a source of danger: 'I have been on the move more than 3,000 miles in this apparition. I feel these points needed ventilation or I would not have stuck my neck out.'

Later he supplemented Josephine with an armour-plated bicycle. This formidable campaigning vehicle weighed 140lb because the placards plastered all over it concealed an iron bedframe and a camera attached to the handlebars, from which he photographed errant motorists – evidence to enable him to bring them to justice.

As Boaks himself put it: 'The classic case was Lady Attlee's. I wanted her charged for dangerous driving. But no one would allow it. Then I went after the Queen and Prince Philip. Cars kill impartially. I don't care whether the driver's a duke or a bloody dustman.'

In 1960 Boaks sought summonses against Lady Attlee at Amersham magistrates court for dangerous and careless driving and causing death by dangerous driving. He said he was appearing on behalf of ADMIRAL, an all-women organisation dedicated to campaigning against road hogs, established by him 'to wage a cold war on the potential killer in charge of a vehicle'.

Lady Attlee's car had skidded on a wet road and crashed into two oncoming cars. It was her seventh car accident in five years. The public prosecutor charged only one of the other drivers, whose passenger had been killed in the accident. Boaks thought that everyone should be charged and that the prosecutor had pre-judged the case by placing the blame on only one party. 'My case is to see that sharing of the blame shall be assessed by a jury.' The magistrates threw out Boaks's case as they could find no authority that any person like him, unconnected with an accident and not having certain defined interests, was entitled to take out a summons. Boaks appealed to the High Court but lost there also.

Far from being discouraged by his failed attempt to arraign the wife of a former Prime Minister, Boaks decided to spread his net wider to catch still bigger fish. He did not have long to wait. Admiral of the Fleet HRH the Prince Philip, Duke of Edinburgh KG, KT, OM, GBE, PC, had been driving his Rover with the Queen as passenger when he collided with the Ford Prefect of a Mr William Cooper of the White Hart Caravan Site, Holyport, Berkshire.

Cooper was later prosecuted for careless driving, driving on a provisional licence unaccompanied and with no 'L' plates. Boaks then tried to issue a summons against Prince Philip for alleged careless driving. As an afterthought, as a believer in female equality, he followed this up by serving a notice of intended prosecution on the Queen herself for aiding and abetting.

Needless to say, this got short shrift and Boaks was probably lucky not to be sent to the Tower.

However, by now he had acquired a taste for litigation and his next move was to sue the Postmaster-General for libel because he received a letter franked with the slogan: 'Accidents are caused by people like you.' Alas! Boaks was balked again as the Post Office was then a Government department and the Crown was held to have immunity from claims of that kind.

In the late 1950s Boaks took his interest in law enforcement to its logical conclusion and applied for the vacant post of Chief Constable of Berkshire. In support of his application he announced that he was at that very moment trying to prosecute the Home Secretary as the accomplice of a police-car driver, whom he accused of committing six traffic offences whilst going around Parliament Square en route to the House of Commons. His special qualifications for the job were: 'For five years my interest has been road accident prevention. I contend the remedy lies in tracking down the road hog before he is involved in an accident.' He did not get the job.

However, whilst trying to instigate court cases against others, Boaks was frequently in the dock himself. In 1955 he was convicted and fined for wilfully obstructing the highway. Just as thousands of cars were leaving the England v Scotland match at Wembley Stadium, Boaks stopped his car at a red traffic light in Kilburn High Road. The lights turned green but Boaks stayed put. The lights changed and changed back time after time. Still Boaks refused to move. Very soon, absolute pandemonium broke out as the hundreds of irate drivers blocked behind him started hooting their horns and yelling at him to get out of the way. Boaks paid no attention. He had learned patience on wartime Atlantic patrols searching for the *Bismarck*, awaiting precisely the right moment to strike. Now he was determined to wait for as long as necessary, until all the tens of thousands of football fans who wanted to cross the road had cleared the area.

The police were soon on the spot. He was arrested and taken away, as much for his own safety as anything else. As he explained to the court later: 'The point at stake is my right to stop my car any time I wish to do so to offer courtesy to any road user. I contend quite firmly that the person who arrives at the crossing point before you is the person who has the right of way. The Highway Code shows quite clearly that you must go on only if the road is clear. The inconvenience to people behind is a secondary matter.'

On the same day he was also separately prosecuted in a different court for a second offence committed only two hours after the first. He had driven his car halfway round the extremely busy roundabout at Cambridge Circus in the West End when he suddenly stopped, got out and asked people who wanted to cross the road to do so, this time immobilising the centre of London.

In 1972 he fell foul of the law again. This time for riding his eccentric campaign bicycle with inefficient brakes, obstructing the highway and staying on a pedestrian crossing longer than necessary. All this occurred directly outside the police station at London Road, Norbury. The bicycle had built over it a metal frame superstructure 6ft tall and 2ft 6in wide, covered with signs which encouraged road users to report traffic offences to the police and institute private prosecutions against motorists. Unfortunately, as Boaks was committing traffic offences himself at the time, he became a victim of his own advice: he was parked on the footway a few feet from a zebra crossing, blocking the view of approaching motorists. By now Boaks was well known as a crank and nuisance. Sergeant John Clark, prosecuting, denied Boaks's suggestion that he was the envy of every other policeman in London for 'knocking off Commander Boaks'.

In yet another case Boaks stopped in Battersea High Street at traffic lights which were still green to let two small children cross the road. Understandably, the driver of a car coming the other way was taken by surprise and could not stop in time despite slamming on the brakes. One of the children was knocked over. Boaks now found himself in very hot water indeed. The magistrate told him sternly, 'If anybody is to blame for that little girl being injured it is you. It may be you have some curious idea about behaviour on the roads but you might easily have caused that little girl's death and it is time you were stopped.'

Boaks was also concerned about safety in the air, which may well have been triggered by his experience of taking part in the *Daily Mail* London–Paris Air Race on roller skates. Convinced that Richmond lay in peril of an air-crash because it was on the flight-path to Heathrow, he strongly supported resiting the airport at Maplin, Selsey or even Bodmin Moor. In fact he wanted all inland airports closed and resited on the coast with passengers brought in by squadrons of helicopters to pick-up pads sited every few hundred yards in parks and open spaces. They could also be used as a rescue force in emergencies and, in a stunning piece of lateral thinking, even supplant undertakers, winching up the body from the bereaved family's garden and dropping it in the sea.

Whilst living in Streatham he badgered Lambeth Council to finance excavation of his garden ('it was huge, the size of *Invincible*'s deck') to turn it into an underground hangar for eight civil defence helicopters. This was a scheme too far, even for a council later renowned for its 'looney tunes'. When the council could take no more from him, it issued a compulsory purchase order on the house and garden and put up a block of flats instead.

Having been moved out of Lambeth, he resited himself in Wimbledon at the prosaic-sounding 188 Kingston Road SW20. From here he patrolled the streets around Wimbledon with a pram loaded with bricks, ever ready to plunge without warning on to pedestrian crossings virtually under the wheels of approaching cars. In line with his radical approach, his new house was to be no suburban 'Dunromin' or 'Myrtle Villa'. Instead, Boaks' writing paper proudly announced its forward-looking name – 'Beggar's Roost Heli-flight Station'.

Boaks also gave evidence to the public inquiry into Rotorport Ltd's proposal for a heliport at Vauxhall. He produced separate proposals for twelve floating helicopter stations along the river between Vauxhall and Tower Bridge and aimed to get them built for £60,000 each at HM Dockyard Sheerness, which was currently underemployed. He also proposed setting up a road-safety HQ on a landing craft, which could also be used as a station for a helicopter and for traffic observation. In a similar proposal for Sheffield, where the river was not ideal for the purpose, his answer was to site a heliport on platforms on a local lake.

Boaks soon realised that his ideas were so innovative that the normal, limited bureaucratic mind was incapable of grasping the grandeur of his conceptions. The only way to make real progress was for him to become a Government Minister himself. In 1970, immediately after the Conservative victory, he arrived in Downing Street clad in gumboots and on his pushbike, as usual plastered with placards demanding road safety. He then came away and announced to the world's press that he had given the new Prime Minister a note asking that he make him Minister of Public Safety with a seat in the House of Lords. As he said: 'For years I've been the unpaid Minister of Air Safety and Road Safety. There's no-one else to do the job.'

Having given the Conservatives a free run by not standing in the 1970 election himself, Mr Heath's polite refusal was a poor reward for his selfless offer. This meant that the gloves were off and, in the February 1974 General Election he stood in three constituencies simultaneously. He polled 240 votes in Wimbledon, 45 votes in Streatham, 35 in Cities of London and Westminster. Showing how unfitted he was for a career in politics, he registered his disappointment candidly: 'I failed miserably.' He put the blame on motorists: 'My policies would have curbed the rights of the motorists and they obviously rebelled.' But looking on the bright side again: 'If I had been elected I think I would have been the next Prime Minister.'

He had set out his political testament: 'I call myself democratic because I want to reform Parliament on democratic lines. Scrap the division lobbies and have secret ballots. The MPs could vote as they thought best, free from pressure groups and their paymasters. White Resident is exactly what I am. Sometimes, when I'm being nominated I find a black, give him a pound and tell him to find another 149 people to do the same so he can stand against me as a Black Immigrant. No one has ever taken me up. More people have been killed on the roads this century than in war. One Remembrance Day I went to the Cenotaph and laid a wreath to road accident victims. People thought it was in poor taste. I was deadly serious.' More controversially he declared himself against fireworks and wanted homosexuals hounded out of public life.

Although Boaks endured several decades of public rejection he steamed ahead. At Glasgow Hillhead in March 1982 his result was notable for two reasons. He secured only five votes, which was remarkable, as he had had to find ten voters to get on the ballot paper in the first place. Secondly, in an earth-shattering performance, Tarquin Fintimlinbinwhimlin f'Tang f'Tang Ole Biscuit Barrel, standard-bearer of the Raving Loony Party, scored forty-five times as many votes. Undaunted, the Lieutenant-Commander returned to the fray at Peckham in October and, in a massive revival of popular support, clocked up a respectable 102.

A by-election was held at Birmingham Northfield on the same day and, shortly before close of nominations, it seemed the constituency was destined to be Boaksless. Political analysts and commentators were agog to know, 'Where was Boaks? Has he hung up his bicycle at last?' One journalist called on him at home to be told, 'Actually I hadn't heard of that one.' But he added firmly, 'The one I'm interested in at the moment is – well, I can't remember the name of it just now, but I'll definitely go in for it if it comes up.'

He was often asked whether the expense in lost deposits was worth it. He was categoric: 'It is worth the money. I have never canvassed. Whenever people get into the polling booth they are either sympathetic or not. I do not believe I ever lose an election – they do.'

Nevertheless, his public-spirited candidatures caused him some privation on his small naval pension. On one occasion his bicycle was hijacked to Aberystwyth and he was immobilised because he could not afford the £20 for essential repairs because he had lost too much money on election deposits.

His campaigns had a freshness wholly lacking in those of the conventional parties: 'I have never bothered about votes. The thing which matters is to give people a chance to vote; it is a matter of complete indifference to me how they vote as long as they have a choice. All that I stand for in is those six words on the ballot paper. I give thinking people the chance to vote for public safety. If they don't think, they will just vote Labour anyway.

'Once I'm nominated I don't go back to the constituency. For one thing I can't afford to. More to the point it would be unethical for someone who holds two commissions (as an RAF pilot as well as the Royal Navy) to go knocking on doors in support of Her Majesty.'

DAVID JAMES

MP FOR BRIGHTON KEMPTOWN 1959–64, NORTH DORSET 1970

'Have almost found the monster.'

In 1964 John Hare, then chairman of the Conservative Party, blamed the 1964 General Election defeat on David James: 'It's all that silly bugger David James's fault. The fool spent most of the three-week election campaign in Scotland looking for the Loch Ness monster.'

The tabloid press was full of it. Every other candidate in the kingdom was pounding the doorsteps and pressing the flesh in his own constituency, but in Brighton Kemptown things were different. Every so often, a telegram along the following lines would be sent by the Tory candidate, David James, from some godforsaken Scottish village, addressed to the Tory agent in Brighton: 'Have almost found the monster. Hope all goes well with the campaign.'

In the event, Labour won Brighton Kemptown by only seven votes and Denis Hobden became Sussex's first Labour MP ever. This was important in the national context as Labour won the 1964 General Election nationally with only 317 seats in a House of Commons of 630 MPs. Hare summed it up with commendable brevity: 'Seven fuckin' votes and we're lumbered with Harold Wilson.'

He had a point, even if it was slightly overstated. Within three months Labour had lost one of its seats in a by-election. So, if

James had won Kemptown it would have been level pegging at that point.

James founded the Loch Ness Phenomena Information Bureau, which conducted an annual hunt for 'Nessie', the monster. In 1964 he organised a conference-expedition on the shores of Loch Ness, to which he invited more than twenty people who claimed that they had seen the elusive creature, along with some of the world's leading biologists and zoologists.

The Bureau was given £7,000 by the Field Enterprise Educational Association of Chicago, which was used to build underwater detection devices. These were used for the first time during the 1964 expedition, which was due to end on 15 October. Unfortunately for James that was also polling day in the General Election and Loch Ness is 600 miles from Brighton.

James had many qualities of value to the House of Commons. For example, he twice escaped from a German POW camp. On the first occasion he resourcefully adopted the identity of a fictitious Bulgarian naval officer, Lieutenant Buggeroff. This improbable disguise served him well for a time, but he was eventually picked up by the Gestapo.

James' absence from the election need not have affected his result that much. By a curious quirk, Hector Hughes, the Labour MP for Aberdeen North since 1945, also lived in Brighton, the better to serve his constituents. He contested Aberdeen again in 1964 and won by a massive 17,478 votes. It is a conceit to believe that the more chance the voters have to see you, the more they will like you and the better your result will be. Shortly afterwards Hughes was prosecuted for shoplifting from a Brighton supermarket – but charges were dropped because, although a sitting MP, he was heard to have no idea what he was doing by virtue of his advanced senility.

4TH LORD AVEBURY

LIBERAL MP FOR ORPINGTON 1962–70;
PEER 1971–

'A dog's dinner.'

Eric Lubbock created a national sensation when he captured one of the Conservatives' safest seats for the Liberals in a by-election, at the nadir of Harold Macmillan's Conservative Government's fortunes in 1962.

In the Commons he was uniformly predictable and dull personally and politically. But, once translated to the Lords as Lord Avebury, eccentricity began to blossom. He became a Buddhist and added a codicil to his will requesting that his body should be given to Battersea Dogs' Home and used as a dog's dinner.

Very appropriately, most people thought he was barking. 'It's a terrible waste to cremate bodies. It's a nice gesture to give doggies a good meal,' he said. 'I don't want to waste heat and energy. I don't want my body to go to waste when there are hundreds of homeless dogs who need a good meal.'

Unfortunately for him, Battersea Dogs' Home looked this gift human in the mouth and refused the offer. The manager said, 'As a vet I am sure there's a lot of nutritional value in the noble lord and the dogs aren't fussy. But we just could not do it – it's not ethical.' The marketing manager of Winalot Prime dog food commented disdainfully on tinned Avebury as potential competition, 'He looks far too tough. Those poor animals could be in for a chewy time.'

Disappointed, but not downhearted, Avebury then announced he would continue his crusade to become pet food, even if every dogs' home turned him down. 'If the dogs can't have me, then perhaps the cats will.' Alas! there were no takers there either.

The remaining option appeared to be burial at sea – outside the twelve-mile limit there was apparently nothing to stop him becoming food for the fishes. This was not so satisfactory, however: 'I'm not so fond of fish as I am of dogs, but burial at sea remains one option.'

Another suggestion was put forward by an eco-admirer. Had he thought of becoming tree fertiliser, combining bio-degradability with the creation of a long-lasting living memorial? The idea was to be buried without a coffin with a broad-leaved sapling planted directly above. Avebury was enthused: 'If the idea caught on it would solve the problem of the hardwood forests in this country which have been depleted over the years. It could only work if enough people did the same, but the idea of a whole series of burial parks in towns and open to the public makes a lot of sense.' Unfortunately, he proved to be barking up the wrong tree – it is currently illegal to be buried without a coffin.

Disposal of human remains had been a preoccupation for Avebury for some time. For seven years he kept his mother's ashes on the mantelpiece as an ornament but, in the end, he decided to dispose of her on a day trip to Stratford-upon-Avon. 'We saw a show at the theatre, then hired a boat and sprinkled the ashes on the river. She was very fond of Shakespeare.' It would be fitting if her favourite play was *All's Well That Ends Well*.

WOGAN PHILIPPS,
2ND BARON MILFORD

PEER 1962–93

'Even though the Communist Party no longer exists,
I am still a Communist.'

1962 saw the conquering of the pinnacle of British political eccentricity. The Communist Party acquired its sole Member of Parliament – in the House of Lords – when the 2nd Baron Milford took his seat literally and metaphorically on the red benches. He inherited his title from his father and automatically became the leader of the Communist peers. There were no others.

Gilbertian events like this go far to explain why revolutions have passed Britain by. Milford quickly sought to use his place in the Lords to make nature imitate art and transform into reality the song from Gilbert and Sullivan's *The Gondoliers*:

> The Chancellor in his peruke –
> The Earl, the Marquess and the Dook,
> The Groom, the Butler and the Cook –
>   They all shall equal be.

> The aristocrat who banks with Coutts –
> The aristocrat who hunts and shoots –
> The aristocrat who cleans our boots –
>   They all shall equal be!

On arrival in the citadel of aristocracy and class privilege, Milford (educated at Eton and Oxford) felt the warm embrace of old friends and contemporaries, fellow members of the best club in Europe. The House of Lords is well accustomed to eccentricity, which (being the politest place in the world) it tolerates benignly. But it was in for a shock when, in July 1963, he made his maiden speech.

The occasion was the Peerage Bill, which would permit reluctant peers to cast off the ermine and disclaim their titles, thereby qualifying for election to the House of Commons. It all arose out of Tony Benn's successful campaign to divest himself of his unwanted viscountcy, whose inheritance had wrenched him from the Commons.

Milford began uncontroversially by announcing that he was against the Bill. It seemed as though the new peer was a diehard reactionary, like other peers who regarded it as an act of apostasy and breach of a sacred trust to undermine the full rigour of the hereditary principle. But then he threw to the winds the convention that a maiden speech should not be controversial. Their Lordships were shattered to discover a blood-curdling Marxist-Leninist in their midst.

He declared that he opposed the Bill only because it was likely to make the unelected Chamber more acceptable and, hence, make it more difficult to abolish. 'I could never support any measure which helps perpetuate this Chamber.' At this point what passes in the House of Lords for a demonstration took place. The Lord Chancellor, unlike the Speaker, has no disciplinary powers and does not enforce order. The Lords, unlike the Commons, has never seen the need for any rules of order. As gentlemen they are so naturally well behaved they do not need them.

Courtesy and correctness are maintained by low rumblings of dissent from other peers, occasional shouts of 'Question!' if there is too much rambling and, in extremis, someone will propose a motion 'that the Noble Lord be no longer heard'. As Lord Milford warmed to his theme it was too much for some of his listeners. There was a noise like the low rumbling of distant thunder. When he started, 'May I ask...' he was promptly rebuked by many peers crying 'No, no; this is a maiden speech.' Undeterred, he announced, 'My party and I are for complete abolition of this Chamber, which is such a bulwark against progress,' at which came the unanswered query, 'Which party?'

The former Labour Prime Minister, Earl Attlee, supplied the answer in the very next speech. Noting that, by convention it fell to him to congratulate Lord Milford on his maiden speech, he observed, 'There are many anomalies in this country. One curious one is that the voice of the Communist Party can only be heard in the House of Lords and not the Commons. That, of course, is the advantage of the hereditary principle.' (Laughter)

Lord Milford recalled in old age: 'Many of the other peers were friends from Eton and Oxford, you see, and so they regarded this as a class betrayal. When I left the House there was a tense silence.'

After a conventional upper-class upbringing, Milford married the Bloomsbury novelist Rosamond Lehmann in 1928. This opened his eyes to a new world of leftish intellectualism. The marriage did not, however, survive the Spanish Civil War, where he went to fight for the Republic against Franco. Badly wounded when the ambulance he was driving was blown up by a bomb, he failed on medical grounds to get into the Merchant Navy for the Second World War. As a result, in true Orwellian spirit, he knuckled down to life as an agricultural labourer in Gloucestershire.

In 1944 he got married again, this time to a Communist of impeccable lineage, whom he had met in Spain – Cristina, Countess of Huntingdon and daughter of the famous hostess of the inter-war years, the Marchesa Casati. Milford recalled the misty-eyed romance of their courtship: 'We read a lot of Marxism together. We found we agreed on it.' She divided her time between making mosaic tombstones for her friends' pets and espousing the cause of Communism.

As a result Milford, up to this point prospective Labour candidate for Henley-on-Thames, joined the Communist Party. This produced problems with his family. With masterly understatement he said, 'My father conformed so terribly – as self-made men do. He minded my not conforming.' In fact, his father disowned him entirely, leaving his enormous fortune to his more conventional brothers, and he hardly spoke to him ever again.

After 1945 he reached the summit of his electoral success and, very improbably, became the first Communist member of Cirencester Rural District Council. In 1950 he stood for Parliament as the Communist candidate for Cirencester & Tewkesbury, unfortunately losing his deposit with only 423 votes, less than one per cent of the total.

Because of the Royal Agricultural College, Cirencester, the town was full of scions of the lended gentry. When some 'Hooray Henrys' heard there was a Communist candidate in the election, they turned up in force at Milford's first public meeting to chase him out. They were about to do their worst when Milford opened his mouth. Their leader suddenly pulled up with a start and shouted out: 'Hang on chaps, he's a gentleman.' Communist or not, they paid Milford the deference properly due to an heir to a peerage.

Deference had worked in Milford's favour in an earlier context also. During the war, Milford had, as a Communist, been an object of suspicion to the security services, who regularly tapped his telephone. Milford would occasionally get exasperated by this and bark out at the eavesdropper, 'Oh come on, constable, do get off the line.' The constable would jump to attention, reply obligingly, 'Sorry, sir,' and put the receiver down.

In 1959 his godson, Nicholas Ridley, was selected as Conservative candidate for the same constituency. Ridley was told by his agent he had heard that Milford was going to stand against him as a Communist, a prospect which delighted them, as it would split the Labour vote. When Ridley rang to check if this was really so, Milford said: 'I'll stand if you can lend me the £150 deposit.'

Sadly for Lord Milford, the British Communist Party ceased to exist after the collapse of the Soviet Union in 1990. The House of Lords has been said to be concrete proof of the existence of life after death. In the case of the Communist Party this was perfectly true, as Milford continued to represent it. On his ninetieth birthday in 1992 he declared, 'Even though the Communist Party no longer exists, I am still a Communist.'

SCREAMING LORD SUTCH

NATIONAL TEENAGE PARTY CANDIDATE FOR STRATFORD-UPON-AVON 1963, LATER BAN THE OLD FOGEYS PARTY AND LEADER OF THE MONSTER RAVING LOONY PARTY 1983–99

'Thatcherism may come and go, but Loonyism will go on for ever.'

Plain Mr David Sutch, pop singer of Wembley, emerged from the chrysalis of obscurity by two simple expedients – changing his name (by deed poll) to Lord David Sutch and scraping together the £150 deposit needed to stand for election to Parliament. Thus, he made an outstandingly successful career out of electoral failure.

In the 1950s Sutch decided to give up plumbing for rock and roll. Attending a talent contest at a Soho coffee-bar, he saw that the nineteen aspirants in front of him were all dressed alike as Elvis Presley. So was he, and he drifted away to devise a different image. In fact very different. He bought a pair of buffalo horns in a junk shop, and fixed them onto a fur-covered crash helmet with bobbles got up to resemble a coronet. He put this contraption on his head, draped the rest of his body in a leopard-skin and returned to Soho. 'I woke 'em up!' he said later.

He later refined his act by growing long hair and arriving on stage in a coffin, from which he would emerge with the buffalo horns on his head and a lavatory seat around his neck. To the accompaniment of his leopard-skinned group, the Savages, he would set fire to his hair and scream songs with ghoulish lyrics

219

such as: 'Last night I was diggin' in the cem-et-erry/ When up jumps a man all black and hair-ry'.

However, it is not music which will guarantee his fame but eccentric politics and, as if to prove this, in 1998 transatlantic record-buyers voted his early 1970s album, *Lord Sutch and Heavy Friends*, the worst rock LP of all time.

In 1963 the Profumo scandal changed his life. Profumo resigned as MP for Stratford-upon-Avon and Sutch decided to stand in the by-election as the National Teenage Party candidate. The candidate's deposit (forfeited if he won less than one eighth of the votes cast) was only £150, a figure unaltered since 1918. If it had kept pace with inflation it would have been over £2,000 and it is unlikely that Sutch would have become a national political institution.

Before Sutch fringe candidates tended to be dull and worthy. He changed all that forever. At Stratford his slogan was 'No Political Bug. Vote Sutch. Gain Much.' The by-election gave rise to a lot of dubious jokes, for example 'Life is better under a Conservative' and 'You've never had it so often'. Sutch garnered 209 votes with his common nonsense approach ('I think we all understand perfectly the big questions. The trouble is we don't know the answers. But does anybody?') and at the count provoked a walkout by the Deputy Mayoress because he sat on the mayoral chair in an extravagantly silly outfit.

In 1964 he announced that he would stand in Huyton against Harold Wilson, who was widely expected to become Prime Minister as a result of the General Election. His programme was fighting discrimination against long hair and knighthoods for the Beatles. Unfortunately, Sutch's nomination papers were not in order so his name did not appear on the ballot paper. Wilson had at first had a sense-of-humour failure and refused to shake his hand. However, he later gave him a cigar, whilst stealing his programme: he gave the Beatles the MBE.

In 1966 Sutch managed to get his nomination papers in order and duly clocked up 585 votes. He campaigned for a Beatles Memorial College and foreign policy of enforced birth control to combat the population explosion – as he put it, 'to restrict the product, not the pleasure'. When the council turned him out of the deserted house which served as his committee rooms he retaliated. He parked his campaign van in the chairman's parking place at the council offices to force them to find him alternative accommodation. Wilson congratulated him for 'livening up the election'.

Emboldened by this success, in 1970 he stood for Westminster as the Young Ideas Party candidate on a programme of building council flats in the gardens of Buckingham Palace as a boost to Prince Philip's finances. He scored only 142 votes.

In 1972 he did nearly end up in 10 Downing Street – but was arrested just before reaching the front door. He was wearing a loincloth and top hat and was accompanied by five naked girls. Arriving by double-decker bus in Whitehall, the girls tore off their clothes and ran screaming up to the residence of Britain's best-known bachelor, Prime Minister Edward Heath. Unfortunately, he was at Chequers, but they left an invitation for him to be guest pianist at a rock concert at Wembley a few days later and protested against the lack of rock music on BBC programmes.

In October 1974 he contested Stafford & Stone for the GB – Go to Blazes – Party. His programme combined logic with a dash of lunacy. For example, he demanded to know: why was there only one Monopolies Commission? His favourite slogan 'Vote for Insanity – You Know it makes Sense', was supported by 351 electors of sound mind (they must have been sane, as lunatics are not allowed to vote).

Following the 'winter of discontent', Sutch sat out the 1979 Election, no doubt concluding that, as the country appeared to have gone mad, he did not need to campaign. But in 1980 he derived great comfort from the election of Ronald Reagan as President in the USA, telling the Americans: 'If you elected a B-movie actor, we can all make good, you know.'

In February 1983 Sutch stood in the Bermondsey by-election, joining fifteen other candidates, the largest number to stand in a single constituency up to that time. This was the election at which the Monster Raving Loony Party (MRLP) was born –

Sutch's own attempt to match the mood set by the SDP's clarion call to 'break the mould of British politics'. On 24 February he romped home in sixth place with 97 votes. No doubt this triumph owed something to the support given in the last three days of the campaign by the former chairman of the Cambridge University Raving Loony Society, Tarquin Fintimlinbinwhimlin Bus Stop f'Tang f'Tang Ole Biscuit Barrel.

Tarquin (as he was known for convenience) had changed his name by deed poll from something tediously normal, in order to contest the 1982 Crosby by-election, where he scored a very creditable 223 votes in a fierce fight with the Social Democrat, Mrs Shirley Williams. She won (and lost it again the following year), leaving the MRLP to exact a terrible revenge at Bootle in 1990, when it drove the SDP candidate into sixth place and the party into oblivion.

A month later he was in action again. In the Darlington by-election on 24 March he improved his showing with a swing of well over 100 per cent, with 374 votes. Here for the first time he saved his deposit – not by getting more than 12.5 per cent of the poll but by betting £50 at 3–1 with William Hill that more than 250 would vote for him. As luck would have it Sutch happened to see Michael Foot, then Labour leader, getting into his car outside Darlington's Labour HQ. Wearing top hat, leopard-skin jacket and shiny leather trousers, he thrust a piece of paper through the car window and Foot amiably obliged with his autograph. Sutch promptly replied that he would 'take it to a chemist and get a prescription for my headache'.

Emboldened by the swelling tide of support, he resolved to storm the ultimate citadel in the General Election ten weeks later, taking on Margaret Thatcher herself in Finchley. He failed, however, to bend the Iron Lady's constituency to his will and departed with 235 votes, coming fifth out of eleven candidates.

By now he was not just an eccentric Independent but a national party leader. He had merged the MRLP with the Green Chicken Alliance and was fielding eleven candidates around the country. These included Flying Officer Kite (Bradford North 194 votes), Masked Man (Oxford West & Abingdon 267 votes) and Dick

Vero – 'More Dick in Dulwich' (99 votes, indicating that most Dulwich electors had no interest in Dick).

Nevertheless, Sutch was delighted by the monster publicity he attracted and was accustomed to finishing well ahead of other 'fringe' candidates. He was still, from time to time, thrown off course by the technical detail which a raving loony ought to be able to ignore. For example, in the Southgate by-election of 1984 he was disqualified for proposing his dog, Splodge, as well as himself.

Only three years later a disaster struck which threatened the whole credibility of the Monster Raving Loony Party – it won a seat! Fortunately it was only on the parish council at Ashburton in Devon, where its candidate Alan Hope, a publican, had been elected unopposed. As though exhausted by this achievement, Sutch preferred to rest on his laurels in the 1987 General Election. Whilst he put together a Rainbow Alliance of fringe parties, he sat the election out personally. He boldly declared, nevertheless: 'We are quite confident we'll get 400–500 seats' and, indeed, one of his candidates did manage to garner as many as 747 votes.

1990 was Sutch's annus mirabilis. In the Bootle by-election in May he scored a massive 1.2 per cent of the poll – 418 votes, compared to 155 for the Social Democrat. This result caused Dr David Owen to conclude that time was up for the SDP, which he promptly closed down. To show there were no hard feelings and that men of goodwill ought to be able to bury petty disagreements and foibles, Sutch then proposed a merger between the two parties. Sadly, however, Owen 'gave a sad little smile and turned down the offer'.

On the fall of Mrs Thatcher shortly afterwards, Sutch wrote to the *Daily Telegraph* 'as the longest serving party leader in Britain' exulting that he had seen off his fourth Tory leader since he began in politics in 1963. 'Her departure proves only one thing – Thatcherism may come and go, but Loonyism, which we believe represents the true spirit of the British people, will go on for ever.'

Notwithstanding this declaration of independence he then promptly paid £10 to join the Conservative Party – but only to qualify himself to stand for the vacant leadership. By an eccentric quirk, the Conservative Party's constitution does not require one to be an MP to do this. It would have been entertaining to see how Sutch, if he had succeeded, proposed to lead the country from the Commons' Public Gallery. He would not have been alone, of course, in looking down on the MPs. But sadly, Sutch fell at the second fence, failing to find two MPs loony enough to propose and second him.

He was less than impressed by the three candidates who did actually emerge: John Major, Douglas Hurd and Michael Heseltine. 'The Loony Party think it very wrong that the Iron Lady with her steel fists has been replaced by three wimps who probably wear rubber gloves. They are the sort of men who do the washing up at home.'

The *Telegraph* got itself into hot water for its excellent news coverage of Sutch and the Tory leadership contest. One irate Green supporter expostulated:

> As a member of Britain's fourth largest national political party, I find it incredible that a serious newspaper should devote a mere three column inches to a report of the Green Party's AGM, while the Monster Raving Loony Party is apparently worthy of almost a whole column plus photograph.
>
> Is it any wonder that the Green Party remains on the fringe of politics while the mass of the electorate is familiar with the rantings of Screaming Lord Sutch?

Between 1963 and his untimely death in 1999, Sutch stood for Parliament thirty-nine times. He polled over 15,000 votes, forfeited over £10,000 in lost deposits and incurred over £85,000 in election expenses. He fought one Euro-election in 1989 but found it impossible to outflank the far more thoroughgoing Euro-lunacies of the 'serious' parties.

In 1993 Sutch celebrated the thirtieth anniversary of his first defeat by dressing in leopard-skin tails and top hat and leading a conga dance across Westminster Bridge. Over a generation he had not only become a national institution but inspired a worldwide explosion in political lunacy. In the early 1990s alone Italy saw the election to Parliament of a porn star called La Cicciolina; Poland voted sixteen candidates of the Beer Lovers Party into the Sejm; and six million Russians voted for Vladimir Zhirinovsky, whose programme was to cut the price of vodka in half and blow nuclear waste over the Lithuanian border to discourage moves for independence.

Perhaps Sutch's strangest by-election failure came when he failed to be nominated in the December 1994 Dudley by-election because he mistakenly threw away his £500 deposit with some rubbish at home. His strongest electoral performance, however, had already come in the Rotherham by-election the previous May. He polled 1,114 votes and came dangerously close to saving his deposit, an event which would have totally destroyed his incredibility.

The party had already experienced an unwelcome brush with political responsibility when its chairman, Alan Hope, won his seat on Ashburton parish council in 1987. He declared, 'There is a definite swing towards lunacy in this country. I intend to take my duties very seriously.' By the early 1990s there were five Loony councillors – two in Cornwall, one in Devon, one in Manchester and one in Birmingham.

In 1989, flushed with electoral success, Sutch was blown up in a public lavatory in London and it seemed that he might have become a target for assassination because of his growing threat to those unofficial loony parties, the Conservatives, Labour and the Liberal Democrats. In flushing the loo he had mixed two volatile brands of chemical cleaner. There was a loud bang and Sutch was engulfed in clouds of ammonia. Coughing and spluttering, he staggered to a nearby hospital 'overcome and in a state of shock'. There being no psychiatric unit available, he was discharged after a thorough physical examination.

In the 1992 General Election he demonstrated his even-handedness by standing in the constituencies of all three party leaders simultaneously, scoring 728 votes against John Major, 547 against Neil Kinnock and 338 against Paddy Ashdown.

Psephologists are still scratching their heads over the riddle of whether the Loony leader's votes varied directly or inversely with the sanity of the other leaders' policies.

A remarkable number of Sutch's manifesto ideas were eventually implemented by one government or another. In 1963 he proposed abolishing the eleven-plus, legalising commercial radio stations, votes at eighteen and the pedestrianisation of Carnaby Street. All were swiftly realised. For a self-confessed loony he had some very sane ideas, recalling George II's reply to those who told him that General Wolfe was a madman: 'Mad is he? Then I wish he would bite some of my other generals.'

Other Loony policies have yet to find favour – for example, abolish winter and improve the weather by encasing London in a plastic dome, using heaters to recreate the tropics; introduce a 'Parliament on wheels, so that it can be carted off to make room for a funfair'; make dogs eat luminous food so you can see their mess in the dark; create a competitor for the Monopolies Commission; demote John Major to John Private; swap the House of Lords with London Zoo 'and see if anyone notices the difference'.

Most parties set up think tanks to keep up the flow of new ideas. The Loonies preferred a drink tank at chairman Alan Hope's pub, the Golden Lion in Ashburton. The intellectual ferment this engendered has occasionally caused rifts and splits in the party over major policy issues. For example, Hope once proposed scrapping the Channel Tunnel in favour of another from Britain to the Channel Islands to convert the whole country into a tax haven. This important matter was left undecided at Sutch's death.

In 1987 a Loony European policy was developed – to turn the EEC butter mountain into a giant iceberg and float it to the South Sandwich Islands near the Antarctic, where it could remain frozen to save storage costs. It was also suggested that water-skiing might take place on the wine lakes and that herrings might be put in them so that they came out ready pickled.

When the BSE crisis destroyed consumer confidence in British beef Sutch, as a responsible political figure, did his best to reassure the public: 'There's nothing wrong with British beef,' he said. 'I've been eating it for years, and look at me!'

He was also (unintentionally) responsible for one serious policy change – raising the Parliamentary election candidate's deposit from £150 to £500. This threatened to cause Sutch severe financial problems and by 1995 he was in very straitened circumstances, with Barclays Bank threatening to foreclose on a loan of £194,000.

Fortunately, William Hill, the turf accountants, exhibited the philanthropic spirit for which their profession is renowned. They came to the rescue, offering to finance his election deposits whilst the bank, in turn, agreed to reschedule the loan payments – two public-spirited actions which frustrated the boring parties' anti-democratic designs.

The increase in the deposit was recommended by the House of Commons Home Affairs Select Committee, in an attempt to exclude from Parliamentary elections all but 'serious candidates'. The *Daily Telegraph* wryly commented at the time: 'This is a concept which comes more readily to MPs than the rest of us.' Sutch retaliated characteristically by announcing that, in the first Queen's Speech after he came to power, the law would be changed again – to ensure that only frivolous candidates would be allowed to stand in future.

In the 1992 election Sutch managed to cross the threshold of fifty candidates and qualified for the right to make a party political broadcast. It was a runaway success. He explained, 'Most punters switch off as soon as the announcer says the dire words "There now follows a Party Political Broadcast..." But millions watched ours. I think our big coup was tracking down the provincial supermarket where Elvis Presley had recently been spotted by *Sunday Sport* readers, and persuading the King to make a guest appearance on our behalf.'

The MRLP was not just distinguished from the major parties by differences of policy. It steadfastly abjured the muckraking and personal abuse which so disfigures modern politics. After the mould-breaking win of a seat on Ashburton parish council, victorious Alan Hope commented, 'We fought a clean election with no smears. Not that we didn't have dirt to throw if we had wanted to. We had conclusive proof that Michael Heseltine had been having an affair with his mirror for the last 20 years. But we didn't tell the *Sun* about it.'

Sutch appears to have changed Parliamentary elections, in particular by-elections, forever. As he once truly said, 'During a General Election people would vote for a goat that 'ad a sticker on it. There's ravin' loonies in there now, an' you know it an' I know it. Parliament is already the longest-running farce in the West End, so a working majority of genuine Loonies there is wholly in keeping with the place.'

JOHN, 4TH EARL RUSSELL

PEER 1970–87

'The House of Lords is indisputably Marxist!'

Lord Russell made the strangest speech ever delivered in the House of Lords. In 1978 he took part in a debate on the victims of crime and apparently advocated anarchy.

He started by proposing that the police should be disbanded and replaced by the Salvation Army, who should give lawbreakers cups of tea. 'If a man takes diamonds from Hatton Garden, you simply give him another bag of diamonds to take with him.' All prisons should be abolished as 'kindness and helping people is better than punitiveness and punishing them'.

When these remarks gave rise to protests he asked his fellow peers: 'What are you? Soulless robots? The police ought to be totally prevented from ever molesting young people at all or ever putting them in gaols and raping them or putting them into brothels or sending them out to serve other people sexually against their wills.'

Warming to his theme, he continued, 'Working is wrong, being in any case the curse visited by God upon Adam...Upper classes are right and should be restored to vogue...everybody should become a leisured aristocrat.' He confused some of his listeners when he asserted, 'Aristocrats are Marxist. The Lord Chancellor holds the Order of Lenin. The fulfillment of industrial life is Tonga and the South Sea Islands and not the satanic mills at all. Shops ought to supply goods without payment so that all motive for stealing vanishes.'

More controversially he went on, 'Women's Lib would be realised by girls being given a house of their own at the age of twelve, with three-quarters of the wealth of the State being given to the girls in houses of their own to support them; so that marriage would be abolished and a girl could have as many husbands as she liked.' As for Men's Lib: 'The men should receive the remaining quarter of the national wealth and can, if they like, live in communal huts.'

Moving on to the Cold War he contended that 'Mr Brezhnev and President Carter are really the same person. What makes it abundantly clear is the saying of "little Audrey" who laughed and laughed because she knew that only God could make a tree.'

Talking of religion, a further thought occurred to him: 'There should be revolutions throughout Latin America, in accordance with the wish of His Holiness the Pope. Since the so-called Protestants who govern Britain are spiritless papal bum-boys, if they cannot take charge of themselves and find the spirit, the confidence and power to remove British arms and all Protestants from Ulster, they should find the said confidence and power to remove them... All soldiers and police throughout the Northern Hemisphere should disappear. They and their functions are no longer necessary and are out of date.'

Summing up the argument so far, his Lordship said: 'These points are the chief requirements for the future of the human race. They should be realised briskly and with discipline. Since the police and bourgeois bosses are and have been anti-aristocratical, the House of Lords is indisputably Marxist and inherits the banner of the Red Army of the Soviet Union.'

Musing on the desirable characteristics of the Ancient Greeks he recommended 'Naked bathing on beaches or in rivers ought to be universal. Is it not better to defend the city before it is fallen? Better than to arrive too late and defend only what would have been, if it had not already gone.' Quite!

SIR NICHOLAS FAIRBAIRN

MP FOR KINROSS & WEST PERTHSHIRE 1974–83, PERTH & KINROSS 1983–95

'A scarecrow from Hell – all tartan, mad hair and watch-fobbery.' (The Guardian*)*

'A SEXY MISTRESS IS BETTER THAN A BORING WIFE' screamed a *Daily Mirror* headline in 1982. Hardly surprising, perhaps. In fact, pretty typical *Mirror* fare. But what raised an eyebrow or two (in those days at least) was that this on-the-record quote came from a Tory MP. What's more, there were lots more. Breathless confessions tumbled out:

My attraction to women began when I was eight years old. I was infatuated with a beautiful school matron whose desirability wasn't lost on several of the masters.

I'm one of those who finds intimacy with a woman one of life's greatest pleasures. Just as in the past, we have MPs today who simply cannot bear the pain of sexual deprivation. Their sexual urges are so dominant as to be in need of frequent satisfaction. Away from home there is an inevitable risk they will look for another woman. It becomes a necessity for them. It's more than a temptation.

My view is that a virile MP who lives with a dozen sexy mistresses will thereby be no better and no worse at his job than one tied down to a boring impotent partner – but probably better.

The virile MP in this instance was the technicolour eccentric Tory MP, Sir Nicholas Fairbairn – also a distinguished QC and former Solicitor-General for Scotland. He was a man of parts, very few of which were private. In *Who's Who* he described himself as:

Author, painter, poet, TV and radio broadcaster, dress designer, landscape gardener, bon viveur and wit.
Education: Loretto and Edinburgh University, educated in spite of both.

Fairbairn could hardly have been more untypical of the Scottish Tory Party in 1974, when chosen as an improbably exotic successor to Sir Alec Douglas-Home as MP for rural Kinross & West Perthshire. He confessed, 'In this rather staid place I feel rather like a hot-cross-bun in a deep freeze.'

Boring and conventional lawyers and politicians list their unremarkable recreations in *Who's Who* as 'gardening, opera, book-collecting' etc. In 1973 Fairbairn listed his as 'Making love, ends meet and people laugh.' He explained: 'I think most people, if they were honest, will admit that those were their main recreations – apart, perhaps, from Ted Heath [then Tory leader], who would probably miss out on the first and third.'

Fairbairn entertainingly reinvented his recreations almost every year:

1975: Creative
1976: Creating
1977: Bunking and debunking
1979: Upholding what's right and demolishing what's left.
1980: Giving and forgiving
1981: The cure and eradication of British tick fever
1983: Being blunt and sharp at the same time
1984: Philanthropy and philogyny
1986: Ornitholatry
1987: Serving queens, restoring castles, debunking bishops, entertaining knights, befriending pawns

1988:   Snookering the reds and all other proctalgias (Greek scholars will translate this Fairbairnism as 'pains in the arse'.)

1989:   Draining brains and scanning bodies

1990:   Growling, prowling, scowling and owling

1991:   Loving beauty and beautifying love

1993:   Drawing ships, making quips, confounding Whigs and   scuttling drips

1995:   Languishing and sandwiching

Always supremely self-assured, he firmly believed he was a lineal descendant of the Scottish enlightenment and a Renaissance Man: 'I was born in the year Hitler came to power, although he wasn't as good a painter as I am.'

He was cold-shouldered by at least a dozen constituencies before finding a billet in Perthshire. This was no surprise as he had offended just about every susceptibility in the Scottish character. He upset the Presbyterian Church by founding a birth-control clinic for unmarried women; and outraged 'refained' Morningside by enthusiastically defending a young lady who appeared naked at the Edinburgh Festival. He scandalised the legal establishment by campaigning against the murder conviction of Patrick Meehan.

Recalling Sydney Smith's apophthegm ('It requires a surgical operation to get a joke well into a Scotch understanding'), his most obvious obstacle in finding a seat was perhaps his wit. Perth & Kinross, to its credit, saw beyond the joke and stood by him through many times when he found it difficult enough to stand himself.

He introduced the Commons to his eccentricities without delay. Shortly after his arrival he designed an outfit for himself which resembled a workman's smock, embellished with special brass buttons bearing the Fairbairn crest and motto 'Nothing but the best'. The design was a protest against Shiny Bottom Syndrome – a condition brought about by MPs' long hours sitting and shuffling on the green leather benches. The smock prevented the seat of his well-tailored trousers coming into contact with the bench.

He announced winningly: 'A lot of Members wander about in suits which at best look as if they were issued on demobilisation day and at worst were worn by their fathers before them.' In a parting sally he said 'I know I look like a bloody ironmonger, but I don't want my suits to glitter like the others.' Typically, in those few words he succeeded in offending not just his Parliamentary colleagues but the ironmongery trade as well.

On high days and holidays he dressed even more strangely. On Budget Day in 1977 he sported a double-breasted scarlet jacket hung with a gold watch-chain and pink shirt. When knighted by the Queen he turned up in full Highland fig – Glengarry, stroboscopic tartan kilt, *skhian dubh* and sword. His flamboyance was less well received by a *Guardian* 'wimmin's page' interviewer, who described him as a '58-year-old scarecrow from Hell – all tartan, mad hair and watch-fobbery'.

In speech and debate the flamboyant Fairbairn relished practising his hobbies of 'being blunt and sharp at the same time' and 'making quips and scuttling drips'. Political incorrectness held no fears for him – he was, for example, one of the few to oppose fellow-Tory MP Janet Fookes' Bill to outlaw kerb-crawling. Speaking against it in the House of Commons he ridiculed a clause which made it an offence for a man to solicit sex from a woman 'in a manner which causes her fear' and said 'I must tell Miss Fookes that I have always been attracted to her. I have never actually dared ask her whether she would go to bed with me, but after the introduction of the Bill I must ask myself how I am to put it to her so that it does not cause her fear.' The rather proper and somewhat matronly Miss Fookes rose to the occasion: 'What I really think is unprintable – but I would rather go to bed with a cold cod than my hon. Friend.'

In the same speech he got into hot water again, alleging that 'a person who occupied a grand office but who, for reasons of chivalry I shall not name' had chatted up and made libidinous suggestions to Mrs Thatcher, then Prime Minister, when she was attending the General Assembly of the Church of Scotland at the Palace of Holyroodhouse. Musing upon whether such an exchange would be an offence under the Bill, Fairbairn revealed that the propositioner 'had taken grandly of wine and, in words which I shall not use, told the Prime Minister he had always fancied her, to which she replied, "Quite right. You have very good taste, but I just don't think you would make it at the moment."'

A newspaper later claimed the mystery man was another leading eccentric, Sir Iain Moncreiffe of that Ilk. The Ilk and Mrs Thatcher both denied the tale, but a small detail of that kind would never have stopped Fairbairn from retailing a good story. He always found it easier to keep hot coals inside his mouth than a witticism.

Sometimes he employed the bludgeon, at other times the rapier. After incautious remarks about salmonella infection in eggs, the Junior Health Minister, Edwina Currie, was forced to resign. In a subsequent debate Fairbairn informed her, 'The hon. Lady should remember that she was an egg herself once; and very many Members on all sides of this House regret that it was ever fertilised.' Currie, humourless and self-absorbed, failed to see the joke. But the House, which disliked her hard-boiled eggo-centricity, roared.

Less successful was his intemperate response to a feminist student in an Edinburgh University debate: 'You are a silly rude bitch and, since you are a potential breeder, God help the next generation.'

In the Commons he could be just as offensive but slightly more deft. When Solicitor-General for Scotland he was asked by Labour MP John Maxton if he appreciated that the 'alarming spread of glue-sniffing among fourteen- and fifteen-year-olds is due to the lack of employment caused by his government and their consequent sense of uselessness?' Fairbairn responded, 'Glue sniffing is not a habit normally indulged in by children above the age of sixteen. It is a criminal offence to employ a child below that age. But if glue-sniffing induces a sense of useless-ness, it amazes me the honourable Member has not taken up the habit himself.'

Fairbairn was not universally popular, perhaps especially on his own side – following the old dictum that your opponents sit across the floor in front of you whereas your enemies sit behind you. Sir Patrick Cormack (Tory MP for South Staffordshire) criticised Fairbairn's 'eccentric and ridiculous utterances, bad manners and eccentric garb'. Unfazed by such criticism, he responded in kind: 'His manners are always appalling and his dress sense is worse. He is a squit.' Not a way to win friends – but he wasn't bothered about that; 'The play's the thing.'

He would rarely consider a day well spent if he had not shocked somebody, especially if his offensive crack was aimed at some sacred (Willie Whitelaw) or profane cow (Edwina Currie): Willie Whitelaw was 'the living person I despise most – sanctimony, guile, false ingenuousness, slime and intrigue under a cloak of decency, for self-advancement – it's called hypocrisy'.

Despite his recreation of 'philogyny' his enthusiasm did not extend to women MPs: 'They don't give me feelings of femininity. They lack fragrance. They're definitely not desert-island material. They all look as though they're from the 5th Kiev Stalinist machine-gun parade. As for Edwina Currie – well, the only person who smells her fragrance is herself. I can't stand the hag.'

Fairbairn did not fit snugly into 'the party of the family' for his views on chastity and marital fidelity made Alan Clark's look somewhat conventional: 'Christian monogamy and its assumption of fidelity is as fallacious as the Catholic concept of the chastity of priests. I am sure that polygamy and harems worked better. We live in a priggish and prim age.'

On the attractions of marriage: 'Apart from the depth of the relationship, you remember when you turn over in bed who you're with – and you don't have to get up at dawn and get out.'

Fairbairn's reputation was as a libertine, but he was more a libertarian. A good illustration of this is his stand against compulsory mass medication by adding fluoride to the water supply. He participated in many long-fought-out debates throughout all-night sittings. During one such debate in the House he was making a serious point when he was suddenly interrupted by his *bête noire*:

'Fluoride is a potent catalase poison which is cumulative. Nobody on any side of the argument denies that it is toxic.'

Edwina Currie, a manic believer in telling people what is good for them, interrupted: 'Fluoridation has been nothing but good. Anything is a poison if we take enough of it. Were we to spread-eagle my hon. Friend on the floor of the House and pour absolutely pure H_2O into him it would kill him in hours.'

Fairbairn, face expressionless, responded devastatingly, 'All the poison that my hon. Friend suggested I would happily take, rather than be spread-eagled on the floor of the House by her.'

He was a regular attender in both the Chamber and the Smoking Room and sometimes, if he visited the latter extensively before the former, it could induce a soporific effect. He once very publicly fell asleep in the Chamber during a boring debate. Whilst Fairbairn snored, Labour MP Dennis Canavan sarcastically pleaded with the Speaker for medical assistance. The appeal was rejected and the slumber continued, punctured by occasional grunts and rhythmic purrs. Canavan was then moved to inform the House that he thought his slumber had been induced, not by the tedium of the proceedings, but patriotism – because he had been 'anaesthetised by one of Scotland's biggest exports'. Shortly after this, Fairbairn was suddenly roused by loud heckling accompanying the speech of SDP MP Charles Kennedy. He immediately rose to his feet and, without a moment's reflection or having heard a word, announced: 'I apologise to the House that the greatest mistake I made this evening was not to fall asleep but to wake up. I have never heard such rubbish.'

One of the more interesting things about the modern House of Commons is the survival of the little-known perquisite of MPs, who are entitled to demand a pinch of snuff as they enter the Chamber. The Principal Doorkeeper maintains an official snuff-box for the purpose, although this harmless eccentricity will no doubt fall victim to political correctness and anti-tobacco paranoia. Sir Nicholas Fairbairn was the last known habitual devotee of the privilege. On one occasion in 1990 he snorted a rather generous pinch, only to be sent into a convulsive fit of coughs and splutters. But a worse disaster followed. He instinctively flung away the excess, which apparently caught Offa, David Blunkett's guide-dog, right between the eyes, causing the normally docile animal to go completely berserk dragging his unfortunate blind master off in confusion.

Fairbairn was adept at getting into scrapes. One of his colleagues said of him after whatever was the latest controversial incident: 'Nicky's in his element again – hot water!' I know what he meant as I got in some myself for writing a verbatim account of an 'interview' Nicky gave me shortly before he died in 1995. This was published in *The Scotsman* just before the Perth by-election and produced a major sense-of-humour failure in the Tory establishment which, unaccountably, nourished the illusion that the Party was still taken seriously in Scotland.

Neil Hamilton: Hello.

Nicholas Fairbairn: Hello, yourself.

NH: I am a little startled to find you are able to speak to me.

NF: Not nearly as much as me.

NH: I thought you'd be in Hell. I thought all Tories go there.

NF: No. Everyone goes to Heaven if they repent. I repented thoroughly at the last moment.

NH: Not of your Conservatism, I hope.

NF: Heaven is a Conservative idyll. There are no Lefties here, or rather they have recanted.

NH: Your death has traumatised Scottish Tories. You left them in terror at the by-election.

NF: I know. I exercised my mortality to perfection. Even the time of my passing was elegantly done – in the middle of a slow news weekend. I surpassed myself.

NH: You had said you thought the candidate chosen to second you was a complete plonker. Do you still feel that?

NF: What I feel is compassion for the poor fellow. He is a timorous man not used to the rough justice of politics. He has my blessing for a quiet and prosperous retirement.

NH: Why promote someone so unhappy in his role?

NF: It is not really his fault. The party usually selects the opposite of the previous MP. I was thought too independent. They selected someone incapable of independent thought. I was thought dodgy; he is thought safe.

NH: I sense contempt for the Scottish Conservative Party.

NF: Blended with affection. Those outside can never believe the degree to which it is simply not political. It is all about respectability and golf. The sheer smugness of Scottish Tories is exasperating. In all my time I never heard one original policy idea. Only rarely do you hear a good joke... and then it's always stolen.

NH: Presumably you have insight into by-election results?

NF: No heavenly advantage, but from this altitude it is obvious the SNP will win it.

NH: I feel a bit parochial talking about Perth and Kinross when you can see Heaven's vistas.

NF: One of my surprises was to find how like Perthshire Heaven is.

NH: Are you wiser after you have sloughed off your body.

NF: I am almost as cocky... but I am changing. Souls do more feeling than thinking. In one sense the absence of thought makes it not unlike the Scottish Tory conference but there is a peace they do not have.

NH: Is God in favour of the European Union? It strikes me as the embodiment of evil and waste.

NF: The free trade bits are fine. God favours open market so the creatures of His Creation can trade between themselves. The bureaucracy of Brussels, the dominant force, is pure malignancy. This is why Mr Blair and his angelic host will win the election – 12 October this year by the way – the Tory party will then awaken from its trance and support an independent Britain.

NH: I thought you'd tell me such squalid matters are beneath consideration in Elysium.

NF: No, no. The life of the world plays out as rather more than a soap drama. The folly of mankind is mostly at the personal level. The only important rule is to do as you would be done by – you must all be kinder to each other – but personal virtue safs nothing of the great collective venture of civil government.

NH: You don't sound like yourself anymore. You sound a bit like a spokesman.

NF: Look, this is important. I think they only allowed the seance so I could get this across. James VI was correct. Kings have their power by Divine Right. The sovereignty of the United Kingdom was not Mr Heath's to cast aside. Britain must trade as openly and as freely as it can with all of mankind... not just 11 neighbouring states. The European Union is opposed to this primary principle. It is a transient nonsense. The Tory party must renounce it.

NH: Er, so will you be attending the Scottish Party Conference this week in spirit?

NF: I think I can haunt proceedings without being there. Sir Michael Hirst needs to learn to relax and accept his fate. He has a kinder heart than he shows. The silly billies could win Scottish seats if they only said what they believed and stopped being limp socialists. Scottish Office ministers do as their civil servants tell them... not as the party wants.

NH: You seem as politically committed as you were before your death.

NF: I can see more clearly – 99 per cent of mortal activity is pure folly. I bitterly regret drinking too much. I took venereal pleasures far too seriously. I was vain and fractious. Things I then thought marginal I now see as crucial. I wish I had alerted Margaret Thatcher earlier that her lieutenants were going to betray her. Rifkind gave me the Historic Buildings Council as a consolation prize. I can see now it was my greatest opportunity.

NH: Any parting message?

NF: I was born a Tory. I lived my life as a Tory. I died a Tory. Vote SNP!

Fairbairn remained the life and soul of the party even in death, which few would say of the modern Conservative Party itself.

ALAN CLARK

CONSERVATIVE MP FOR PLYMOUTH, SUTTON 1974–92, KENSINGTON & CHELSEA 1997–9

'The most dangerous man in the Commons.'

Alan Clark was the most 'politically incorrect, outspoken, iconoclastic and reckless politician of our times' (Norman Lamont). Tony Benn said he was 'an independent man who said what he thought and meant what he said – and that isn't all that common in the present House of Commons.' Both, nevertheless, rather underestimated the eccentricity of the man.

In 1984 a number of Tory MPs were libelled by a BBC *Panorama* programme entitled 'Maggie's Militant Tendency', which alleged that the Tory Party was secretly being assailed by a right-wing version of Militant Tendency, a Trotskyist organisation which had been worming its members into positions from which it could take over the Labour Party. The Tory militants supposedly formed a tightly knit group of racist and militarist extremists and I was falsely named as one.

This programme was broadcast only six months after my election as an MP for a constituency with which I had had no previous connection. It was a highly damaging libel and I was extremely concerned about its effect on my career. Alan pooh-poohed this and was at pains to tell me it didn't matter a damn. In order to reassure me further he told me enthusiastically, 'You needn't worry about any of that. I am a Nazi. I AM A NAZI. I've never made any secret of it and it hasn't done me any harm!'

At the time I thought he was being frivolous, protected from reality by his extreme wealth and the independence it gave him. I now know he was quite serious. After an interview he gave to the *Guardian*, readers wrote outraged letters to the paper protesting about his 'fascist' views. Clark was, in turn, outraged by these monstrous libels on him: 'I'm NOT a fascist,' he declared. 'Fascists are shopkeepers who look after their dividends. I'm a Nazi.' He was nothing if not consistent. In the preface to his book on Operation Barbarossa (the German attack on Soviet Russia in 1941) he wrote in 1964, 'I have tried to suggest a reassessment of Hitler's military ability. No truly objective historian could refrain from admiring this man.'

He relished the controversy generated by saying outrageous things. He once referred to Africa in a meeting with officials as 'Bongo-Bongo land', knowing it was bound to be leaked, with the inevitable hue and cry from the hypocritical tabloids. As a result of this, Douglas Hurd advised Margaret Thatcher not to appoint him Minister for Trade. Clark's candid view of Hurd, vouchsafed in his published diaries, was appropriately robust: 'Might as well have a corn-cob up his arse.'

President Bongo of the tropical African Republic of Gabon took a more amused and tolerant approach and sent Clark one of his election posters with the slogan 'Gagnez avec Bongo' – a trophy which Clark enthusiastically displayed at election meetings in Plymouth in 1987.

He was singled out by the whips as 'the most dangerous man in the Commons'. Unhappily, this was the verdict of Conservative whips on his recklessness rather than Labour whips fearing his expertise. His very first outing as a Minister in the Commons in July 1983 proved the accuracy of the assessment.

As bad luck would have it, he had to pilot through the House late at night an anti-sex-discrimination law under some European Directive. Clark was, of course, both militantly anti-feminist and anti-European. He had also, according to his diaries, made the mistake of spending the evening beforehand tasting a variety of irresistibly magnificent first-growth clarets, which predictably boosted his confidence whilst reducing his ability to justify it.

He got up at the Dispatch Box to the ritual cheers which always accompany a Minister about to make his first official speech to the Commons. The House was quite full, not least because most Tory MPs, astonished at his appointment and expecting it all to end in some vast indiscretion, anticipated some entertainment. They were not disappointed.

Clark had hardly glanced at the convoluted and congealed text prepared for him by his civil servants. In addition, the alcoholic clouds occluding his eyes made it even more difficult for him to read it out intelligibly. His diary records, 'I found myself dwelling on, implicitly sneering at the more cumbrous and unintelligible passages.' He dragged out his words as if each had a ball and chain attached, adding uncalled-for emphasis which was interpreted as sarcasm. Very soon uproar ensued. Tories laughed and cheered whilst Labour MPs jumped up and down complaining that the Minister was mocking his own legislation. Eventually, Clare Short, then a humourless Mme Defarge, rose on a point of order to suggest Clark was drunk: 'It is disrespectful to the House and to the office that he holds that he should come here in this condition.' On and on and on the tumult roared until it seemed as though the business would collapse in confusion. Happily, things were ultimately patched up behind the scenes, but there was much tut-tutting and 'I told you so-ing.'

In April 1984 Clark got into even more serious trouble, requiring the personal intervention of Mrs Thatcher to keep him in the Government. As an anti-American protectionist representing a naval constituency, he understandably disagreed with the Government's decision to buy an American missile in preference to the British 'Sea Eagle'. Contrary to all the rules of Ministerial behaviour he attacked the decision on the BBC's *Question Time*. A great public row followed and Defence Secretary, Michael Heseltine, demanded his head for stepping out of line. However, he was told that the Lady was standing by him despite the gaffe – as she always did.

As a result of this sympathy, Clark survived several fracas which would have meant instant death to others. He flattered her femininity. In spite of his diary revelation, 'For me, girls have to be succulent and thus really under 25', he thrilled to his Leader's trim legs and tiny ankles. But she also recognised his value as a free spirit. 'Margaret would always let me see her and she always listened. She let me take liberties. Other people at meetings would gasp and say ooooh er, conceited little shit, he's gone too far. But she liked it.'

His most enjoyable job was Minister of State for Defence Procurement. But he was disappointed that, despite their mutual devotion, she would not promote him to the Cabinet, where she had promoted so many 'spastics'. When asked why she had overlooked his military expertise and not made him Defence Secretary she replied simply, 'Would you put Alan in charge of a nuclear weapon?'

Clark left the Commons in 1992, expecting that John Major would lose the election and not relishing the prospect of life in Opposition at the age of 64. Out of the House he suddenly became even more controversial than before. The candour of his diaries created a sensation. His former boss, Tom King, was described as 'an awful person to work with – indecisive, blustering, bullying, stupid and cunningly cautious even when he didn't need to be'. Kenneth Clarke was 'that podgy life-insurance risk' or 'a pudgy puffball'. Michael Heseltine, 'a jerky wild-eyed zombie' and a 'charlatan'.

Then, a much greater furore was caused by the revelations of his role in covert arms sales to Iraq – the Supergun and Matrix Churchill affairs. Britain was committed to selling arms to neither side in the Iran–Iraq war but Clark had regarded the export sales guidelines as 'tiresome and obtrusive'. In 1988 he met executives from the Matrix Churchill machine-tool company who were frustrated at delays in getting licences for sensitive exports. Clark, as Minister for Trade, suggested specifications implying the machinery 'would not be suitable for military purposes'. Subsequently, Matrix Churchill executives were prosecuted by the Government for making false statements in order to breach the arms embargo, despite their defence that Clark had given them official encouragement. Clark denied on oath to Customs officers and in Court that he had advised on how to circumvent the embargo. But documents were produced which proved the opposite. At this point Clark admitted he had been 'economical with the actualité', the trial collapsed and the Government was greatly embarrassed.

He soon realised his 'colossal mistake' in giving up his seat in 1992 and pined to return to the Commons. Not surprisingly, he was blackballed by Central Office from standing in any by-elections but, amazingly, he was selected at the age of 69 to fight Kensington & Chelsea – one of the Tories' safest seats, which became vacant when its MP was deselected for outrageous conduct!

Clark 'did not give a toss' what people thought about his private life and the Kensington selection meeting loved it when he replied to the inevitable question 'Are there any skeletons in your cupboard?' 'Whole graveyards full!'

As the whole world now knows from his famous diaries, he was a louche philanderer who somehow managed to combine extreme promiscuousness with extreme loyalty to his long-suffering wife, Jane, whom he had married when she was only sixteen and he was thirty. The most celebrated episode in his Don Juan existence was his coup of conducting an affair simultaneously with a mother and her two daughters, Valerie, Alison and Josephine Harkess. This highly attractive trio he described as his 'coven' and its revelation to an astonished world provoked the cuckolded husband, James Harkess (who was well-known to Clark), to pronounce that he should be 'horse-whipped'. He rushed from South Africa to administer the corrective. Although Clark did not submit to this, he agreed that his conduct throroughly deserved such a punishment.

Jane he described as 'rather wonderful about the whole episode.' She did harbour resentments about his strings of affairs and said, 'I don't forgive him and he knows it.' This was not surprising as, remarkably, he even invited one of his girlfriends to join them on their honeymoon. In response to an incredulous television interviewer Jane said, 'Yes he did, amazingly. But she was nice, the others have been pretty good rubbish since then. We could have had a Bunuel situation on the honeymoon and done away with him. I have often been tempted since.'

Sometimes her wrath did boil over and she once threw an axe at him. 'As it left my hand I hoped it would hit him, but it missed and I am glad that my aim was so bad. I know he is an S-H-One-T, but I still think he's super.' China, books and other artefacts followed the trajectory of the axe in many other recriminatory scenes. Despite her anger, she always clove to her errant partner because 'I know he adores me, we're lovers and soulmates. We're the other half of each other.' Her comment on the Harkesses expresses it succinctly: 'Quite frankly, if you bed people of below-stairs class, they go to the papers don't they?'

They both delighted in shocking the bourgeoisie. Jane once said the peacocks they kept at Saltwood Castle, their Norman pile in Kent, fought themselves 'when they see their reflections in the Porsche. We drive around with blood all over the car. We tell people we ran into a charity cycle race.' Their favourite dogs were rottweilers, one of whom was called Hanna (after Hitler's favourite test pilot, Hanna Reitsch) and the other, Leni, after the Nazi film-maker, Leni Riefenstahl.

As soon as he got back to Westminster he was in trouble again, suggesting that the only way to deal with the IRA was to kill six hundred people in one night. He was the only Conservative MP to abstain in the leadership contest which elected William Hague and he volubly criticised the party's desperate attempt to jettison the party's Thatcherite past.

ROY JENKINS

SOCIAL DEMOCRAT CANDIDATE FOR WARRINGTON 1980

'It's no fun being called Roy Jenkins.'

The Warrington by-election was the electoral birthplace of the Social Democrat Party (SDP). Roy Jenkins, former Labour Chancellor of the Exchequer, former President of the European Commission and founder of the SDP resolved to attempt to break the mould of British politics by standing as the first SDP challenger to the established parties.

But he was not the only Roy Jenkins on the ballot paper. Annoyed by Jenkins' patrician 'Smoothichops' air, wobbly 'r's and claret-drenched, well-fed rotundity, Douglas Parkin of the West Yorkshire Single Persons Homeless Aid in Batley decided to introduce some confusion into the contest by changing his name to Roy Jenkins and putting his hat into the ring as a Social Democrat candidate too.

Roy Jenkins II exhibited certain characteristics which would identify him as an unlikely substitute for the sainted centrist plutocrat. First, he was a beer-drinker. Second, he had no teeth and third, he pronounced his new name as 'Roy', not 'Woy'. He acquired this new name by the simple expedient of visiting the Manchester Stamp Office and executing a deed poll for the price of 50p.

At lunch immediately afterwards he announced: 'It's no fun being called Roy Jenkins. I doubt if I'm going to keep it. I don't like it. It's not my style. I'm sticking to Tetley's bitter until the working class switches to claret.'

Much to Woy's annoyance, Roy II came ahead of him on the ballot paper, because Roy II was described as 'Roy Jenkins, Social Democrat' whilst Woy I appeared as 'Rt. Hon. Roy Jenkins, Social Democrat with Liberal Party support'. Like Woy, Roy II was also annoyed – but with himself for missing a trick at the Stamp Office and neglecting to acquire Rt. and Hon. as two extra Christian names, which would have created even more confusion.

It was suggested to Woy by irreverent journalists that he could solve the problem of potential confusion by following Mr Parkin's example and changing his name by deed poll too – perhaps to 'Doug Hoyle (Labour), the Labour candidate'.

The ballot paper eventually contained two Roy Jenkinses, three Social Democrats, two candidates called Keane (one of whom was a Social Democrat too), an English Democrat (who removed his shirt at the nomination ceremony to reveal coffee-stained underwear) and a United Democrat (standing on a policy of castration).

With all this confusion, a whiff of sanity was introduced by the arrival, breathless and twenty minutes late on the coach from London, of 77-year-old Commander Bill Boaks of the Air, Road, Public Safety, Democratic Monarchist, White Resident Party. He was pushing a shopping trolley carrying a large notice: 'Zebra Pass £100; Burial £500', and announced he opposed the Consenting Adults Bill. It was (he believed) his twenty-first by-election. The Conservative candidate was called Stan Sorrell, but the pantomime nature of the contest was maintained by the arrival of Willie Whitelaw, who announced he was 'delighted to be in Warrington to campaign for my friend, Stan Laurel'.

The rest is history. Woy nearly won in Wawwington and Roy, weawying of the wancour of politics, wetired fwom the fway.

DAVID ICKE

GREEN PARTY 1988–91, EX-MESSIAH

'Jesus's was the last mission. Mine is the next one.'

Icke was a goalkeeper for Hereford United but rheumatoid arthritis forced him to retire when only twenty-one. In the 1970s he acquired celebrity as a BBC TV sports presenter, most memorably as anchorman at snooker tournaments. Then he decided to enter politics. It was a natural progression. His life has been dominated by balls – catching them, commentating on their use and, finally, talking it.

He set up home on the Isle of Wight and expressed an interest in being selected as Liberal candidate for the 1987 election, when the sitting Liberal MP had decided to retire. He chose the Liberals chiefly because the party was keen on environmental issues and he had already joined Greenpeace. The Liberals were initially keen on Icke too, as he was a famous celluloid character who possessed an attractive blandness coupled with a windy fluency in woolly rhetoric. He was ideal material.

Unfortunately it was not to be. Icke fell out with the island's Liberals because he was urged to accept a compromise on some unvouchsafed issue. Icke said, 'I was sickened by the political scene and I thought I don't want any of this. I'm interested in spreading the truth.'

The Liberals responded: 'David thought he was going to walk into the seat. Icke's very arrogant sense of what he should be due was outraged that he should have to submit to a competitive selection process with other candidates. Within a couple of days of it being announced, he was banging off to the local press, running the Liberals down with real vitriol and spite. It's quite funny that someone so aggressive should now be carrying on about love being the healing balm of the planet.'

Icke and his wife, Linda, then formed the Isle of Wight Green Party. Within six months he was one of the Party's four national spokesmen. He started his own environmentalist pressure group on the Isle of Wight, called Islandwatch, and rapidly became more radical and aggressive. At a meeting to discuss the development of a car-park in Ryde, bouncers tore the microphone away from an elderly Tory councillor. He led a belligerent demonstration of poll-tax refuseniks (though Isle of Wight Radio later reported that, having encouraged others to risk going to prison, he quietly paid his own).

Within a short time, however, he moved beyond mere terrestrial concerns. In March 1990 he visited for the third time a Brighton spiritual healer and medium called Betty Shine, searching for relief from his long-term arthritic pain. Suddenly there occurred a blinding revelation. Shine made contact with a Chinaman who had been dead for 800 years and who informed them, 'Socrates is with me.' Socrates then came on the line and told her that 'Icke is a healer who is here to heal the earth and he will be world-famous.'

'Jesus's was the last mission. Mine is the next one. I feel a sense of awe and honour. I feel immensely privileged to be part of a team working in many universes. It is hard to say you are the son of God without being described as arrogant.' Sceptics were easily dismissed. Jesus was assailed by the Pharisees and Sadducees. 'It is just history repeating itself.'

Icke claimed that other missions had preceded his. A-taurus, an archangel, had sabotaged a previous attempt by the citizens of the lost city of Atlantis to use the 'power-point at Stonehenge' to restore the cosmic balance. As a result King Arthur and Merlin (who were also archangels) had to flee to Britain and 'turn off Stonehenge' to prevent the demon using it.

The universe is full of good and bad energy, creating vibrations ordinary mortals cannot see. Humans, unlike Godhead and archangels, were on the whole bad and their evil thoughts produced bad energy. The people who had lived in 'the glorious, golden age of Atlantis' had tried to produce better energy and found that their pure bodies had become considerably lighter than ours in the process. The Earth was created at the same time as the planet Venus and another called Vulcan (one of two planets in our solar system we have yet to see). At that time a bad thought arrived from the planet Sirius, disrupting the Earth from the start.

Good energy was now trying to restore the balance and threatened to destroy much of humanity in the process as it surged through energy channels setting off volcanoes, earthquakes and tidal waves.

Good energy resonated with turquoise, which led Icke and his followers to wear turquoise tracksuits. 'I am a channel for the Christ spirit. The title was given to me very recently by the Godhead.'

He was the son of God, he explained. By 'God' he meant 'the spirit in the highest frequency which has the most perfect balance between the polarities'. Having been abroad 'clearing blocked energy points' in the Middle East, Italy, the USA and Canada, he returned to Britain to say that he was continuing the work of Jesus Christ and that, in fact he was more powerful than Jesus, who lacked the advantage of worldwide media!

He followed up these personal revelations with some blood-curdling prophecies. By Christmas 1991 Greece, Cuba, Teesside and the cliffs of Kent would be underwater after being hit by earthquakes measuring eight on the Richter scale. Much of China and Sicily would fall victim to 'disruptive thought vibrations' caused by the Tiananmen Square massacre and the Mafia. The first sign of the cataclysm would be the explosion of Mount Rainier in the USA. Then the Channel Tunnel, Texan oilfields and Naples Cathedral would go as the Godhead 'tried to restore the balance on earth'. Martinique would be almost destroyed, as would Las Vegas and parts of Los Angeles. A hurricane would destroy Londonderry and the Arctic Circle would begin to move southwards.

Some months later, when none of his forecasts of doom had been fulfilled, Icke solemnly announced, 'I have said things in

the past year and when I was saying them I knew they were
crazy. But it was a karmic experience which was being set up for
me. I had to experience extreme ridicule so that I could emerge
stronger and wiser. My predictions were meant to be wrong on a
massive scale because I have always previously been scared of
ridicule. If you have not experienced hot and cold you cannot
know what lukewarm is.' He still believed he was Socrates in a
previous life and that Sir Francis Bacon asked him if he wanted
to endure being 'Son of God'. In a final blinding flash of insight
he revealed: 'Turquoise is an important colour but you do not
have to wear it all the time.'

LATTER-DAY POLITICAL ECCENTRICS

1900–PRESENT

'I am retiring from the House of Commons to devote more time to Politics.' (Tony Benn MP)

Going into politics is a pretty strange thing to do in itself. Although most politicians are idealists, the public generally takes the Ambrose Bierce view that politics is 'a strife of interests masquerading as a contest of principles'. Many, even more cynical, would define an honest politician as 'one who, when he's been bought, stays bought'. Sadly, MPs are not respected as a class and their motives are suspect. However, only a fool would choose politics as the means of acquiring wealth. The clever or quick-witted can make vastly more outside. A newspaper editor, for example, will be paid at least twice as much as a Cabinet Minister, can be more effectively opinionated and lead a private life relatively free from media intrusion and invention.

Furthermore, it has always been a source of wonder to me how many people who are basically shy or lacking in social skills end up in the Commons and even make it to the top of the 'greasy pole'. Take, for example, **SIR EDWARD HEATH (Conservative MP for Bexley 1950–83, Old Bexley and Sidcup 1983–2001).** Sara Morrison was made vice chairman of the Conservative Party with the admittedly difficult brief 'to turn

Ted into a human being'. At a Conservative agents' annual dinner she noticed that the conversation between Heath and the chief agent's wife had dried up. She wrote on her napkin: 'For God's sake say something!', folded it neatly and passed it through the diners to the top table. Heath received it, opened it up, glanced at the message and wrote on it: 'I have', and passed it back.

Julian Critchley reports a similar story. He was dining in the House of Commons one evening with Norman Fowler, David Walder and Jim Prior when, midway through the pudding, Heath arrived. He greeted Prior warmly. 'Good to see you,' he said, followed by lots of shoulder-shaking bonhomie. But by no word, glance or gesture did he acknowledge the existence of the other three at the table. As he left, Prior (who had been Heath's PPS) said to them despairingly, 'What on earth can I do with him?'

Very few of the extraordinary individuals in this book were conscious eccentrics or publicity-seekers. Most exhibit the characteristics of Charles Waterton, an intrepid traveller who rode a crocodile for fun and pirouetted on one leg on the head of the angel atop Rome's Castel Sant'Angelo. Edith Sitwell said of him: 'He was an eccentric only as all great gentlemen are eccentric, by which I mean that their gestures are not born to fit the conventions or the cowardice of the crowd.'

SIR WINSTON CHURCHILL certainly came into that category. He was not, of course, an eccentric in the normally understoood sense of a 'whimsical oddity'. But he did have a decidedly strange Parliamentary career – **Conservative MP for Oldham 1900–6, Liberal MP for Manchester North West 1906–8 and Dundee 1908–22, Free Trade Liberal candidate for Leicester West 1923, Independent Anti-Socialist candidate for Westminster Abbey 1924, elected as Constitutionalist MP for Epping 1924 and sat as a Conservative 1924–45, Conservative MP for Wanstead & Woodford 1945–64.**

First elected as a jingoistic Conservative MP for Oldham in the 1900 'khaki election' during the Boer War, by 1904 he had crossed the floor to become a Free Trade Liberal. For a decade or

Sir Winston Churchill.

so he rose through the Liberal ranks to high office but, during the First World War, he became increasingly independent, as the Liberal Party was rent into factions by the caustic personal dispute between Asquith and Lloyd George. Defeated by an Independent Prohibitionist at Dundee in 1922, Churchill stood as a Free Trade Liberal at Leicester West in 1923 and then as an Independent Anti-Socialist in a by-election in Westminster in early 1924. After a campaign in which a sitting Conservative MP ran each of his committee rooms, he lost by only 43 votes to the Conservative candidate in what should have been one of the Tories' safest seats. Within a few months he was elected as a 'Constitutionalist' at Epping in the 1924 General Election, rejoining the Conservative Party immediately afterwards, when Baldwin made him Chancellor of the Exchequer. He joked about his unconventional switches of allegiance: 'Anyone can rat. It takes a real amount of ingenuity to re-rat!'

In the 1923 General Election Sir William Jowitt was elected to the House of Commons one day as a Liberal and moved to the Lords the next as the new Labour Government's Lord Chancellor. Churchill, discussing this manoeuvre with friends expressing critical views, was indulgent: 'Poor fellow. He didn't know how to do it. Now, if he had come to me, I could have instructed him in the technique of tergiversation.'

What place is there for strange characters in Cool Britannia? None whatever, I should think, as the essence of both major party leaders appears to be to sift out anyone threatening the monochrome uniformity dictated by the spin-doctors. As more and more MPs are lobotomised by the control-freaks running the party machines, it is hardly conceivable that the likes of Tony Benn, Tam Dalyell, Alan Clark or Nicky Fairbairn would ever again slip through the official winnowing fans.

The House of Commons in modern times has had few enough strange characters whose passing 'eclipsed the gaiety of nations and diminished the public stock of harmless pleasure'. Even the buffoons sometimes had much to contribute – for example, **SIR GERALD NABARRO (Conservative MP for Kidderminster 1950–64, South Worcestershire 1966–73)** who, in the 1960s,

Daily Mirror,
1 January 1963.

Worcester Evening News and Times,
19 January 1965.

News of the World,
10 October 1965.

Dundee Evening Telegraph,
1 April 1966.

was better known than most of the Cabinet and possessed many characteristics which were a gift to cartoonists. He was instantly recognisable by his enormous handlebar moustache, (combed four times a day and claimed to be soft and downy because he had never shaved his upper lip since it started to sprout when he was fourteen). He was instantly recognisable on the road by the number-plates of his cars (he owned NAB 1 to NAB 10 and founded 'autonumerology'). He was a rampant self-publicist whose eccentricities endeared him to a wide public through constant appearances on TV and radio. His broad shoulders, large head and moustaches made him seem larger than life on the small screen. This sometimes led people, when they met him in the flesh, involuntarily to express surprise that he was actually quite short – to which he invariably responded, 'Great men usually are.'

One of the last MPs habitually to wear a top hat in the Chamber – which he did regularly on Budget Day – he was regularly voted one of the ten best-dressed MPs. He disapproved of coloured shirts and ties but did not dislike colours as such. He regularly sported garishly coloured braces, which he wore to the House of Commons as occasion demanded. 'Normally they are unseen,' he said. 'But from time to time they are displayed to irritate my political opponents on the benches on the other side of the House. If there is to be a noisy debate I wear red.'

One of his most famous campaigns was not at all strange, but exposed the multifarious absurdities of one of Britain's most eccentric taxes. He achieved this by asking three Parliamentary Questions every Tuesday and Thursday for four years, of which the following are entertaining samples:

On 13 February 1958 he asked the Chancellor of the Exchequer if he was 'aware that a nut cracker is liable to Purchase Tax at 15 per cent, whereas a door knocker over five inches in length is free of tax; and that there is an increasing practice of supplying nut crackers with screw holes so that they can theoretically be used as door knockers, so making them free of tax?' He went on to ask the unanswerable: 'What is the justification for this invidious distinction between door-knocking nut crackers and nut-cracking door-knockers?'

This was followed by others in the same vein: 'Why are blinds fitted with three-inch circular peepholes free of tax whereas those without peepholes are not?' On being told that the tax was charged only on blinds for domestic and office use and blinds with peepholes were used only in shops, he continued: 'Does not this fiscal discrimination encourage the sale of blinds with peepholes and, as the presence of these peepholes is incitement to offences under the Justices of the Peace Act 1361 – the Peeping Tom Act – will the Government remove Purchase Tax from all blinds so as to give a modicum of comfort to all law-abiding people?'

He discovered that straps for supporting double chins and caps for projecting ears were taxed at 90 per cent while wrist and ankle supports were tax free; that Australian opossum, undyed and sold in strips less than nine inches by one inch was tax free but, if longer and wider, taxed at 50 per cent as furs; that a pottery piggy bank used for saving was taxed at 30 per cent as a toy, but if painted with the words 'razor blades' it paid only 15 per cent as a salvage receptacle.

Among hundreds of other Questions which brought the House down, he asked the Chancellor: 'Is he aware that a horn regarded as a wind musical instrument is subject to Purchase Tax at 30 per cent, whereas a musical motor car horn attracts no tax even if occasionally used for theatrical performances?' and 'Why are eyelash curlers liable to tax at 50 per cent whilst eyebrow combs are chargeable at 25 per cent?'

His outsize personality allied to relentless ridicule ensured that the tax was gradually simplified and reduced.

Another relentless questioner was **ARTHUR LEWIS (Labour MP for Upton 1945–50, West Ham North 1950–74, Newham North West 1974–83)**. He was known for eccentric outbursts, such as when he called for a group of youths to be shot for beating up a Scottish woman so badly that she needed 168 stitches: 'I would shoot them. I would be prepared to take the gun and do it myself.'

But he was best known for asking more Parliamentary Questions than any other MP. He regularly asked around 2,000 or so a year, his best score being 2,222. Between 1970 and 1974 alone it cost the taxpayer £105,000 (well over £500,000 at today's values) in civil servants' time to answer them.

Some questions were decidedly strange adornments of the House of Commons Order Paper:

To ask the Secretary of State for the Environment – 'When is he to hold an official party and reception to celebrate the 50th anniversary of the foundation of the Government Hospitality Fund; who will be invited and at what costs to public funds; and whether those Members of Parliament with 25 years and more of membership who have never been invited to participate in expenditure from the Fund will, on this special occasion, receive an invitation to be present?'

To ask the Lord President of the Council – 'why were there were no cheese rolls available to Members in the Members' self-service cafeteria on 27 March 1971; and whether, since the cost to members of making a cheese roll from cheese and roll and butter supplied is 33p, and since heat, rates, light and other equipment are supplied, he will list the factors which go to make up this cost?'

Despite the best efforts of the homogenisers, a few other true individuals have managed to retain their place on the Commons benches in recent years. **SIR PETER EMERY (Conservative MP for Reading 1959–66, Honiton 1967–97, Devon East 1997–2001)** when appointed a member of the Scottish Grand Committee against his will as an English makeweight, immediately adopted a strange plan to get off it. He turned up at the first meeting of the Committee unannounced in full Highland dress, including dirk and sporran which he had hired from a theatrical costumier – an act which gave offence to Scots of all political persuasions. The Government Whips, however, thought it a splendid wheeze and Emery was duly excused service.

SIR JOHN STOKES (Conservative MP for Oldbury & Halesowen 1970–4, Halesowen & Stourbridge 1974–97), a bristly-moustached defender of all tradition, might have been a twentieth-century soulmate for Colonel Sibthorp. The political editor of the *Guardian* described him as '100 per cent wholemeal reactionary, for whom the twentieth century has been a mistake'. In 1983 he reminded Cecil Parkinson, the Tories' chairman, that 'in the past the Tory Party has always preferred the landed to the moneyed interest'. He believed the Conservative Party was 'the national party of the duke and dustman' and was a stout defender of local working people who, he always averred, thought just like him.

A strong supporter of General Franco, Stokes began his political career in 1937 by being narrowly defeated by Edward Heath, the anti-Franco candidate for the chairmanship of the Oxford University Conservative Association. As a personnel consultant, he proposed a drastic solution to strikes at British

Leyland in the 1970s – 'shoot a few ringleaders!' 1980 was a typical year for him. Among other blows for reaction, he opposed a Bill allowing Catholics to marry into the Royal Family, opposed artificial insemination, attacked Viscount Cranborne MP for criticising the survival of hereditary peers and advocated improving the police by attracting more public-school entrants.

DAME ELAINE KELLETT-BOWMAN (Conservative MP for Lancaster 1970–97) clutched an iron-clad handbag into which she stuffed the dog-eared notes which she scribbled incessantly. She screeched like a demented parakeet across the Chamber.

ANTHONY CROSLAND (Labour MP for South Gloucestershire 1950–5; Grimsby 1959–77), like many Socialist intellectuals (following Karl Marx's example), was extremely arrogant and especially rude to women. Paul Johnson recounts a story of Crosland attending a party in Kensington whilst a member of Harold Wilson's Cabinet. Dressed casually in carpet slippers and shirt-sleeves, he became bored by the company and, although not drunk, decided to lie full-length on the floor just outside the ladies' cloakroom. This meant that any lady wishing to get her coat had to walk around or over his recumbent form. A tall, plain, shy girl did this with some difficulty, causing Crosland to revive. He looked up at her and snarled, 'Hello, ugly face!' The girl retreated in tears and, on asking 'Who is that horrible man?', was told 'That is Her Majesty's Secretary of State for Education.'

TOM HOOSON (Conservative MP for Brecon & Radnor 1979–85) cut his political teeth in Caernarvon and probably holds the record for long-distance electioneering. Strangely, he was chosen as prospective candidate for Caernarvon in 1960, just as he was about to leave for a job in America. He did not resign the candidature until three years later. In the meantime, he spoke to his constituents through the ether. He would make a ranting soliloquy into a microphone in the USA and post a tape of his oration to his agent in Caernarvon. The agent would then solemnly bear it around the constituency to play his disembodied voice to huddled gatherings of the faithful in various remote and draughty halls. He is perhaps best remembered now for introducing a Bill to allow tenant farmers to shoot rabbits by night.

JOHN RYMAN (Labour MP for Blyth 1974–87) was the last Labour MP regularly to hunt foxes and wear a bowler hat to the House. He made his maiden speech on the surprising topic of Church of England worship and doctrine. In 1974 he attacked the West German Chancellor, Helmut Schmidt, as a 'patronising Hun' for trying to keep Britian in the EEC.

TONY BENN, formerly the Hon. Anthony Wedgwood Benn, formerly the Viscount Stansgate (Labour MP for Bristol South East 1950–60 & 1963–83, Chesterfield 1984–2001), whose name got shorter and shorter as he got older and older and 'prolier than thou'. Harold Wilson said of him, 'he immatures with age' – an unfair judgment on one of the last true House of Commons men. Courteous and erudite, he carries on almost alone the greatest traditions of Parliamentary oratory and political independence. His eccentricities were commonplace only a short time ago, before the House of Commons became degraded by 'spin' – he thinks for himself and is not controlled by cosmic forces transmitted by electronic pagers. In May 2001 he retired from the House of Commons to devote more time to politics.

SIR CHARLES IRVING (Conservative MP for Cheltenham 1974–92) was, on paper, a strangely unsuitable choice as MP for the red-faced retired colonels of Cheltenham. Camp as Julian Clary, he was ultra-liberal, anti-hanging-and-flogging, anti-pâté de foie gras, tolerant of prostitution and opposed the ban on unions at GCHQ. He had no pretensions to military capabilities himself. When he tried to join the Army in World War II he was turned down on grounds of being insufficiently robust. Relegated to the Home Guard, he was no more successful there and the highlight of his career there was the accidental stabbing of a retired lieutenant-general with a bayonet in the backside.

He loved Cheltenham and was forever dropping in on constituents. He resolved to continue doing so after his death –

by directing his ashes to be propelled in a rocket to a great height and then scattered over the town.

Sir Charles seems to have started a bit of a trend. When the **7TH LORD NEWBOROUGH** died in 1998, he left instructions for his ashes to be shot out of an eighteenth-century cannon into his estate at Rhug, in North Wales. This was a fitting end for a peer who was once fined £25 for firing a nine-pound cannonball from the ramparts of his other estate, Belan Fort, and damaging the sails of a yacht in the Menai Strait. A great practical joker, he built a folly in his park, to which he would send guests to see a mythical Mr and Mrs Jones. When they rang the doorbell they activated a bucket, which would douse them thoroughly with water.

The Palace of Westminster contains that strangest of all legislative Chambers, the House of Lords – hitherto a kind of game reserve for strange aristocrats. It is entirely appropriate that the only representative of the Communist Party to sit in Parliament since 1950 was a hereditary peer, the **2ND BARON MILFORD**. Sadly, the phasing out of hereditary peers will substantially reduce the scope for eccentricity in the future. But we can still glory in the past.

In 1935, for instance, *The Times* reported 'The House of Lords has lost, at the age of 91, one of its most picturesque personalities in the **19TH EARL OF MORTON**. He had a great gift for silence and, during all the years that he attended at Westminster as a Scottish representative peer, his voice was never heard in debate.' His example recalls Disraeli's advice to a young MP who, as he had been a silent Member of the House for some time, asked whether it was not time to make his maiden speech: 'Sir, it is better that we should wonder why you do not speak, than why you do.' It is a pity more Members in that 'other place' do not profit from such wisdom today.

In former days, not only were there many MPs who felt no desire to detain the House with their opinions, some even slept in the Chamber. **SIR GEORGE HUME (MP for Greenwich 1922–45)**, addressing his constituents in 1936, said that people need not be surprised at a good deal of sleeping going on in the

House of Commons. 'You get weary at times, and in the atmosphere of the House, it is very difficult to keep awake. But the public do not seem able to appreciate our difficulties. Some of the best Members are the silent ones.' It is not immediately obvious that the Commons has improved with the growing garrulity of its Members.

In fact, the opposite may be true. As the House has become more and more populated with hyperactive professional politicians, less and less notice seems to be taken of anything said there. In a more innocent age MPs were looked-up to – despite the sometimes quaint naïveté of yesteryear's amateur politicians. Who can doubt the good sense of **CAPTAIN R. G. BRISCOWE (MP for Cambridgeshire 1923–45)**? Speaking at a bowls dinner in Cambridge in 1938 he said, 'If only Hitler and Mussolini could have a good game of bowls once a week at Geneva, I feel that Europe would not be as troubled as it is.'

A generation later the **14TH EARL OF HOME**, Secretary of State for Commonwealth Relations, also went to the heart of the matter when he introduced the Prime Minister of Pakistan by recalling his greatest distinctions in life: 'He coxed his college boat at Oxford – and I'm told he sings Gilbert and Sullivan in his bath, which immediately makes us take him to our hearts.'

A few years later Home, having disclaimed his peerage, brought his talents back to the Commons as Prime Minister. Although he had been an MP from 1931 to 1951 and was a Cabinet Minister in the Lords from 1955 to 1963, he remained at heart an amateur with some notable eccentricities. His approach to solving economic problems was to have 'a box of matches and start moving the matchsticks into position to illustrate and simplify the points'. Years later, as a young politician on the make, this gave me an opportunity to say sycophantically in a vote of thanks for a speech of his at the Carlton Club, 'if the story were true I feel sure that the brand of matches must have been "England's Glory".' As a Welshman I ought to have realised this would not necessarily be taken as a compliment by a Scot!

In the 1964 General Election, Harold Wilson made much political capital by contrasting the Tory 'grouse-moor' image with the 'white-heat of the technological revolution', supposedly represented by Labour. Wilson attacked Home as a 14th Earl and an anachronism, to which Home tartly and effectively responded: 'Well, I suppose, when you think about it, Mr Wilson is the 14th Mr Wilson. Why should criticism centre on this? Are all men equal, except peers?'

In comparison with Home some members of the Upper House really were out of touch. For example, the perils of travelling without a valet were illustrated by the experience of 'Bert', **10TH DUKE OF MARLBOROUGH**, whilst staying with one of his daughters in the 1950s. She was surprised to hear him complain that his toothbrush 'did not foam properly' so would she please buy him a new one? After an investigation she was able to remind him gently that, without the aid of toothpaste, usually applied for him each morning by his valet, no toothbrush foamed automatically.

Whilst at Blenheim, the Duke was accustomed to provide entertainment for his guests by throwing raspberries to the ceiling of the fabulous dining room and catching them in his mouth. 'I know by the applause when he's at it,' the Duchess told a breathless gossip columnist.

However strange, most hereditary peers nevertheless had some useful attributes to help guide the nation's destiny. As **LORD WINSTER** once put it: 'I have heard it said of the "backwoods" peer that he had three qualities. He knew how to kill a fox, he knew how to get rid of a bad tenant and he knew how to discard an unwanted mistress. A man who possesses these three qualities would certainly have something to contribute to the work of the House.'

We live now in an age of excessive familiarity, when the Prime Minister invites people whom he has never met before to 'call me Tony'. It is perhaps worth regretting the demise of 'correct form', a code of conduct which may today appear to be just an aristocratic eccentricity, but which was once a stabilising influence on society. In the 1960s **LORD TREDEGAR**'s 'gentleman's gentleman' recounted a perfect example of it in his memoirs:

> I remember the morning when his Lordship was taken exceedingly ill. Instead of the usual nod of the head to me on my arrival, he spoke. 'Cronin,' he said, 'I think I'm dying.' The habit of the years could not be broken in me and I knew that Lord Tredegar in his more collected moments would not wish it to be. So, correctly, I replied, 'Very good, my lord.' – and thereafter the normal silence between us was re-established to our mutual satisfaction.

Actually, such codes of conduct applied in Victorian times throughout all levels of society, a universality evocatively caught by T. H. White. Describing rank and station in the servants' hall, he wrote in *Farewell Victoria*:

> The gradations of service formed a regular social service, which was of the greatest importance to the servants, giving them dignity and ambition. They possessed hopes of feasible advancement and relished their ranks to the full. Each lieutenant lorded it over his inferiors and exacted the respect which he gave willingly to those above. The caste-ladder was polite and gentlemanly. It gave pleasure to all, for even the boot-boy could snub the cowman and he, presumably, could kick the cows. Not that there were any kicks; only a superiority, abetted by both parties. It was a system of manners, which had been the discovery of the preceding century.'

So perhaps it was not so strange after all.

Despite the last paragraph, this book has no pretensions to sociological analysis or as literature. Its sole purpose is to entertain by recalling some of the strangest characters who flitted through the Palace of Westminster or who would have liked to do so – and to remind us that, whilst political jokes may amuse, all too often they get elected. For the rest of us, that may sometimes be no laughing matter.